4

940.04395
Logan, F. Donald

The Vikings in
history

DATE DUE

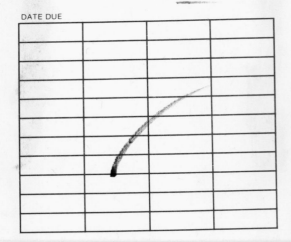

4

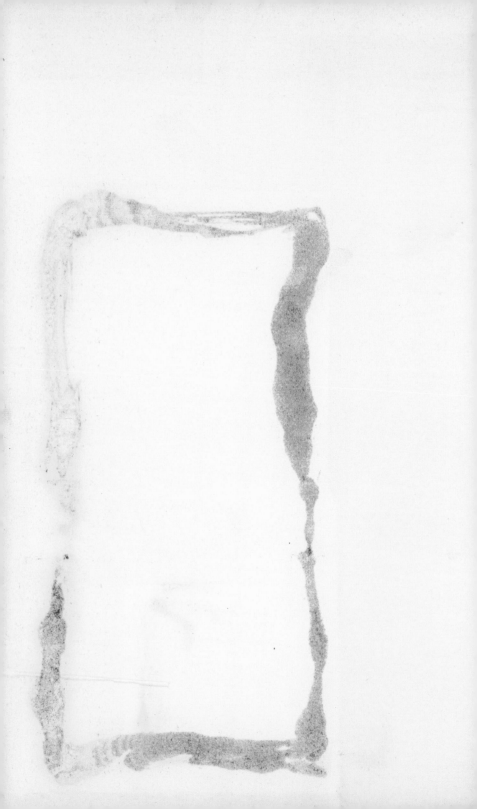

The Vikings in History

The Vikings in History

F. Donald Logan

BARNES & NOBLE BOOKS
TOTOWA, NEW JERSEY

First published in the USA 1983 by
BARNES & NOBLE BOOKS
81 ADAMS DRIVE
TOTOWA, NEW JERSEY, 07512

© F. Donald Logan 1983

Library of Congress Cataloging in Publication Data
Logan, F. Donald
   The Vikings in history.
   Includes index.
   1. Vikings.   I. Title
DL65.L63   1983   940'.04395   82-25533

ISBN 0-389-20384-X

For Patti and Jeff

Contents

Maps, illustrations and tables

Maps

Illustrations

(between pages 96 and 97)

The Jelling stone, erected by Harald Bluetooth in memory of his mother and father
Part of the Cuerdale Hoard, found near the River Ribble in Lancashire
The Kensington stone, an alleged Viking remain found in Minnesota
Two sides of a Norse penny, found at Goddard's farm, near Brookline in Maine
Thingvellir: the site of the Icelandic general assembly, the althing

(between pages 128 and 129)

Excavation of the Gokstad ship from a burial mound in Vestfold, Norway
Site of the largest house excavated at L'Anse aux Meadows, Newfoundland
A ring-headed pin of bronze excavated in a house site at L'Anse aux Meadows
Spindle whorl of soapstone from L'Anse aux Meadows
Stone lamp from the Viking site at L'Anse aux Meadows

Tables

Acknowledgements

The author and publishers would like to thank the copyright holders below for their kind permission to reproduce the following material:

Thingvellir, the Icelandic general assembly, by permission of Scandinavian Airlines System.

The Jelling stone, by permission of the Nationalmuseet, Copenhagen.

Excavation of the Gokstad ship, from Geoffrey Ashe (ed.), *The Quest for America* (Pall Mall Press 1971), reproduced by permission of The Phaidon Picture Library.

The Cuerdale Hoard, copyright the Trustees of the British Museum.

The Kensington stone, reproduced by permission of the Department of Anthropology, Smithsonian Institution (photo no. 38110 A).

Two sides of a Norse penny, copyright the Maine State Museum.

Photographs of the site at L'Anse aux Meadows, from Anne Stine Ingstad, *The Discovery of a Norse Settlement in America* (Universitets Forlaget 1977), and copyright Helge Ingstad.

Map 11, from R. A. Skelton, T. E. Marston, and G. D. Painter, *The Vinland Map and the Tartar Relation* (Yale University Press 1965), copyright © 1965 by Yale University.

Preface

A word of explanation to the reader for the intrusion by an historian of the late middle ages into the holy places of early medieval history.

Fewer epochs are of more genuine interest to the historian than the epoch of Viking-age Europe. Into the consciousness of western Europe came hordes of northmen, spilling out of the lands of Scandinavia, lands hitherto vaguely known and little considered. It is a period which invites the professional historian with other research interests to investigate its general lines of development, to search out results of recent specialized scholarship, and to identify the historical problems being addressed and still to be solved. It is a story worth telling, and the story told here is focused on the Viking expeditions, the Vikings on their way across seas, through river systems, and even overland; the Vikings abroad. The contact of the Vikings with the outside world during the period roughly 800 to 1050 has given a European – perhaps, some might say, even a world – dimension to their story and has given rise to the Viking age. Such a period, it is fervently hoped, can profit from a fresh look by an outsider.

Steering this outsider from perilous shoals and hidden reefs are good friends and faithful guides. Chief among these is Dr Janet Nelson, who read the text throughout and provided me with the benefit of her broad knowledge of the period, her acute historical judgement, and the encouragement needed to persevere. It is a debt only partially repaid by a much improved text. Professor Henry R. Loyn has read the manuscript twice for the publisher, and his perceptive comments and enthusiasm for the project are greatly appreciated. Parts of the text were generously read by Dr Marlyn Lewis, Mr A. F. O'Brien, and Dr David Smith.

Information concerning the Goddard coin was supplied by Dr Bruce J. Bourque of the Maine State Museum in Augusta, Maine. Numerous inquiries to the staff at the Emmanuel College Library were greeted promptly and cheerfully with accurate information, particularly by Cynthia J. Whealler and Judith K. Narosny. Infelicities of style persist despite the advice of Cynthia Jobin. Professor J. J. Scarisbrick, who originally suggested that I write this book, has shown enthusiasm for the project at every stage, and the publisher, Claire L'Enfant, has assisted me throughout with kindly forbearance and high professional expertise. The onus of proofreading and indexing has been eased by the kind assistance of Dorothy Walsh Fleming, a former student, and Pamela Johnson, a present student of this college.

The errors that remain – *errata et corrigenda residua* – are due to personal limitations of knowledge and (alas!) defects of character.

F. Donald Logan
Emmanuel College
Boston, Massachusetts

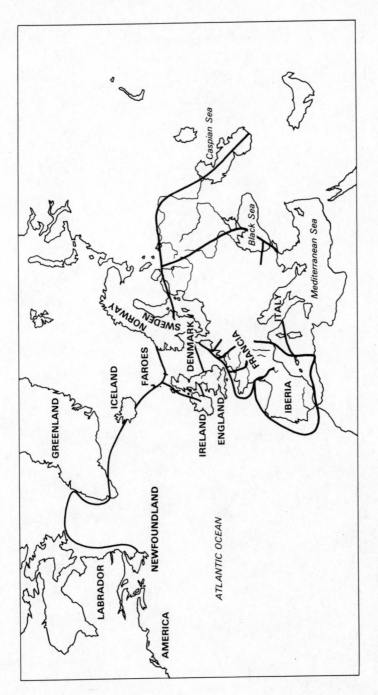

1   *The Viking expeditions*

1 The Vikings on the eve

A furore normannorum, libera nos, domine. (From the violence of the men from the north, O Lord, deliver us.)

This might well be taken as the epitaph chiselled by general historical opinion on the Viking gravestone. The phrase – there is absolutely no evidence that it was ever added to the monastic litanies – sums up the hostile treatment usually given to the Vikings by historians of the early middle ages: the wild Vikings proved a temporary threat to the progress of western civilization. They belong, it is said, on the periphery of events, far removed from the central events of the ninth, tenth, and early eleventh centuries. They were, like the Magyars and the Moors, irritants, negative and destructive, hostile to Francia, the historical centre of Europe at that time. The traditional story begins or, at least, rises to a high pinnacle with the coronation of Charlemagne at St Peter's in Rome on Christmas Day in the year 800. We are told variously that this event was the central point of the early middle ages, that it was the first attempt by the Germanic peoples to organize Europe, that it was the event which provides a focus for European history till the eleventh century and beyond. Political theorists have taken this event, however they may interpret it, as a landmark in the struggle between 'church and state' (to use the anachronism still, alas, alive among us). And, we are told, the main lines of European history follow. Charlemagne established an empire or, at least, a large area of western Europe under Frankish control: from the Danish March to central Italy. This so-called empire collapsed under his son and his grandsons. With the treaty of Verdun in 843 there began, so the story runs, the dismemberment of this empire, and within a hundred years the once united empire of Charlemagne had been fractured and left in hundreds of pieces, some tiny, others large, all virtually separate and autonomous units. Then the East Franks in Saxony slowly began to rebuild and Otto I took the imperial title in 962. His successors developed a strong East Frankish state; in 1049 this development reached its climax when Henry III placed Leo IX, who started the work of papal reform, on the papal throne. The promise of Charlemagne was now fulfilled. Thus, in this accounting, the story of European history from the beginning of the ninth century till the mid eleventh century is the story of the rise and fall of the Carolingian empire and the rise of its German successors. Who can doubt this?

Doubt should arise, for this traditional view has as its focus Francia; the rest of Europe, while not forgotten, is thrown out of focus and placed on the margin of events, peripheral to what was happening in the lands of Charlemagne and his successors. The nationalist historians of the nineteenth century, particularly the French and Germans, in search of their national origins have set the historiographical agenda for the twentieth century. Thus, this Charlemagne – Otto I – Henry III school of historical writing. The Viking invaders, to them, were merely a negative, destructive force which accelerated the decline of civilization in the west. Relying overmuch on the monastic chronicles, the nationalist historians seem to have forgotten the other destructive forces at play in the Europe of the time. What of the internecine wars among the Irish tribes or the Anglo-Saxon kingdoms or the Frankish peoples? The Vikings have become a convenient whipping boy.

This book argues that the traditional focus is misplaced: if there is to be a single focus, it should not be centred on the Carolingians and their successors but, rather, on the Scandinavian peoples of northern Europe, and on the peninsulas of the north where the dynamic forces of Europe were to be found. The Viking civilization of the north, vibrant, untamed, and raw, had a strong and unmistakable impact on much of the rest of Europe and on lands across seas and oceans. While Charlemagne was receiving the imperial crown in the year 800, the Vikings were harassing the coasts of England, Scotland, and Ireland and setting up bases in the Orkneys and the Western Isles. Before the death of Charlemagne in 814, they had interdicted the northward progress of the Franks. To the court of his son, Louis the Pious, there came with an embassy from Constantinople in 838 Vikings who had undoubtedly reached Byzantium through Russia. While the grandsons of Charles were carving out their petty kingdoms, destined to be carved into smaller and smaller pieces, the countryside of Francia was almost constantly raided by these people from the north. Within a hundred years of the death of Charlemagne the Vikings had set up kingdoms in Ireland, in the north and east of England, and in Russia as well as an overseas settlement in Iceland. These warrior–seamen of Scandinavia were to travel as far west as the shores of North America and as far east as the Volga basin and some even beyond.

An uncritical obsession with a European history with Francia and, later, the empire and the papacy at its centre has caused the historian to think of the Viking only in passing. This franco-centric view has, strangely enough, caused attention to be placed on the decline of a prematurely organized state with its tedious list of soubriqueted kings. The dynamic and vital forces in Europe are not to be found in a decaying civilization but rather in the exuberant, at times destructive, young warrior–seamen who sailed out of the fjords of the northern European peninsulas and whose legacy can be traced in lines through Normandy, Sicily, the Crusades, and an Anglo-Norman state whose laws have come to form the basis of legal systems in North America and elsewhere. Let us look to the north.

Scandinavia

It was from the northern European peninsulas that the Vikings came: from the Jutland peninsula and its easterly islands and from the Norwegian–Swedish peninsula and the Baltic islands offshore. The three lands from which they came – which we would now call Norway, Sweden, and Denmark – cover vast areas. If one leaves the northern tip of Scandinavia at Cape North and travels to Rome, one is only half-way when southern Denmark is reached. Yet, in a sense, this is misleading, for this land was not thickly settled in the Viking period: we are dealing with a very large area with a scattered population. These three places face the sea in different ways: the face of Denmark to the west and southwest; the face of Norway to the west and, so to speak, to the far west; and the face of Sweden to the east and southeast. If we are to look for a key to the geography of these places, it is in the mountains and fjords of Norway, the dense forestland of Sweden, and the size of Denmark.

Norway, a vast land, then as now mostly uninhabitable, extends over 1600 miles along its coast and 1100 direct miles from its southern tip, The Naze, to Cape North, well above the Arctic Circle. The same northwestern European highlands which can be seen in Donegal and across Scotland stretch through almost the full length

2   *Viking-age Scandinavia*

of this land, which looks like the upturned keel of a ship (thus, the name of these mountains, The Keel), and leave Norway with an average altitude of 500 metres above sea-level. Its western shore is punctuated by fjords; some of these long, deep-water inlets (for example, the Sognefjord) extend over a hundred miles into the interior. Fertile lands can be found in the southeast, in the lands near the waterways around the head of the Oslofjord and north from there on a line through Lake Mjøsa and the Osterdal and Gudbrandsdal valley systems to Trondheim. West of this fertile land is high plateau country reaching out towards the Atlantic and a coastline ragged, island-dotted, and indented by deep fjords. Fertile lands can also be found in narrow rims between the mountains and the sea and along narrow, glaciated valleys. The favourable Atlantic climate usually keeps the western fjords ice-free throughout the year; today the mean January temperature at Lofoten, above the Arctic Circle, is 24°C (43°F). Although access to Sweden was possible through tortuous mountain passes, the normal internal and external means of communication was over the seas. By sea, Bergen lies nearer to Scotland than to Sweden. Settlements were scattered along these fjords and, perhaps, there were also nucleated settlements in the southeast. From fjord settlement to fjord settlement it was the highway of the sea that joined people together. Any national (i.e., Norwegian) feeling would be a long time in becoming crystallized, and the political organization of these people would have to wait for Harald Finehair (c. 890). Even then, the extent of effective political control under him might have been limited only to parts of this large and sparsely settled land.

Much less mountainous than Norway, its neighbour Sweden had, at the beginning of the Viking period, a few large settlements. The one at Uppland, inhabited by the Swedes (Latin, *Suiones*), was centred on Old Uppsala. Its land formed the northern edge of the central European plain and, although at one time thickly forested, by the eighth century Uppland was sufficiently cleared to maintain its people. South of Uppland, separated by dense forests, Götaland lies in an area which contains perhaps the most fertile land on the peninsula. To the north of Uppland, again separated by forest and bogland, large areas of which were impenetrable, were the very thinly settled regions of Hälsingland and Medelpad, and beyond, in another world, the arctic regions of Norrland and Finnmark. The Baltic island of Gotland (to be carefully distinguished from the mainland Götaland), probably the ancestral homeland of the Goths who descended upon the Roman world in the late fourth century, was ideally situated along trade routes to the littoral of the Baltic and beyond to the heartland of what was to become Russia. Separated peoples all; their primary identification was local and particular, rather than national. Although Uppland was clearly the most powerful part of Sweden by the eighth century, the extent of the hegemony of its kings over the peoples of Gotland and Götaland is not clear.

Much more homogeneous geographically and politically was Denmark, consisting of the other northern peninsula, Jutland, and the islands, particularly Fyn and Zeeland, to the east. It should be remembered, also, that the extreme south of modern Sweden (Skäne, Halland, and Blekinge) belonged in this Danish orbit during the Viking period and for a long time thereafter. The neck of the peninsula, largely barren in our period, provided a barrier between the Danes and their southern neighbours the Saxons and the Slavs. Most of Denmark was fairly flat and lent itself, where cleared, to the growing of grain and the raising of livestock. Its maritime nature made fishing in the neighbouring waters a fruitful industry. In about the year 800 Denmark had a strong king in Godefred and was perhaps the most politically advanced of these northern European countries.

The Scandinavians inhabiting these lands lived mostly in scattered settlements and farmsteads, yet three major trading centres existed, one in each of these lands: Kaupang in Norway, Hedeby in Denmark, and Birka in Sweden. Situated on the western shore of the Oslofjord (*The Vik*), Kaupang was the smallest of the three. It was visited in the late ninth century by Ohthere, a Norwegian from Helgeland. He said that the place was called Sciringesheal and that it was a market. Its modern name, Kaupang, means a market. Recent archaeological evidence has clearly identified this site. The water-level has dropped two metres since Viking times, and aerial photography and a keen archaeological imagination are necessary to see in the modern remains a market-place situated on a bay and sheltered at its back by hills and at its front by islands and shoals, many of them then submerged but now visible. Excavations in the market and in the hinterland, particularly rich in graves of the Viking period, reveal objects from the British Isles, the Rhineland, and the eastern Baltic. The commodities traded at Kaupang probably included iron, soapstone, and possibly fish. Yet, Kaupang ought to be viewed more as a stopping-off point for traders on their way from Norway to the Danish town of Hedeby than as a terminal market.

Ohthere, a traveller from Norway, when he called at Kaupang, was, in fact, on his way, to Hedeby, five days' further journey. The largest of the towns of Scandinavia, Hedeby had a life almost coterminous with the Viking period. It probably came into existence in the late eighth century when three small communities combined at a point in the neck of the Jutland peninsula where a stream enters a cove of the Sleifjord. Extensive excavations since the late nineteenth century have revealed a town facing east towards the fjord, its back and sides protected by a semi-circular rampart, two-thirds of a mile long, which in the tenth century rose to a height of nearly ten metres. The sixty acres within the rampart contained dwelling places of both the stave-built (horizontal as well as vertical) and the wattle-and-daub varieties. In about 950 an Arab merchant, al-Tartushi, from the caliphate of distant Cordova, visited Hedeby and recorded his vivid impressions of the place.

Slesvig [i.e., Hedeby] is a large town at the other end of the world sea. Freshwater wells are to be found within the town. The people there, apart from a few Christians who have a church, worship Sirius. A festival of eating and drinking is held to honour their god. When a man kills a sacrificial animal, whether it be an ox, ram, goat, or pig, he hangs it on a pole outside his house so that passersby will know that he has made sacrifice in honour of the god. The town is not rich in goods and wealth. The staple food for the inhabitants is fish, since it is so plentiful. It often happens that a newborn infant is tossed into the sea to save raising it. Also, whenever they wish, women may exercise their right to divorce their husbands. An eye makeup used by both men and women causes their beauty never to fade but to increase. . . . Nothing can compare with the dreadful singing of these people, worse even than the barking of dogs.

How barbaric it all must have seemed to this man from the magnificent splendour of Islamic Spain. Did he know, one wonders, that it was the Danes, some perhaps from Hedeby itself, who, a century or so earlier, had sailed up the Guadalquivir and attacked Seville in the heartland of this mighty caliphate? Even at the time al-Tartushi was writing Hedeby's days were numbered. In the middle of the eleventh century it died: burned by Harald Hardrada in 1050, ravaged by Slavs in 1066, and, in the end, probably abandoned as the water-level receded.

Birka in central Sweden may have been the wealthiest of the northern trading centres. Although there is evidence of commercial connections between Birka and Dorestad in modern Holland and with the Rhineland, its main trade was with the east, particularly with Moslem traders whom Swedish merchants would meet among the Bulgars at the Volga Bend. Coins found from the Islamic east in excavated graves on the site at Birka are seven times more numerous than coins found from the west. Situated on an island in Lake Mälar on the way to the open sea from Uppsala and nearly fifty miles west of modern Stockholm, Birka had its rampart to its back and sides. The Black Earth, so called because human habitation has coloured the earth, was the settled area; over it a commanding hill stood watch. Over 2000 graves in the cemetery have provided archaeologists with the richest Viking site so far known. The demise of Birka, unlike Kaupang and Hedeby, came, it would seem, from neither plunder nor natural causes but occurred when its trade link with the Arabs was broken by Svyatoslav's assault upon the Bulgars at the Volga Bend in about 965.

Important as it is to stress the separate settlements of the north, the isolation of thinly settled areas from one another, and the sense of localness of the peoples, it would be a gross error to think of the Scandinavians as having nothing in common save their northern lands. They were united by links stronger than those of politics and frequent human commerce: they shared a common language, a common art, and a common religion.

Runic inscriptions of the eighth to the tenth centuries, which have been found in widely distant places in each of these lands, show a sameness of language. Spoken language, no doubt, differed from the written language and dialects of spoken language were inevitable, but these were the normal differences found in any language which is living and is used to communicate human needs and feelings. The primitive Nordic language (*dönsk tunga, vox danica*) was still in use among these Nordic peoples at the beginnings of the Viking age. The Vikings in Vinland and the Vikings at the Volga Bend would have been intelligible to one another. Only later did the *dönsk tunga* give rise to the distinct languages characteristic of Norway, Sweden, Denmark, and Iceland.

Likewise, a common art was shared by the Vikings in the north. Art historians try to refine our knowledge of Viking art and distinguish six different styles: Style III (Oseberg), Borre, its near contemporary Jelling, Mammen, Ringerike, and Urnes. The surviving examples of these styles undoubtedly represent only a small fraction of the artistic output of the Viking period. It would seem better to stress the similarities of these styles rather than their differences. No doubt dependent on earlier Germanic art and influenced by and, in turn, influencing Irish, Anglo-Saxon, and Carolingian art, the distinctive art of the Vikings was an applied art found principally on wood and stone and, to a lesser extent, on metal. The semi-naturalistic ornamentation of functional objects made use of motifs with animal heads and their ribbon-like bodies, which interlaced in patterns of slow curves. Examples have been found in places as far removed from one another as Oseberg in Norway, where there are the fine wood carvings of the ninth-century royal burial ship, Jelling in Jutland, where an exquisite silver goblet was found, and Källunge on Gotland, where a weather vane of graceful decorative design was discovered. Of course, local variations occurred, such as the preponderance of picture (i.e., representational) stones on the island of Gotland, but the general line is clear: a basic Viking art, common in motif and design, throughout Scandinavia.

The pantheon of gods in the Scandinavian religion was peopled by anthropomorphic deities, each with his own symbol: among them, Odin, the god of the aristocrats, with a spear; Thor, the thundering god of the peasants, with a hammer; Frey, the fertility god, with an erect phallus. Their cult was not uniform: Thor rather than Odin had the place of honour in the temple at Old Uppsala as described by Adam of Bremen. The slain warriors of Odin, it was widely believed, were conducted by the valkyries, those princesses of legend, to Valhalla, their heaven-like abode. Votive sacrificial rites were held usually in the open air, in groves, near holy trees, although occasionally a farm building (*hof*) might have been used for convivial rites. With expected local variations, with regional emphasis on different gods of a common pantheon – local 'saints', as it were – and with the scattered nature of the archaeological evidence, it is still possible to attribute to the Scandinavians a religion common to them and, although some analogues with the religions of other Germanic peoples can be found, a religion peculiar to them.

The law system prevailing in these northern lands is known to us chiefly from later codified collections and by overly romantic attempts of whiggish historians to look for the origins of northern European democratic institutions. Throughout Scandinavia, it seems clear, the social distinction between king, *jarls* (noblemen), freemen, freedmen, and *thralls* (slaves) had an effect on the general administration of society. In a society with this social stratification and with scattered settlements what else might one expect than for the local men of property (the power elite) to make local decisions – their assembly was a *thing* – and for the greater men of a region to make regional decisions in a *thing* of that region? This pattern prevailed during the Viking age throughout Scandinavia and its colonies in the North Atlantic. It is impossible to say that the substance of law was uniform throughout the Viking world: it probably was not, given the ability of the powerful men locally and regionally to make decisions and given, too, the variety of precedents thus emerging from each *thing*. Outlawry, probably with similar, if not always exactly the same, consequences, existed as a penalty throughout the north. In West Götaland the law of manslaughter left the initiative in prosecution to the deceased person's heir. The laws of Gotland contained a schedule of fines, curious in its scaling, for the touching of a woman: for touching her wrist or ankle, 4 ounces of silver; her elbow or her leg between knee and calf, $2\frac{2}{3}$ ounces; her breast, 1 ounce; higher above the knee, the 'touch dishonourable' or the 'fool's clasp', no fine payable since most women tolerate it when it goes that far. Diverse as specific laws such as these might have been throughout the Viking world, the same basic procedural system did prevail and Scandinavian laws, when they appeared in fuller light in the thirteenth and fourteenth centuries, modified by new influences including canon law, reflected a common past.

The northern explosion

The eruption of the Vikings out of their homelands in the late eighth and early ninth centuries remains a puzzling historical phenomenon. Without exaggerating the numbers involved we must say that it surely was more than an accident of history that in the 790s Norwegians were attacking the eastern and even the western coasts of Britain, the islands to the north and west, and Ireland; that the Danes between 800 and 810 repulsed the expansionist forces of Charlemagne and began to extend themselves along the Frisian coast; and that the Swedes had already crossed the Baltic into Latvia and by the early ninth century had travelled as far as Lake Ladoga. It was as if a fierce convulsion went through these northern lands, followed by other convulsions, and for nearly two centuries Scandinavia sent streams of emigrants to the west and south and east, first as seasonal raiders, then as more permanently situated raiders, and, finally, as settlers. How does one explain this phenomenon? The historian faces here an historical problem beyond the power of his sources and his talents to provide an absolute answer. He is thrown into the penumbra where partial evidence and assumption meet to produce conclusions far from certain, conclusions which must be couched in subjunctive moods, and where we are, unhappily, never free from nagging doubt. Some might call this an uncharacteristically humble position for the historian. So be it.

The word 'cause' at this stage must be stricken from the historian's vocabulary and replaced by the more convenient 'factor'. That there was a population factor involved in the Viking explosion has been the view of many historians since the late nineteenth century. Scandinavian society was a male-dominated society; its idea of virility included the siring of large numbers of children, particularly male children, and an heroic sense of adventure connected with the seas and the discovery of new places overseas. If we can believe the somewhat hostile account of Adam of Bremen, polygamy was widespread in Sweden, limited only by one's wealth. Other accounts suggest that chieftains might have had as many as forty women. It does not require much imagination to see the effect this could have on population growth. A man might have sired twenty sons, ten of whom survived to manhood, each of whom in turn might have sired twenty sons with ten surviving, etc. Harald Finehair had at least nine sons – some accounts say twenty – who reached manhood; his son Eric Bloodaxe had at least eight surviving sons. And so it would go. Or, rather, so it would go till the crunch point was reached, which, as population grows in this pattern, could happen swiftly and with little warning. It must be quickly added that the relation of male polygamy to population growth need not in itself be dramatic, for the number of children depends in the final analysis on the number of impregnated women and not impregnating men. Yet, even when this is considered, in a society, such as the Viking society, which was male-dominated and in which a man could have many wives simultaneously and serially, polygamy must be considered a positive, if not predominant, factor in the population picture.

Population growth need not be dependent on polygamy: even a

society wholly monogamous in its marriage customs, which the Viking society clearly was not, can know the pressures of increasing numbers of people. Other elements become involved. The Viking age in Scandinavia witnessed optimal climate, which, in turn, enabled much land, previously used for grazing, to be used for growing crops, some for animal consumption but a remarkably increased amount, particularly high in protein content, for human consumption. New farming implements (for example, the mouldboard wheel plough) led to more productive use of tillage land. At the same time attempts were made to use new lands, less favourable lands, particularly uplands; also, attempts to clear (i.e., assart) forestland were probably made. Such changes both stimulated and responded to population growth and, at the point in time when they failed to satisfy the needs of this burgeoning population, the next step would have been emigration. (Who can forget the millions who, faced with hunger, fled Ireland in the late 1840s?) A thousand years before Malthus was to describe emigration as a safety valve for excessive population, the reality seems to have occurred in the lands of Scandinavia.

Emigration creates its own inner dynamic. Those who leave in the first instance to search for a means of subsistence – even if getting it requires looting and killing – might intend theirs to be a temporary, seasonal emigration. Before long overseas colonies become established, to which not only those fleeing hunger and want but also the adventurers, outlaws, and political exiles would go. The momentum was already there.

No doubt, the existence of known trade routes facilitated some of this outward expansion. Knowledge of these trade routes gave rise to knowledge of foreign places. Remote though Scandinavia was, its peoples had contacts with their neighbours. External trade did exist, yet its importance as a factor in Scandinavian migrations of the ninth and tenth centuries should not be exaggerated. Most of the evidence refers to the Swedes and their mercantile connections in the east – Birka was at one end of a trade route that extended to the Volga – and, to a lesser extent, to the Danes and their contacts with Frisia, especially with Dorestad. This latter contact became intensified by the construction of the Danevirke at the neck of the Jutland peninsula. This earthwork, in places five metres high and thirty-eight metres wide, was to serve as a defensive barrier against attacks from the south and as a road joining the River Trene in the east with Sleifjord in the west at Hedeby. A portage of only eight

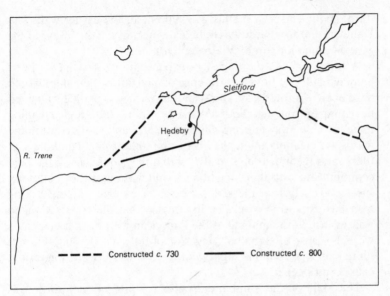

3   *Danevirke*, c. *800*

miles replaced the long voyage around Jutland. The inclusion of the construction of the Danevirke as an element in the increased trade of the early ninth century argues from the assumptions that it was constructed at one time in the early ninth century as a result of an order of King Godefred in 808 and that its existence intensified the Danish trading connection with Dorestad in Frisia. The *Frankish Chronicle* for the year 808 states that

> Godefred determined to protect the border of his kingdom with Saxony. To this end he had constructed a defensive rampart extending from an inlet in the east (Ostarsalt) as far as the sea on the west along the northern bank of the Ejder River. The rampart was interrupted by only one gate for the use of horses and carriages.

It has become easy to use only this foreign source and, thus, to attribute the Danevirke to Godefred and its construction to the opening decades of the ninth century. The careful investigations of modern dendrochronologists give us a fuller view which reveals three distinct steps in the construction of this earthwork. As early as about 730 a first wall was built; another wall was built about 800 and is referred to by Danish archaeologists as the Kovirke; and a third, about 960, was mainly a rebuilding of the earlier wall. The Danevirke of Godefred might be evidence, in a minor way, to the general phenomenon of Viking emigration.

Without ships the Viking expansion would have been unimaginable; without a knowledge of navigation their ships would have been of limited use. The Scandinavians were people who lived near and by the sea. The very name Viking, although meaning raider or adventurer during this period, probably has its root in the word *vik*, meaning inlet; they were the 'inlet folk'. The boat was their natural companion and ally: with it they could fish, trade, and communicate with their neighbours, and without it they could not survive. To say that the sailing vessel was a cause of the Viking overseas expansion would be like saying that the covered wagon was a cause of the making of the American west or that elephants were the cause of Hannibal's invasion of Italy. The Viking ship was quite simply a *conditio sine qua non* for this outward migration: causes run deeper.

The skill of the shipbuilders and seamen of the north was legendary. About AD 90 Tacitus, the Roman historian, remarked on the vessels of the north:

Their ships are different. With a prow at either end they can easily land. Also, they do not use sails nor do they fasten their oars in banks along the sides.

This absence of a sail at a time when sails, long since in use in the Mediterranean, were being used off the coasts of Gaul is strange. It is usual to say that the Scandinavians came late to the use of the sail, that the sail was a development of the seventh or, more likely, the eighth century, and that the full sail came into use only at the end of the eighth century, thus making possible the Viking raids which began at that time. This may well be true, but it is based on the negative conclusion, always the most hazardous kind of historical conclusion, that the sail was not used by Scandinavian seamen until this period because no evidence for its earlier existence survives among the sparse extant sources. Fresh evidence could overturn this conclusion. Also, it should be borne in mind that in Scandinavia the development of sails did not replace the rowing boat: the two coexisted throughout the Viking period and for a long time thereafter. The question that remains must be: how long did they coexist before the Viking period? The picture stones of Gotland provide early evidence, even from the seventh century, that the sail was in use in the Baltic Sea. It would be a rash historian indeed who would state categorically that the sail was unknown in the north before the seventh century. Yet, whatever its prior history, by the end of the eighth century the sailing vessel with a developed keel existed among the Scandinavians and made possible their overseas expeditions.

Archaeological excavations in the past one hundred years have revealed a number of Viking ships: the classic examples are the Tune ship, probably of the late ninth century, excavated in 1867 from a burial mound on the eastern side of the Oslofjord; the Gokstad ship, again probably late ninth century, excavated in 1880 at a burial site on the western side of the same fjord; and the Oseberg ship, also on the western side of that fjord, which was found in 1903. These three famous ships, all exhibited at the Viking Ship Museum at Bygdøy near Oslo, were burial ships, whose ritual purpose was to speed the departed to another world. The text of *Beowulf* speaks of the ship–funeral of a Scandinavian chieftain:

There at the quay stood a ring–prowed ship,
The radiant and eager ship of the lord.
They laid down the beloved lord,
The giver of rings, in the bosom of the ship.
The lord lay by the mast. They brought from afar
Many great treasures and costly trappings.
I never heard of a ship so richly furnished as this,
With weapons of war, armour of battle,
Swords and corslets. Many treasures lay
Piled on his breast.

Although this text does not refer to a burial in an earth mound, it reflects the common motif of the great man, his life here over, being borne by ship to paradise. It is in the ships still preserved in hundreds of burial barrows scattered throughout the north that we may find answers to many of our questions about the types and the dating of the Viking ships. Another form of archaeological activity raised five Viking ships from the muddy bottom of the Roskildefjord at Skuldelev in Denmark in 1962, but more of these later.

There was no such thing as *the* Viking ship: there were, indeed, many kinds of Viking ship, varying not only in size (from about six metres to about twenty-five metres) but also in means of power (oars or sail/oars) and in purpose (local, North Atlantic, fishing, commerce, warfare). The classic features of the Viking sailing ships can be seen in the Gokstad ship: light in the water, graceful to the eye, speedy at full sail, and easy to beach. This virtually complete Viking ship was found by archaeologists under a five-metre mound at Gokstad. It was preserved by the blue potter's clay in which it was buried and with which it was filled. Although probably buried in the late ninth century, the Gokstad ship could have been fifty years old at that time, which would mean that it could be a ship of the early Viking period. The ship measures 23.33 metres long, 5.25 metres broad amidship, and 1.95 metres from the keel to a line from starboard to port gunwale amidship. Built entirely of oak, except for the decking, mast, and yards, she probably weighed as much as 18 tonnes and probably drew 90 to 95 centimetres, a very shallow draught. The most remarkable part of this ship is her keel; carved from a single oak timber, it measures 17.6 metres long and tapers in depth from 42 centimetres amidship to 37 centimetres at its ends. The oak tree from which the keel was shaped must have been at least 25 metres high and, of necessity, straight. Craftsmen fashioned this keel so that it formed a gentle arc about 25 centimetres deeper in the centre than fore and aft and they created thereby a shallow ship. The pressure of water against the keel countered the pressure of wind on the sail and, thus, the keel kept the sailing vessel from capsizing. Once the keel was laid, then the bow and stern posts, each a single piece of oak, were affixed to it by wooden nails. With the keel and endposts in place, it appears that the siding was then attached to them and, only after that, nineteen frames and cross-beams were stretched across the ship to keep the sidings in place. Each side was constructed of sixteen strakes (planks), each overlapping the one below it (i.e., clinker-built). The oar-strake on each side had sixteen circular oar-holes, which could be closed by wooden shutters when the ship was under sail. Above the topmost strake a thick gunwale was placed. A shield-rack along the gunwale permitted thirty-two shields to be hung overlapping on the outside: the remains of all sixty-four shields were found at the Gokstad site. Decking was placed on, but not attached to, the cross-beams. The ship was steered by a long rudder, which was not placed at the bow but, rather, was fastened to a piece of wood, called the wart, on the starboard (steer-board) quarter. The mast has not survived in its original state, and its height and, consequently, the height of the sail are not known with any certainty. Whatever its precise height –

somewhere between 10 metres and 13 metres – the mast was set into a heavy housing on the keel amidship; from this housing it could be removed as conditions required. The sail was rectangular in shape or, perhaps, close to being a square (possibly 11 metres square). Probably checked or striped and made of coarse wool, the sail hung from a yard; lines attached from the bottom of the sail to points along the gunwale provided the necessary ability to reach (i.e., sail across the wind) and to tack (i.e., sail on the wind).

A replica of this magnificent ship was made in 1892–3 – its oak keel-timber had to be transported from Canada – and under Captain Magnus Andersen *The Viking* as she was called sailed from Bergen on 30 April 1893 and twenty-eight days later arrived at Newfoundland. Captain Andersen praised the lightness of the ship in the water, comparing her to a seagull. Her flexibility permitted the hull-frame to twist as much as 15 centimetres from its true shape. The side rudder, he felt, was infinitely preferable to a stern rudder for this kind of ship. The Gokstad replica handled well in adverse weather, and at top speed she was as fast as contemporary cargo steamers, averaging on 15 and 16 May a speed of 9.3 knots over 223 sea miles and attaining speeds of 11 knots. Oars were used only in becalmed waters and in places (for example, narrow parts of fjords) where the sail could not be used easily.

Very large ships were occasionally built during the Viking period. The most famous of these, the *Long Serpent*, was built by Olaf Tryggvason, king of Norway, near Trondheim probably in 998. Contemporary poets lauded her, and she quickly sailed into the sea of Scandinavian legend. Centuries later Snorri Sturluson, the Icelandic historian, using earlier poetic material, described in a memorable passage in *Heimskringla* the building of this dragon-style Viking longship:

The winter after King Olaf came from Halogaland he had a great vessel built at Ladehammer, which was larger than any ship in the country and the beam-knees of which are still to be seen. The length of the keel that rested upon the grass was seventy-four ells. Thorberg Skafhog was the name of the man who was the master builder of the ship; but there were many others besides – some to fell wood, some to shape it, some to make nails, some to carry timber. All that was used was of the best. The ship was long and broad and high-sided and strongly timbered. While they were planking the ship, it happened that Thorberg had to go home to his farm upon some urgent business, and, as he remained there a long time, the ship was planked up on

both sides when he came back. In the evening the king went out with
Thorberg to see how the vessel looked, and everyone said that never was
there seen so large and so beautiful a ship of war. Then the king returned to
the town. Early next morning the king returned with Thorberg to see the
ship. The carpenters were there before them, but all were standing idle with
their arms crossed. The king asked, 'What is the matter?' They said that the
ship was ruined, for somebody had gone from stem to stern and cut one
deep notch after the other down one side of the planking. When the king
came nearer, he saw it was so and said with an oath, 'The man shall die who
has ruined the vessel out of envy, if he can be discovered, and I shall bestow
a great reward on whoever finds him out.'

'I can tell you, king,' said Thorberg, 'who has done this.'

'I don't think,' replied the king, 'that anyone is so likely to find this out as
you are.'

Thorberg said, 'I will tell you, king, who did it. I did it myself.'

The king said, 'You must restore it all to the same condition as before or
your life shall pay for it.'

Then Thorberg went and chipped the planks until the deep notches were
all smoothed and made even with the rest. The king and all present declared
that the ship was much handsomer on the side of the hull which Thorberg
had chipped. The king bade him to shape the other side in the same way,
and afterwards he gave him great thanks for the improvement. Thorberg
was the master builder of the ship until she was entirely finished. This ship
the king had built after the fashion of the ship he had captured in
Halogaland, but this new ship was larger and more carefully put together in
all her parts. She looked like a dragon, and the king named her the *Long
Serpent* and the other the *Short Serpent*. The *Long Serpent* had thirty-four
benches for rowers. The head and the arched tail were as high as in
sea-going ships. This ship was the best and most costly ever made in
Norway.

Wide berth must be given here to poetic licence and to the
conventions of saga 'history': the ship thus described would have
been of exceptional length, probably 37 metres, longer than any
other Viking ship now known. Yet it is clear that Olaf Tryggvason
near the end of the tenth century built an impressive Viking
longship.

The five wrecks rescued from the Roskildefjord near Skuldelev
by a remarkable feat of underwater archaeology demonstrate
plainly the varied nature of Viking ships. In 1957 frogmen
discovered that what had been thought to be a fifteenth-century
wreck was, in fact, something quite different: a stone pile 50 metres
long and 14 metres wide which, when the encrustations were

washed off by means of pressurized fire hoses, were found to be covering the wreckage of five Viking ships of the early eleventh century. They had been laden down with boulders and sunk in such a way as to block entrance to the harbour of Roskilde. The ships were two warships (Wrecks 2 and 5), two cargo boats (Wrecks 1 and 3), and one small coastal vessel (Wreck 6). (Note that there is no Wreck 4.) Of these Wreck 2 is the largest and, indeed, it is the largest Viking ship yet discovered: 28 metres long and probably about 5 metres wide amidship. Wreck 1 is the larger of the two cargo boats and probably plied the North Atlantic route. A deep vessel which drew about 1.5 metres with a full load, she had a clearly defined cargo space amidship and had quarter decks fore and aft. The smaller cargo boat (Wreck 3) might have been used on the Baltic trade route, while the smallest of all these ships (Wreck 5) might have seen service as a fishing or ferry boat. The Skuldelev ships provide us with a vivid reminder that *the* Viking ship did not exist.

The Scandinavian seamen had a common-sense method of navigation. On the open seas they sailed latitudinally, taking their bearings from the fixed points of sun and polar star. As veterans of the seas they could easily identify coastal fish and birds. Their practical powers of observation permitted them to 'smell' land. Longitudinal navigation in the open sea seemed beyond them; they sailed along a fixed latitude until making landfall and then would sail north or south. In arctic areas there are known to exist mirages which by light refraction extend the horizon beyond the 'real horizon' of a few miles to the 'mirage horizon' of forty miles or more. Such arctic mirages, unlike desert mirages, reflect real things. The Vikings sailing in far northern waters might have 'seen' further than the real horizon, but, even if they did (which is far from proved), their navigation could not rely on the chance meeting of the forces necessary for an arctic mirage. Even with their refined navigational and sailing skills the Vikings occasionally experienced disaster in the face of treacherous seas. Eric the Red sailed from Iceland to Greenland, according to the saga, in a convoy of twenty-five ships; some turned back, some foundered and were lost, and only fourteen arrived safely at their new settlement.

These skills and these ships made the Scandinavians ready to sail west to the islands of the North Atlantic, south to the lands of the Franks and their neighbours, and east by river and portage to the world of Byzantium and Islam. Sail on.

Selected further reading

Even in English the literature is vast. An excellent comprehensive study is Gwyn Jones, *A History of the Vikings,* Oxford University Press 1968; also of considerable value despite its age is T. D. Kendrick, *A History of the Vikings*, Frank Cass 1930. Although in serious need of revision, Johannes Brøndsted, *The Vikings*, Penguin 1965, is of particular use for its archaeological summaries. Other general books with archaeological and artistic emphases are Holger Arbman, *The Vikings*, Thames & Hudson 1961, and Eric Oxenstierna, *The Norsemen*, Studio Vista 1966. A summary account in a larger setting is D. M. Wilson, *The Vikings and Their Origins: Scandinavia in the First Millenium*, Thames & Hudson 1980. Although published for the British Museum exhibition on the Vikings, James Graham-Campbell and Dafydd Kidd, *The Vikings*, British Museum Publications 1980, is not a catalogue but, rather, a generously illustrated book with chapters on such 'museum subjects' as settlement, gods, dress, coins, and crafts. For a series of useful essays see P. H. Sawyer, *The Age of the Vikings,* 2nd edn, Edward Arnold 1971. A valuable analytical study of Viking society is P. G. Foote and D. M. Wilson, *The Viking Achievement,* Sidgwick & Jackson 1970.

For introductions to specific topics the following books will be useful: for art D. M. Wilson and O. Klindt-Jensen, *Viking Art*, 2nd edn, Allen & Unwin 1980; for religion E. O. G. Turville-Petre, *Myth and Religion of the North*, Weidenfeld & Nicolson 1964, and H. R. Ellis Davidson, *Gods and Myths of Northern Europe*, Penguin 1964; and for ships A. W. Brøgger and H. Shetelig, *Viking Ships, their ancestry and evolution,* Oslo: Dreyer 1951, and Sawyer, chapter 4.

2 The first raids on the British Isles and their aftermath

' . . . and the heathen came'. The Vikings were not the first foreigners nor, for that matter, the first heathens to attack the British Isles. They were much like the Romans and the Anglo-Saxons before them – heathen, exploitive, persistent – but unlike their invading predecessors the Vikings eventually became assimilated. Moreover, their horizons were different: they reached Ireland and other parts of the British Isles (and places beyond) untouched by these earlier invaders. Unlike the Roman and Anglo-Saxon invaders, the Vikings also had the misfortune, as they would have seen it, of having their deeds reported by a uniformly hostile 'press'. These unlettered Vikings left no contemporary written accounts of these events: nothing left to challenge the native annalists and chroniclers, who naturally viewed these invasions with fear and horror. Bearing this in mind, let us follow the course of the Vikings and their ships through the waters west of Scandinavia.

It is useful to make the assumption that the Norwegian raiders attacked England first and, only afterwards, Scotland and its Northern and Western Isles, and Ireland, in that order. There is a neatness to this scenario that recommends it, a geographical logic that is satisfied by seeing the Vikings working their way from the east coast of England, round the top of Scotland, and into the Irish Sea. The evident logic of the situation might tempt us to infer that a master strategy was at work here, that there were co-ordinated raiding missions, that the raiders were in close communication with one another, and that season by season, in a planned, systematic fashion, they exploited the coasts of the British Isles. We suffer in these considerations from a scarcity of sources for these early years. What unrecorded contacts there might have been before the event described in the *Anglo-Saxon Chronicle* for the year 789, no one knows. And no one knows if in fact the pattern which has been assumed was the actual pattern. It might be profitable to assemble here the earliest known dates for these initial raids on the British Isles: between 786 and 793 Portland in Dorset, in 793 Lindisfarne, in 794 Jarrow, in 795 Iona and Lambay (an island near Dublin). Other attacks, no doubt, went unrecorded. The Western Isles probably served as the base for the attack on Lambay; and we may never know to what extent the Welsh coast was harassed or when the Vikings first raided the Irish mainland and the Isle of Man. The picture that does emerge is that in the last decade of the eighth century a number of Viking attacks with perhaps little co-ordination were made against the islands off the northwest coast of Europe.

England

Three recorded incidents constitute the sum of the known raids by the Vikings on England at the beginning of the Viking period. A reading of the *Anglo-Saxon Chronicle* must strike even the most casual reader with the extent and frequency of the violence wrought by the Anglo-Saxons against one another. With this as a backdrop the three early Viking raids might not seem unusual except for the fact that the attackers were foreigners and heathens. Yet, they were profoundly significant incidents, for they heralded the beginning of what can only be called the Scandinavian period in English history. Even the chronicler recognized this, however dimly, when he said that the attack in Dorset was the first time that the Vikings' ships had come to England. It was not the last. After these initial raids a period of forty years free from Viking raids on England – but scarcely free from internal violence – followed; then came the Danes. The first Vikings to come were, we are told, Norwegians, but even this bears some further consideration.

For all of these early incidents the major, although not the only, source is the *Anglo-Saxon Chronicle*. Something of a misnomer, the chronicle is, in fact, a number of chronicles drawn together in Wessex during King Alfred's reign, sometime after 892, into one major chronicle written in Old English; it exists now in seven versions. Although the chronicle was taken from earlier annals, it is not possible to identify these and, therefore, it is not possible to establish their reliability. The Alfredian compiler (or compilers) knew of the early Viking raids only through these unknown sources and, of course, wrote a hundred years after the events. With this *caveat* in mind let us turn to each of these incidents in order.

4 *Early Viking attacks on the British Isles*

789   In this year King Brihtric married Offa's daughter Eadburh. And in
      his days there came for the first time three ships of Northmen. The
      reeve rode out to meet them and tried to force them to go to the
      king's residence, for he did not know what they were; and they slew
      him. Those were the first ships of Danish men which came to the land
      of the English.

Three other versions of the Chronicle seem to indicate that the
northmen were from Hörthaland, which is in western Norway. The
Annals of St Neots identifies the place where they landed as
Portland (Dorset). Æthelweard says that the slain reeve was called
Beaduheard and that he rode to Portland from Dorchester with a
few men under the mistaken impression that the strangers were
merchants. Several questions arise from these accounts. The first
has to do with the dating of this event. The chronicler puts this entry
under the year 787, but one should read 789, for the chronicle at
this point is two years out of synchronization. He simply says that it
happened during the reign of Brihtric, a West Saxon king who
reigned from 786 to 802. The events at Lindisfarne in 793 are the
next Viking raids described in the Chronicle. These must have
followed the incident on the south coast, since the Dorset attack was
called the 'first'. It seems safe, then, to conclude that the southern
attack took place sometime between 786 and 793.

   It is almost universally agreed that the attackers at Dorset were
Norwegians, but the question of their identity should not, on that
account, be passed over in silence. What do the texts say? All
versions of the *Anglo-Saxon Chronicle* identify them as 'northmen'
and 'Danish men'; three add that they were 'of Hæredalande'.
Æthelweard calls them 'Danes'. What evidence is there for
considering them Norwegians? Simply that three versions of the
chronicle indicate that they came from Hæredalande. These three
versions (D, E, and F) are closely related and should not be
considered in this context as three separate accounts, but merely
one. The usual translation and interpretation is that Hæredalande is
Hörthaland in western Norway. Even if this is true – and it is not at
all clear that it must be – one's mind boggles in trying to determine
how this information could have been acquired. Were formal
introductions exchanged on a Dorset beach? Who acted as
interpreter? And were not the reeve *and his men* slain by the
strangers? There is also the puzzling matter of this having been an
attack on the *south* coast. This location does not fit in with what we

know of other Norwegian attacks: the northeast of England, Scotland, the Isles, Ireland, etc. It seems more probable that raiders along the English south coast would have been Danes. The subsequent Danish attacks were in these parts and in these waters: Frisia in Holland, the east coast of England, and, through the English channel, the south coast of England and the west coast of Francia.

No one can dispute that the other two early raids on England were by Norwegians.

793   In this year dire portents appeared over Northumbria and sorely frightened the people. They consisted of immense whirlwinds and flashes of lightning, and fiery dragons were seen flying in the air. A great famine immediately followed these signs, and a little later in the same year, on 8 June, the ravages of heathen men miserably destroyed God's church on Lindisfarne with plunder and slaughter.

This incident more than the previous incident in the south (given, perhaps, undue emphasis by a Wessex compiler) marked the true beginning of the Viking assaults on Britain. The earlier account of the event at Dorset made no mention of plunder and uncontrolled slaughter: the strangers killed the reeve and his men. The attack on Lindisfarne was an attack on both the body and soul of Christian England. Simeon of Durham, writing in the early twelfth century but apparently using as a source an earlier northern version of the *Anglo-Saxon Chronicle* no longer extant, likened the Vikings in their attack on Lindisfarne to 'stinging hornets' and 'ravenous wolves'; they slaughtered priests and nuns and destroyed everything in sight, including the holy relics, and took with them the treasures of the church and even some monks as slaves. Knowledge of this unexpected attack came to the court of Charlemagne, where Alcuin of York, the most distinguished Englishman of his time, was the educational adviser to the Frankish king. Alcuin responded not once but seven times in different letters to the news of this attack: three times to Æthelred, King of the Northumbrians, once to Æthelhard, Archbishop of Canterbury, to the monks of Wearmouth-Jarrow, to the Bishop of Lindisfarne, and to a priest at Lindisfarne. 'It has been nearly three hundred and fifty years', he wrote in one of these letters, 'that we and our fathers have lived in this most beautiful land and never before has such a terror appeared in Britain and never was such a landing from the sea thought possible.' The cause, Alcuin moralized, was the failure of the monks to live up to their monastic ideal; God was punishing them for their unfaithfulness to Him. Allowing for the rhetoric of the moralist, the possible distortion of events in the transmission, and the piety of a native Northumbrian, it still remains abundantly clear that this event struck deep to the heart of Alcuin, not merely for what it was but also for what it portended.

The third incident occurred at Jarrow where in 681 Benedict Biscop had founded a sister monastery to Wearmouth.

794   And the heathens ravaged in Northumbria and plundered Ecgfrith's monastery at Donemuthan. One of their leaders was killed there, and also some of their ships were broken to bits by stormy weather, and many of the men were drowned there. Some reached the shore alive and were immediately killed at the mouth of the river.

Simeon of Durham identified the monastery as Jarrow on the River Don, a tributary of the Tyne. He confirmed the failure of the heathen Vikings and attributed it to the intercession of St Cuthbert. They were not invincible, then, nor were the Christians merciful and sparing.

In the broad panorama of the Viking age these three English incidents must appear as very minor indeed. They were important because they drew the lines between Christian and pagan, between attacked and attackers, and pointed to two centuries in which England must be seen in the broader, north European context. The Danes were to come in the 830s, but that story belongs to another chapter.

Scotland and the Isles

The view has been presented by some that the attacks on the northeast of England were, in fact, by-products of the colonizing by western Norwegians of Orkney and Shetland in the last half of the eighth century. The evidence for this view is far from persuasive; in fact, it is non-existent. A number of archaeological excavations – the best known at Jarlshof (Shetland) and at Birsay (Orkney) – have produced some early Viking graves, which do not permit precise dating: the safest description of the earliest is 'about 800', permitting a margin on either side. The place-name evidence is scarcely as strong as the archaeological. It is best used for describing patterns of settlement and can have only a very limited use in precise dating. The attempt of some place-name scholars to push the period of settlement backwards to the last quarter of the eighth century has no support. Although Orcadian and Shetland piety might have it otherwise, the safer approach in this matter is still the traditional: there were Viking attacks against these northern islands in the last decade of the eighth century. These attacks belong in the wider context of the well-documented raids during the same decade on Northumbria, the Western Isles, and Ireland. According to the *Annals of Ulster* under the year 794 there was 'a laying waste by the heathen of all the islands of Britain'. Perhaps, as is sometimes said, the Vikings used Orkney and Shetland as bases for the westerly raids. This assertion, for which there is again no substantial evidence, does have the value of satisfying some demands of geographical and even military-naval logic.

The Venerable Bede described the Orkney Islands as being at the back (*a tergo*) of Britain, 'where it lies open to the endless ocean'. The two North Atlantic archipelagos – Orkney (about seventy islands and 389 square miles) and Shetland (about 100 islands and 558 square miles) – lie almost like a loose string of pearls north of Scotland. From the shores of Caithness to the southern tip of Orkney the distance is only six and a half miles across the Pentland Firth at the narrowest point; from the higher elevations on Rousay in Orkney one can see Fair Isle, midway to the Shetlands; and from Fair Isle the southern tip of Shetland, Sumburgh Head, is visible. These islands were inhabited by non-Celtic Picts in the eighth century. Christians since the late sixth century, these Picts had neither vanished, as some would have it, nor were vanishing when the Vikings came. These descendants of the builders of chamber-tombs and brochs were either quickly assimilated or just as quickly destroyed by the Vikings. The similarities in Pictish and Norse houses would support an assimilation thesis. In any case, when Ragnald and his sons came from Norway to Orkney in about the middle of the ninth century, the implication was that they were going to a place safe from their enemies. This argues to a settled Scandinavian presence before that time, a situation consistent with the archaeological evidence for this period. The excavations at Jarlshof between 1934 and 1952 have revealed a fairly full picture of a Viking settlement from the early ninth century to the thirteenth or fourteenth century. For the very early period a small farming community has been uncovered. Its principal building was a 'longhouse' twenty-two metres by six metres; its roof was held up by posts and rafters; its walls bowed inward at the ends and it had four outbuildings including a byre and a smithy. The remains at Birsay, although less comprehensive, reveal a cathedral and a bishop's residence dating from the eleventh and twelfth centuries as well as a number of earlier buildings, some from the early ninth century. It was in this cathedral that the body of Earl Magnus, patron saint of these islands, lay for almost thirty years after his murder. In the three hundred years between the original raiders and settlers and the death of Saint Magnus the Vikings had overwhelmed the Picts, established a thoroughly Scandinavian community with their own Nordic language (*Norn*), returned the islands to paganism, and were themselves, in turn, converted to Christianity. Their descendants are determinedly not Scots and are to be clearly distinguished from their friendly neighbours to the south, with whom they were joined politically as a result of a marriage dowry in the late fifteenth century.

To some extent the immediate neighbour to the south, Caithness, must be excluded from this distinction, for during the Viking period and for some time thereafter it formed part of the Orkney–Shetland world. Norse names feature prominently in Caithness toponymy. Thurso, for example, takes its name from the Old Norse 'Thor's Mound'. A sizeable number of Caithness place-names derive from -*bolstadr* (farm), such as Bilbster, Ulbster, Scrabster, Lybster, and Thrumster. Many places derive their names from Old Norse -*setr* (dwelling) such as Tister and Reaster. Also the many place-names ending in '-dale' (for example, Berriedale, Harpsdale, Weydale) come from the Old Norse -*dalr* (valley). All the place-names ending in '-gill', '-wick', and '-toft' also indicate Nordic origins. The Scandinavian settlers in east Caithness called the Scottish mainland to their south 'Sudland', and so it has remained Sutherland. Excavations at Freswick in northeast Caithness have revealed buildings and artefacts from the later Viking period.

The other islands – the Inner and Outer Hebrides, the Isle of Man, and Anglesey – became, in time, minor parts of the larger Viking world, their connection with Orkney a dominant theme and their proximity to Ireland a constant factor in their history. Wales, apart from Anglesey, escaped the full force and fury of Viking activities and witnessed no successful settlement.

Ireland

Southwest from the Northern Isles the Vikings came inexorably via the Hebrides and the Kintyre peninsula to the western world, the westernmost survivor of the once mighty Celtic lands, which they named 'Ireland'. They also named three of its provinces: Ulster, Leinster, and Munster. It would be an anachronism to consider this island as the basic Irish historical unit at this time, for they were a tribally centred people to whose world belonged the Celtic islands to the north and west and even the western Scottish peninsulas. Irish historians are wont to describe this phase in their history as 'the Viking period'. A tragic view of Irish history would have it that the great achievements of the golden age of Celtic Christianity ended abruptly under the axe and torch of the Viking. The great successes of the Irish monks, it is said, lay not only in establishing monasteries at places like Clonmacnois, Durrow, Glendalough, Clonfert, Bangor, Armagh, and Cork, which kept alive the western tradition of Latin letters, but also in spreading this tradition through Columba to Scotland and Northumbria and through Columbanus to Luxeuil, Saint Gall, and Bobbio on the continent, and through others still further east. Illuminated manuscripts, monastic ruins, and Celtic high crosses are the remaining symbols, we are told, of the great promise and achievement of early Celtic Christianity in Ireland; and the Viking destroyed all this. We meet here, in this tragic view of Irish history, a figure not unfamiliar in Irish historiography, the destructive foreigner, the cause of all evil. This view must be returned to, but first the raids themselves.

The first raids took place, as in England and the Northern and Western Isles, during the decade of the 790s. The remark already referred to in the *Annals of Ulster* for 794 (*vastatio omnium insularum Britanniae a gentilibus*) must mean that in 794 there were widespread attacks in the Hebrides and, perhaps, further south in Iona and even Man. The *Annals* become quite specific in 795: the raiders attacked the islands of Skye and Iona off the west coast of Scotland, the island of Lambay, just north of Dublin, two islands off the west coast of Ireland (Inishmurray, off the Sligo coast, and Inishbofin, off the Galway coast). In 798 Inispatrick, the Isle of Saint Patrick off Dublin, for long mistakenly confused with the Isle of Saint Patrick, Man, was plundered and the shrine of Saint Conna was broken into. In 798 Ulster and the Hebrides were also visited and plundered. The *Annals of Ulster* sum up the year 798 by saying

5   *Ireland in the Viking age*

simply: 'great devastation between Ireland and Scotland'. The *Annals* continue: in 802 and 806 Iona was revisited; the second time sixty-eight were slain and the remnant forced to move to Kells the following year; in 812 the Owles of Mayo, Connemara, and even Kerry in the southwest were attacked; in 813 the Owles were attacked again; in 821 Howth near Dublin was raided and women taken as slaves; in 823 Skellig Michael, the island sanctuary about ten miles off the Kerry coast in the Atlantic Ocean, was attacked and Bangor, Co. Down, was invaded and the relics of Saint Comgall were desecrated; Bangor was also attacked the following year; in in 832 Armagh was sacked three times within a month, and from that time the Vikings were a constant element in Irish history.

The pattern in the history of Irish–Norse relations becomes quickly apparent. First there were these initial years (*c.* 795–*c.* 830) of raids, hit-and-run attacks on coastal and insular places. There followed two periods of settlement, each followed by some degree of quiet and even assimilation: one from the 830s to the 870s, the other from about 914 to the 940s. It is not necessary here to rehearse in detail the story of these two latter stages. This story can be found in the abundant pages of the Irish annals. It is not generally recognized how extraordinarily rich these annals are for this period, richer, indeed, than the Anglo-Saxon annalistic records for the same period. There is, however, a danger of conflating the accounts of the annals with later, less reliable saga accounts. It is enough here to draw the general lines of the narrative.

The first settlement stage began in the 830s and lasted about forty years. Precise dates should not be insisted upon. What is clear is that for the 830s there is evidence of greatly intensified raiding, both from the west and from the east. The rivers gave access to the Irish heartland. The Shannon, in the west, led the Vikings into Connaught, which they harried in 836 (*vastatio crudelissima a gentilibus omnium finium Connactorum*), to Clonmacnois, which they plundered repeatedly, and to other places in the midlands. They were at the mouth of the Vartry River (Wicklow) in 836, and in the following year two large fleets of sixty ships each sailed up the Boyne to the richest lands in the country in eastern Meath and up the Liffey with its fertile valley; they also sailed into Lough Erne. In 839 the Vikings sailed into the mouth of the Lee, where they burned the monastery at Cork. That year they were also in Lough Neagh, which they used as a base for attacks on eastern Ulster. The picture is clear: raids in every province of the land, large-scale, unco-ordinated, extending deep into the interior through the extensive Irish river systems. The Vikings by 840 posed a threat to Celtic, Christian Ireland.

The threat was to take a new form when, in the 840s, the Vikings began to winter and to establish permanent bases in Ireland. Lough Neagh and Lough Rea were two of the early areas the Vikings used for wintering. In 841 the Norse built a *longport* (a protected place to keep ships) in Louth, probably at Anagassan to the south of Dundalk, and, also, at Dublin (*Duiblinn*, 'black pool'). The *Annals* indicate that these were used as centres for plundering. Other such centres were soon established at *Hlymrekr* (Limerick), *Veigsfjörth* (Wexford), *Vethrafjöthr* (Waterford), *Vikingalo* (Wicklow), and in the marshes at Cork.

The Vikings, thus, introduced towns to Ireland. The small settlements already existing near Celtic monasteries could scarcely merit the name 'towns'. Dublin's subsequent illustrious history should not distort its actual importance in the mid ninth century: for its first few decades it was just another of the growing Viking towns. If one of these towns stood out, it was perhaps Limerick. However, Dublin's splendid harbour, its eastward prospect, and its potential for trade were to make it, in time, Ireland's principal town. Four sites of Viking Dublin were excavated in the 1960s: two just south of High Street, one to the south of Christchurch Place, and one to the east of Winetavern Street by Wood Quay. Over 30,000 objects have been recovered; of these very few date from the ninth century. The excavations have produced a picture of a wealthy town with extensive mercantile connections with northern Europe. This Viking town, nestled on the slope rising from the south bank of the Liffey, had houses made of post-and-wattle construction. Tree trunks were hollowed out and split longitudinally to provide at High Street an open wooden conduit, its purpose not altogether certain. What is certain is that Dublin had specialized craftsmen, especially bronzesmiths (700 finely decorated pins were found), combmakers (the large quantities of antler waste suggest workshops at the High Street and Christchurch Place sites), and leatherworkers, probably shoemakers, with shops in High Street. No evidence has appeared to support the suggestion that there was a pre-Viking settlement at Dublin, and no evidence to associate *ath cliath* ('the ford of the wattles') mentioned in the annals with an inhabited settlement on the promontory formed where the Liffey was joined by its tributary, the Poddle, now underground, passing at one point under St

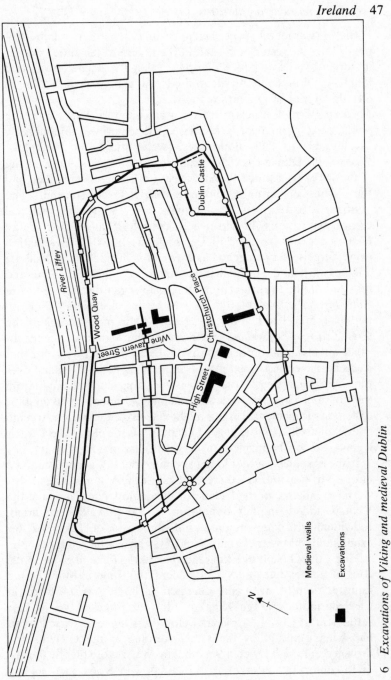

6 *Excavations of Viking and medieval Dublin*

Patrick's Cathedral near Dean Swift's grave. A number of pre-Viking monasteries existed in the region of the Liffey and its hinterland (Clondalkin, Swords, Tallaght, Kilmainham and Finglas), but none on the site of the Norwegian town of Dublin. In 841 the glories of Dublin lay in the future.

The pattern of attack in Ireland was bound to change once the Vikings had permanent bases there. The tempo was undoubtedly accelerated: in 845 alone there were attacks on Teryglass, Clonenagh, Dunamese, Clonmacnois, Clonfert, and Lorrha; the Abbot of Teryglass and the Sub-Abbot of Kildare were killed and the Abbot of Armagh captured and held for ransom. The permanent settlements also brought the Vikings into political contact with the Irish, and it is in the 840s that we first see an alliance between Irish and Viking chieftains. Into this new situation came Turgeis, whom legend has crowned as the great king of all the Vikings in Ireland. His fame is due to the accounts of his deeds and misdeeds in the twelfth-century chronicle-saga *Cogadh Gaedhel re Gallaibh* ('The War of the Irish with the Foreigners'). For the period from 811 to 922 this text relies on chronicles, probably the *Great Chronicle of Ireland* (the principal non-extant source for the other annals), and on oral tradition. From the text we learn that Turgeis arrived in Dublin in 841 and took general command over the Vikings in the east – the Vikings operating in the Shannon from their base in Limerick were independent. Although some doubt is cast upon the incident, Turgeis might indeed have captured Armagh and set himself up as the pagan high priest. Little else in the Turgeis legend, except the incident of his death, has any truth to it.

Irish resistance was not long in coming, but it was not a national effort. Nor was it directed merely against the Vikings. Inter-tribal warfare, endemic to the Ireland of this period, continued and the Vikings added another dimension to the prevailing situation. Individual Irish kings mounted individual attacks. Take 847, for example. In that year Cerball, King of Osraige, attacked the Dublin Vikings; the O'Neill overking faced a Viking force at Skreen; the King of Cashel defeated Viking raiders; the Kings of Munster and Leinster jointly met and defeated a large Viking force at Castledermot; and the King of Munster attacked the Viking settlement at Cork. Two years before that the legendary Turgeis had been captured by the same overking of the O'Neills and drowned in Lough Owel in Westmeath. We are told that by the mid ninth century alliances of Irish factions with Norse factions had brought into existence the 'foreign Irish' (*Gall-Gaedhill*). The historian's appetite for knowledge of these hybrid people is whetted but far from satisfied. The hostile legends portray them as turncoats and opportunists, who joined Turgeis and, with him, plundered Christian monasteries and churches, where they then worshipped Thor. The *Gall-Gaedhill*, it can be said, were a group of Celtic-Norse, some of whom were the offspring of *connubium* between Vikings and Celts, and whose culture and religion probably reflected their mixed ancestry. In 856 their fleet was destroyed by an O'Neill fleet, and after 860 their importance as a separate political force began to wane. There remains the very distinct possibility that the *Gall-Gaedhill* were not Irish at all; that they were, rather, raiders from the western part of Scotland and from the Western Isles, places settled and being farmed by the Norse by this time and where intermarriage had, no doubt, taken place. The later name of Galloway in Scotland derives from these people.

The waters of Irish history were to be muddied even more when other foreigners, this time Danes, probably from England, attacked Ireland in 851. They directed their hostile attentions to their fellow northmen and carried out a successful attack upon Norse Dublin. The Dubliners, eager for revenge, sailed with a fleet of 160 ships into Carlingford Lough to meet the Danes, but after three days of fighting only a handful of the Dubliners escaped with their lives. The Danish days in Ireland were to be brief, and their impact on Irish history slight. In 853 Olaf, a son of a Norwegian king, came to Ireland with a sizeable fleet, quickly routed the Danes, established himself as king in Dublin, and married the Christian daughter of the northern O'Neill. His brother Ivar had taken command of the Vikings in the west at Limerick. The two brothers helped to establish a permanent Norse presence in Ireland. The Norse were there to stay, never to be driven from the island, although defeats were to be suffered. Olaf and Ivar extended the interests of Dublin into western Scotland: Ivar, when he succeeded his brother in Dublin in 871, was called 'the king of the Norsemen of all Ireland and Britain', no doubt an inflated claim, but, at least, a statement of ambition. Although warfare was to continue after Ivar became king, the convulsive years of this phase were now over, and with some justice the annalist can describe the forty years from the death of Ivar in 873 – who might have died a Christian – as 'the forty-years rest', i.e., forty years free from invasions.

Forty years is only approximate: the period of relative peace ended about 914 with the beginning of the final phase (the second settlement stage) of the Vikings in Ireland. The colonization of Iceland in the twenty-five years or so on either side of the year 900 drew away a number of the Norwegians who had settled in Ireland. Likewise, a major defeat of the Vikings at Dublin in 902 caused more to leave, this time to settle in the Isle of Man and in northwest England from the Wirral north to the Solway, where there survive purely Norse names in such places as Ainsdale, Bescar, Meols Cop, Ormskirk, and Scarisbrick. (There is some not unchallenged modern opinion that holds that Cumbria and Lancashire were settled at this period by Norse from the Western Isles of Scotland.) The time was ripe for a renewed external attack by the Vikings on Ireland. It came in 914 and in successive years as large fleets descended upon Ireland. Under the leadership of the grandsons of Ivar they raided over large areas of the country, particularly in Munster and Leinster, and in 919 defeated the O'Neill king of Tara, who fell in battle together with twelve minor kings. The *Annals of Ulster* mourn his passing:

> Sorrowful today is noble Ireland
> Without a valiant chief of hostage reign.
> It is seeing the heavens without a sun
> To see Magh-Neill without Neill.
>
> There is no joy in man's goodness;
> There is no peace nor gladness among hosts;
> No fair can be celebrated
> For his death brings only sorrow.
>
> A tragedy this, O beloved plain of Brega,
> Beautiful, desirable country.
> Thou hast parted with my lordly king;
> Neill, your warrior hero, has left thee.
>
> Where is the chief of the Western World?
> Where is the hero of every clash of arms?
> Is it the brave Neill of Cnucha
> That has been lost, O great land?

In the wake of this stunning victory the Viking kingdom of Dublin was quickly re-established. It soon became the centre of a kingdom which stretched across the Irish Sea and the Pennines to the city of York in the Danelaw in England. That the connection with York existed in the tenth century is abundantly clear. One of the grandsons of Ivar, Ragnald, gained control at York in 919. He was succeeded, in turn, by his kinsmen Sihtric, Guthfrith, Olaf Guthfrithson, and Olaf Sihtricson. The latter, who had married an O'Neill princess, was baptized in 943 and was to die on the monastic isle of Iona. Although crucial details of the Dublin–York connection in the tenth century are lacking, archaeological excavations in both cities, most recently in York, underline their close inter-relationship.

Dublin's importance was as a centre in this Norse axis. Tenth-century Dublin was, in a way, like eighteenth-century Dublin: prosperous, part of a larger world, an international city ruled by non-Irishmen. Although preoccupied with their own eastward sphere, the Dublin Vikings in 921 attacked Armagh, and in 924 and again in 931 they tried to gain control over the Vikings at Limerick. These Limerick Vikings themselves were at frequent odds with the Waterford Vikings. A spate of Viking pirate raids followed along the coasts of the north and the northwest and up rivers such as the Shannon and the Erne. The true history of Ireland at this time was not of a struggle of the Irish against the Vikings but of an internal struggle among Irish kings for the overkingships. The Vikings, by the mid tenth century, had blended into this general pattern and become additional chessmen used by the greater Irish kings in their attempts to establish wider political power. This struggle dominated the Irish scene till the advent of the Normans in 1169. It is with this as a backdrop that the last days of the Vikings as a separate, foreign element must be seen. Their integration and hibernization were eased by their conversion to Christianity, which was slowly taking place from the mid tenth century – some would say from the mid ninth century – by their alliances with native Irish factions and by intermarriages. In fact, for the ninth and tenth centuries there is considerable evidence that the great Norse families and the great Irish families – the ruling elite – frequently intermarried.

What, then, of the Battle of Clontarf in 1014? Was this not the event by which Brian Boru stilled the Viking threat once and for all, destroyed this heathen power, and saved Ireland for the Celt? Legends die hard, and perhaps no legend will die harder than the legend of Brian Boru and the Battle of Clontarf, for there are so many people in Ireland and in the Irish diaspora who claim descent from this legendary hero. As the legend would have it, Brian emerged from the fastnesses of deepest Clare as overking of the south and in time as the High King of Ireland. A cultural patron, a glorifier of the early Christian attainments of Ireland, a rebuilder of monasteries and libraries, an enemy to ignorance and barbarity, Brian stood tall as the national leader to defeat the Norse, who were inimical to all true Celtic values. It was at Clontarf, north of the Liffey near Dublin, that the Celt faced the Norseman, the Christian faced the heathen, and Brian Boru faced Sihtric. The Vikings had summoned a mighty Viking army from virtually the whole Viking world: they came from the Hebrides, Orkney, Normandy, the Isle of Man, and Scandinavia itself to protect their Dublin brothers. On the eve of battle omens were seen across the north as far away as Caithness and Iceland. Brian saw a vision of Saint Senan, who demanded reparations for Brian's attack on his monastery on Inis Cathaig in 977. The ships of the King of Man received ghostly visitors, and iron-beaked and iron-clawed ravens attacked the Manx warriors. The day of battle arrived on Good Friday, 1014, and Brian's Irish army, lacking the Leinstermen, who had gone over to the Viking side, and the northern O'Neill, who had stayed home, posted itself in two flanks parallel to the Liffey on its north side. Brian knelt on an animal skin in Tomar's Wood and refused, himself, to enter into combat on this sacred day. Nevertheless, battle was joined. First, a champion from each side met, but with no decision. The forces of Munster then fell back before onrushing Leinster, but it was only a ploy as the southern O'Neill proceeded to crush Leinster. Sigur, the *jarl* of the Orkneys, rallied about him the remnants of the Viking army and the men of Leinster, but it was too late. They were forced to flee to their ships through a nearby wood. There they saw an old man kneeling amidst a circle of warriors. Brodir, King of Man, asked who this man was, and he was told Brian Boru. Brodir raised his mighty battle sword and smote the High King of Ireland. The day was already lost, however, and the blood of Brian Boru sealed the victory of the Celt over the *Gael-Gaedhill*, of the Christian over the heathen. The Viking age had ended. Or, at least, as the legend runs, the Viking age had ended.

From this tangle of fact and fiction some sifting must be done. Brian Boru had indeed gained hegemony over the south and, at times, over parts of the north. He was never High King of Ireland; there was no such office at that time. He did lead a confederation of some Irish tribes (and even some Viking forces) at a battle at Clontarf on Good Friday in 1014. His principal opponent was not the Vikings: it was the King of Leinster, who had tried to reassert his independence and who, through marriage, had friendly relations with the Viking King of Dublin. Brian Boru's forces were successful, but he fell in the battle. The struggle for hegemony in Ireland continued for a century and a half after Clontarf, which was merely one among many events in that struggle. It did not destroy the power of the Vikings. Nothing so simple as a one-day battle in the spring of 1014 accomplished that. The gradual assimilation of the Vikings had begun over half a century before Clontarf and was to continue after Clontarf. The Vikings as a distinct element gradually faded from the Irish scene in the two centuries or so between 950 and 1169, conversion and intermarriage being the twin agents of this assimilation.

It remains to assess the effect of the Vikings on Ireland during the two centuries when they formed a distinct part of the Irish scene. It has not been uncommon to speak of the Viking experience in Ireland as catastrophic. Even a hasty reading of the great *Annals of Ulster* might tend to confirm this judgement: references abound there to burning and plundering by the 'foreigners'. But before any general judgement is made, one might distinguish between the effects of the Vikings on Irish secular society and their effects on Irish ecclesiastical society. With regard to the former several things should be said. The general political structure of Ireland was not substantially altered by the Vikings: there were still two 'halves' to Ireland, i.e., a northern hegemony exercised at Tara by the O'Neills, alternating between the southern and northern branches of that family, and the south with an overking at Cashel, fluctuating between the Eoganacht and the Dal Cáis. The Vikings, in a sense, discovered the coast of Ireland by establishing along it seaport towns with accompanying overseas trade and other contacts with the outside world. The Vikings gave Ireland the gift of Dublin, without which not only Ireland but the world would be a much poorer place.

The assessment of the consequences of the Vikings in Ireland narrows to their effect on the ecclesiastical side of society. It was the monasteries and the churches of Ireland which were visited by these marauding foreigners. An early hostile verdict was rendered in the twelfth century in the vivid words of the author of 'The War Against the Foreigners' when he said:

If one neck had a hundred heads of hardened steel and if each head had a hundred sharp tongues of tempered metal and if each tongue shouted incessantly in a hundred voices, they could never list the sufferings which the Irish – men and women, laity and clergy, young and old – endured from these warlike, savage people.

Scarcely a friendly appraisal, but such a view, couched in less vivid language, has carried the day: the brilliance of early Christian Ireland (as represented by the Ardagh Chalice, the Book of Kells, the Tara Brooch, etc.) was extinguished by the Vikings. Before the coming of the Norsemen the native Irish respected the holy places, and it was only after these places were violated by the Vikings that the Irish themselves attacked places of Christian worship. This view, however, has been challenged recently by Dr A. T. Lucas, former Director of the National Museum of Ireland. He combed through the extant annals for the period from 600 to 1163 and tabulated the plunderings and burnings of churches and monasteries where the nationalities of the attackers could be discerned. Of the number of such plunderings where the nationality of the plunderers is known there are 139 attributable to the Irish, 140 to the Norse, and fourteen to the Irish and Norse combined. Of the number of burnings there are fifty attributable to the Irish, thirty-seven to the Norse, and five to the Irish and Norse combined. Of the number of instances in which there was both plundering and burning twelve are attributable to the Irish and seven to the Norse. The conclusion drawn is that the Irish themselves share with the Vikings the responsibility and guilt for the devastation inflicted upon the sacred places. The key to an understanding of this conclusion is that these holy places were used as sanctuaries for persons and, especially, for property and that made them attractive targets for attack. Dr Kathleen Hughes has challenged the Lucas view. While not denying that the Irish as well as the Norse attacked Christian churches and monasteries, Dr Hughes maintained that to use the dates 600 and 1163 as terminal dates is not particularly helpful for such a comparison, for these dates begin 200 years before the Vikings were a factor in Ireland and end 150 years after the Viking assimilation was well underway. A more accurate comparison of the destruction by the Irish and Vikings respectively should be narrowed to the years roughly 800 to 1000, or, more particularly, 831 to 980. Before 831 Dr Hughes found only five instances of raids where Irishmen raided holy places in a manner similar to the Viking raids. It is true that in the violence widespread at this time among the Irish other, more limited attacks by Irishmen on churches did occur, but their purpose was specific and their destruction less than total. The Viking raids, however, were aimed at plunder and indiscriminate destruction. For the fifty years after 831, the period of the most intensive Viking hostile activity, Dr Hughes found only ten instances of plundering or burning (or both) by Irishmen compared to eighty-three instances by Vikings. For the period from 881 to 919 there were only six instances of raids by Irishmen and twenty-seven instances of raids by Vikings. Thus, for this almost ninety-year period at the height of the Viking attacks the totals read Irish sixteen, Vikings 100. During the remaining decades of the tenth century the Irish raids grew in frequency and by the eleventh century they outnumbered the Viking raids. The number of recorded raids in which the assailants are unknown is insignificant during the first three of these periods, but for the period 981–1170 the number rises to 162, most of which, Dr Hughes allows, were probably by the Irish: there was, she argues, a gradual erosion of respect for church property among the Irish. The fifty years in the mid ninth century were the crucial years, and old, Celtic Ireland did not recover from the attacks of the foreigners which occurred during those years. And so, according to Dr Hughes, the traditional view, although in need of some modification, still stands.

One might be permitted to wonder aloud, pondering the terms of this scholarly dialogue, how methods of quantification can be confidently used on this material. The reliability of the extant annals is not particularly at issue, rather their completeness. There is no way of knowing how complete these annals are, how many raids by the Irish or by the Vikings took place, and, when the annals speak of 'widespread devastation', what precisely is meant? What percentage of actual raids were recorded in the annals? What percentage of the annals have survived? Until these and similar questions can be answered – and it is difficult to see how they all can ever be adequately answered – the conclusions drawn from the scattered evidence must stress simply that the Vikings menaced Ireland in an extremely violent fashion during the fifty years spanning the middle of the ninth century and that they remained thereafter as one, among many, of the violent forces bedevilling the land in the tribal warfare endemic to Ireland in the centuries before the Normans. In any case, too fine a distinction should not be drawn between the ecclesiastical and secular spheres of Irish society. Monasteries and churches were attacked and plundered not only because they contained material wealth but also because they had a close relationship with the local *tuath*, the regional kingdom. Many of them were tribal monasteries and churches, often with close familial and hereditary ties with the local king. Inter-tribal warfare, then, easily led to attacks on these sacred places, the obvious and vulnerable signs of an enemy's wealth.

The period of magnificent illuminated manuscripts had ended. With the Book of Kells at the end of the eighth century and the simpler Book of Armagh a little later serving as final examples, the tradition of manuscript illumination appears to have left Ireland. Although ornamental metalwork and stonework continued into the tenth century, an age had indeed come to an end. Would it have ended as quickly without the Vikings? Should these artistic achievements of the Irish stand as the basis for judging a society which had so many other (but less dramatic) sides? Let them stand for us as symbols of the tragedy of unfulfilled promise. And strangers came again in 1169.

Selected further reading

The *Anglo-Saxon Chronicle* can be consulted in translations by Dorothy Whitelock, David C. Douglas and S. I. Tucker (eds.), Eyre & Spottiswoode 1962, and by G. N. Garmonsway, J. M. Dent & Sons 1953; the *Annals of Ulster*, pending the promised edition by Gearoid MacNiocaill, in the four-volume edition by W. M. Hennessy, Dublin; HM Stationery Office 1887–1901, and *The War of the Gaedhil with the Gaill* in the edition by J. H. Todd in the Rolls Series, HM Stationery Office 1867. For a general summary of an aspect of recent work see D. M. Wilson, 'Scandinavian settlements in the north and west of the British Isles', in *Transactions of the Royal Historical Society* 5th series, vol. 26 (1976), pp. 95–113. For Scotland see, in general, A. A. M. Duncan, *Scotland: The Making of the Kingdom*, Oliver & Boyd 1975, and, more particularly, A. Ritchie, 'Pict and Norsemen in northern Scotland', in *Scottish Archaeological Forum*, vol. 6 (1974), pp. 23–36. An older work, still of interest, is A. W. Brøgger, *Ancient Emigrants: A History of the Norse Settlements of Scotland*, Clarendon Press 1929. For the Isles the most useful general work is still F. T. Wainwright, 'The Scandinavian settlement', in *The Northern Isles*, Nelson 1962, pp. 117–62. Descriptions of some particular excavations can be found in J. R. C. Hamilton, *Excavations at Jarlshof, Shetland*, HM Stationery Office 1956, especially chapter 6, and C. A. R. Radford, *The Early Christian and Norse Settlements at Birsay, Orkney*, Edinburgh: HM

Stationery Office 1959. Place-name evidence, perhaps in need of some refinement, has been martialled by W. F. H. Nicolaisen in 'Norse settlement in the northern and western isles: some place-name evidence', in *Scottish Historical Review,* vol. 18 (1969), pp. 6–17. The rich grave sites of Man are described and evaluated by D. M. Wilson in *The Viking Age in the Isle of Man: The Archaeological Evidence,* Odense: Odense Universitetsforlag 1974. Of considerable interest is Henry R. Loyn, *The Vikings in Wales,* London: Viking Society for Northern Research 1977. For Ireland the most recent narrative is Donncha Ó Corráin, *Ireland Before the Normans,* Dublin: Gill & Macmillan 1972. Of considerable use are essays by Nora F. Chadwick, Françoise Henry, A. Sommerfeldt, and D. A. Binchey, in *Proceedings of the International Congress of Celtic Studies . . . 1959,* Dublin: Institute for Advanced Studies 1962. A challenging view is presented by A. P. Smyth in *Scandinavian York and Dublin,* 2 vols., Dublin: Templekieran Press 1975–8. For coins see the magisterial presentation by Michael Dolley in *Hiberno-Norse Coins in the British Museum,* British Museum Publications 1966. The excavations at Dublin are described by Brendan Ó Ríordáin in 'Excavations at High Street and Winetavern Street, Dublin', in *Medieval Archaeology,* vols. 15 (1971), pp. 73–85, 16 (1973), p. 168, 17 (1973), pp. 151–2, and anonymously in *Viking and Medieval Dublin: National Museum Excavations, 1962–1973: Catalogue of Exhibition,* Dublin: National Museum of Ireland 1973. For the question of towns see Liam de Paor, 'The Viking towns of Ireland', in *Proceedings of the Seventh Viking Congress,* B. Almquist and D. Greene (eds.), Dublin: distributed by Viking Society for Northern Research (London) 1976, pp. 29–37. The best summary of the Viking effect on Irish art is by Françoise Henry in *Irish Art During the Viking Invasions, 800–1020,* Methuen 1967. The fullest statement of Dr A. T. Lucas's revisionist views can be found in 'The plundering and burning of churches in Ireland, 7th to 16th century', in Etienne Rynne (ed.), *North Munster Studies: Essays in Commemoration of Monsignor Michael Moloney,* Limerick: Thomond Archaeological Society 1967, pp. 172–229. Dr Kathleen Hughes's response is in her book *Early Christian Ireland: Introduction to the Sources,* Hodder & Stoughton 1972, chapter 4.

3 Across the North Atlantic

The island-hopping of the Vikings during the ninth century was almost inevitable. The inner dynamic of the emigration movement, particularly the land hunger, drove these seamen–farmers further and further west. Once Shetland was settled and once Ireland had begun to lose its attraction, the Vikings found other and uninhabited places to settle. Flat maps distort distances in the northern waters; in fact, the North Atlantic islands lie at regular, navigable distances from one another, not like a string of pearls, more like stepping stones of different sizes and shapes. The Faroe Islands are only 190 miles from Shetland; the Faroes, in turn, only 240 miles from Iceland; and Iceland only 190 miles from the nearest part of Greenland. Or, to look at it another way, facing from Norway to the west, the Faroes lie about 350 miles distant, Iceland 600 miles, and Greenland close to 1000 miles. Nothing in history, of course, is truly inevitable, but, given the sailing and navigational skills of the Vikings and their land hunger in the ninth and tenth centuries, it comes as no surprise that the settlement of Shetland was followed by settlements in Faroe, Iceland, Greenland, and even beyond Greenland till the lines were so long, the circumstances so disagreeable, that the westward expansion ended, short-lived, on the shores of North America. That theme belongs to the next chapter. For now, let us consider the Viking achievement in the islands of the North Atlantic, unique among Viking experiences, for here they settled uninhabited lands and their achievements reached a dazzling fulfilment in the great Icelandic age.

Faroe Islands

Northwest of the Shetlands, the Faroes ('sheep islands') comprise an archipelago of twenty-two sizeable islands, eighteen of which are inhabited in the twentieth century. Streymoy (28 miles by 8 miles) is the largest of these; Torshavn, its principal town, is named for the

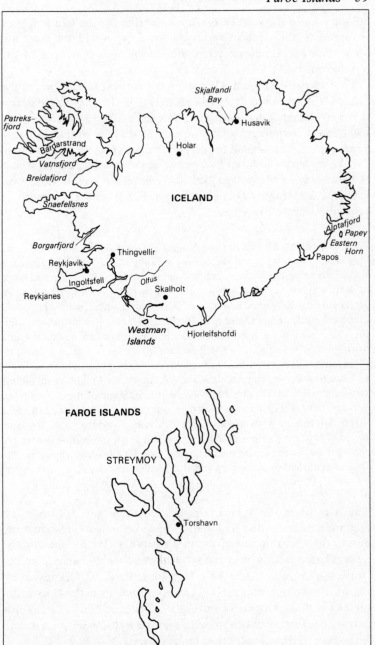

7 *Iceland and the Faroe Islands in the Viking age*

Viking god. In the west cliffs rise sheer from the sea to a height of over 300 metres in places and rocky beaches abound, but there are also inlets and sandy stretches that enabled the beaching of the Viking vessels.

The earliest Viking ships landed in the Faroes probably about the year 800, drawn there from islands to the south. They found in this otherwise uninhabited place Irish monks, whose predecessors had established hermitages on these remote islands over a hundred years earlier. The ideal of the *peregrinatio pro Christo* had sent Irish monks not as missionaries but, rather, as penitential pilgrims whose penance was the pilgrimage itself and whose destination was Christ. The Irish geographer Dicuil, writing in 825 from the testimony of reliable witnesses, reports:

There are islands around our own island Hibernia, some small and some very small. Near the island Britannia are many islands, some large, some small, and some medium-sized. Some are in the sea to her south and some in the sea to her west, but they abound mostly to the northwest and north. Among these I have lived in some and have visited others; some I have only glimpsed, while others I have read about. . . . There are many other islands [besides Thule] in the ocean to the north of Britain which can be reached from the northern islands of Britain in a direct voyage of two days and nights with sails filled with a continuously favourable wind. A devout priest told me that in two summer days and the intervening night he sailed in a two-benched boat and landed on one of them. Some of these islands are very small; nearly all are separated from one another by narrow stretches of water. On these islands hermits sailing from our country Scotia [Ireland] have lived for nearly a hundred years. But just as they were always deserted from the beginning of the world, so now because of the northmen pirates they are emptied of anchorites and filled with countless sheep and a great variety of sea-fowls.

The date when the Vikings first settled there and disturbed the eremitical peace of the Irish monks must be assigned to sometime during the first quarter of the ninth century. Where the earliest settlers came from is uncertain, but they probably came from the Norse settlements to the south (Hebrides, Shetland, Orkney, etc.). During the ninth century settlers were to come from the Norwegian regions of Sogn, Rogaland and Agder. The suitability of Faroe for grazing became quickly apparent, and the fields were soon dotted with sheep. Fishing and other interests were to follow.

The Viking settlement, at first small, grew in size during its first century. The rise of Harald Finehair to a kind of political hegemony in Norway in the 880s or 890s, undoubtedly caused some dissidents and rivals to go into exile, particularly to the Faroes and to Iceland. The political émigrés formed only part of this colonization process: the desire for land, wealth, and adventure were no doubt present among the motives of the early settlers. The *Saga of the Faroe Islanders*, which glorified the role of Olaf Tryggvason in the conversion and prospering of the islands, is not historically reliable. Christianity did come to Faroe through King Olaf about the year 1000. One might think that in their subsequent history the Faroe Islands would have served as a stopping-off point for traffic going between Norway and Iceland, but this does not appear to have been the case: vessels went direct to Iceland by a route which took them through the waters between Shetland and Faroe. Yet, once a shipping route was established between Norway and Greenland, the vessels on this route regularly called at the Faroes.

Iceland

The Viking civilization reached its highest point amidst the glaciers, ice, sandy beaches, lava plains and green meadows of Iceland. Nowhere else did the Vikings establish a sizeable permanent settlement of their own, undisturbed by native peoples, by the necessities of conquest, and by consequent absorption. Iceland was to be the child who outgrew the parent; her mature literary achievements were to be greater than those of the Scandinavian homelands as well as those of the Viking settlers in conquered lands.

Writers of antiquity – Polybius, Strabo, Pliny, and Tacitus – knew of an island a six-day journey from Britain. They called it Thule, the Venerable Bede, in his treatise on time, cited the ancients and described Thule as six days' sailing north from Britain, a place where there is no night at the summer solstice and no day at the winter solstice, and which is one day's journey south of the eternal ice. In 825 Dicuil wrote of Thule in terms which demand its identification as Iceland. He knew these same antique sources but added:

It is now thirty years since clerics, who had lived on the island from the first of February to the first of August, told me that not only at the summer solstice but in the days round about it the sun setting in the evening hides itself as though behind a small hill in such a way that there was no darkness in that very small space of time and a man could do whatever he wished as though the sun were still there, even remove lice from his shirt, and, if one stood on a mountain-top, the sun perhaps would still be visible to him.

Thus, from about 775, the seemingly ubiquitous Irish monks spent the bright (and warm) seasons in Iceland, coming and going presumably in their leather-sided currachs. They were known to the Vikings as *papar,* and such place-names as Papey and Papos in southwestern Iceland indicate names used by the Vikings – surely not by the Irish hermits themselves – to describe the places where the holy men used to stay. The existence of this island must have been known to the Norwegians by the first quarter of the ninth century. By then they were settling Orkney, Shetland, and Faroe, and were familiar figures in Ireland. The traditional accounts place the Viking 'discovery' of Iceland about the year 860, a date which is later than might be expected in view of their presence only 240 miles to the southwest at Faroe since about 800. They might, indeed, have known about Iceland and might have even sighted it before 860, but the sagas are silent about any such 'discovery'.

What the Vikings discovered when they reached Iceland was an island, oval in shape except for a peninsula in the northwest and somewhat larger than Ireland. The land was composed of elements which were very diverse in nature. Basically a tableland, Iceland had – and, indeed, has – an average height of between 600 and 950 metres; desert land of ice-sheets, glaciers, and cooled lava covered a large part of the island. Twenty-five of the more than two hundred volcanoes have been active at various times since the arrival of the Vikings and have made Iceland one of the world's most volcanically active regions. The rims of land along the coast and along some of the river valleys – not unlike the native Norway of many of the Viking settlers – remain to this day the only arable areas where grain and hay grow and where livestock graze. In the Viking age Icelandic waters provided the inhabitants with abundant quantities of fish.

Who was the first of the Vikings to discover this island nestled below the Arctic Circle? The question needs to be asked if for no other reason than that it was an important question to subsequent generations of Icelanders. The *Landnámabók*, about which more will be said, in its various versions associates three men with the Viking discovery: Naddod, Gardar, and Floki. The discovery by Naddod was accidental. To wit:

It is reported that men had a voyage to make from Norway to the Faroes; some say it was Naddod the Viking. They were driven by a storm into the western ocean and found there a big country. They climbed in the region of the Eastfirths up a high mountain where they commanded a splendid view. They looked for smoke or some other sign of human habitation but saw none. They stayed until autumn, and, as they left, returning to the Faroes, they saw snow on the mountain tops, and, thus, they called the land Snowland, which they praised highly.

This alleged misadventure of Naddod does not appear to have greatly impressed the teller of the story. And what of Gardar?

There was a man named Gardar Svarvarsson, by descent a Swede, who set off in search of Snowland at the command of his mother, a seeress. He made landfall east of the Eastern Horn, where there was a harbour. Gardar circumnavigated the land and discovered it was an island. That winter he spent at Husavik in Skjalfandi, where he built a home. In the spring . . . Gardar returned to Norway and praised the land highly. The land was now called Gardarsholm, and it had woods between the mountains and the shore.

Two discoverers, each praising the land highly, and two names for the land. The third 'discoverer' found the place uncongenial, damned it, and gave it a pejorative name, which, in the irony of such events, proved permanent.

There was a great Viking named Floki Vilgerdarson, who sailed from Flokavardi, as it is called now, where Hordaland and Rogaland meet, in search of Gardarsholm. First he sailed for Shetland, where he anchored. . . . They made Horn from the east and sailed along the south coast. When they sailed west beyond Reykjanes, the fjord opened up before them and they could see Snaefellsnes. Faxi said, 'This land which we have discovered must be a big land: these are large rivers.' Floki and his men continued sailing west, crossed Breidafjord, and landed at Vatnsfjord (as we call it) near Bardarstrand. They took so much advantage of the excellent fishing there that they neglected to make hay, and all their livestock died during the winter. A rather cold spring followed. Floki climbed up a high mountain, faced north, and saw a fjord full of ice and called the land Iceland. . . . Floki spent the winter in Borgarfjord . . . and next summer sailed for Norway. When asked about the place, he gave it a bad name.

Whatever ring of truth may sound from any of these stories, they were important stories for subsequent generations, for whom the sighting and discovery of new lands had a fascination and provided the stuff from which heroes were made. The historian also finds the question of the discovery of Iceland fascinating and, at the same time, of very limited significance. If Iceland was 'discovered', then surely the credit must go to Irish monks swept westward in their currachs by winds of self-denial and Christian asceticism. The historian of the Vikings knows that during the 860s some Vikings sighted and explored the coastal regions of Iceland. Whether Naddod, Gardar, or Floki were among them matters little.

The *settlement* of Iceland by Europeans is what does matter. From 870 to 930 an immigration of some size took place: thousands of immigrants sailed from Norway and the Celtic lands with the purpose of settling. These were not voyages of exploration, nor were they summer excursions to the northwest or seasonal raiding parties. These immigrants – the first to feel the *Drang nach Westen* – came to settle in the fertile fjords and coastal plains. As quickly as it had started this immigration ended: sixty years and it was over. Communications, of course, persisted with the old country, but the convoys of ships bringing settlers had ended by 830 and Iceland was on its way to becoming the only independent, self-contained Viking overseas settlement.

Two twelfth-century vernacular sources describe this age of settlement. Ari Thorgilsson, the father of Icelandic history, wrote *Íslendingabók (The Book of the Icelanders)* in about 1125. It is true that this book was written some two hundred years after the settlement, but Ari had been raised by Hallr Thorarinsson, who could remember his baptism in 998, who later served the Norwegian king, and who was reputed to have had a prodigious memory: a close link, albeit one of unwritten tradition, with the settlers and their new-found island and a reliable link, at the least, to the very early national traditions of these people. The second source had a very different intent. The *Landnámabók (The Book of the Landtaking),* probably written down in the twelfth century, is known to us only through thirteenth-century editions. This book reads like a catalogue of early settlers, not really a list – bones without flesh – but, rather, the names of 400 settlers, the places of their origin, some genealogical information, and very frequently stories attached to them, describing the exploits, oddities, and even ironies of such people as Wale the Strong, Osborn the Wealthy, Rolf the Thick, Thorkell the Tall, and Cetil One-Hand. It would be a mistake to view either of these books as completely historical or as fully reliable in the least detail. Yet they stand fairly close to the earliest Icelandic traditions. What do they tell us?

They tell us that Ingolf Arnarson was the premier settler. The story is instructive; its longer version is in the *Landnámabók*.

The foster brothers [Ingolf and Leif] went out in their fully fitted ship in search of the land which Raven-Floki had discovered and which he had called Iceland. They discovered that land and made landfall on the east coast in the southern Alptafjord: the land there seemed to them more fruitful than in the north. After one winter there they returned to Norway. Ingolf then made preparation for a voyage of settlement, while Leif went a-viking to the British Isles. He harried in Ireland . . ., took a sword from a man in a dark underground place and was hence called Hjorleif (Sword Leif) . . . and returned with ten slaves. That winter Ingolf made sacrifices to the gods, seeking signs of his future; Hjorleif did not sacrifice. The signs directed Ingolf to Iceland. Each brother prepared his ship for the journey . . . and they put out to sea.

In the summer when Ingolf and Hjorleif set out to settle Iceland Harald Finehair had been king of Norway for twelve years, there had been 3774 winters since the beginning of the world and 874 years from the incarnation of the Lord. They split up once they reached sight of Iceland. Ingolf threw his high-seat pillars into the sea, vowing to settle where they landed. He reached land at what is now called Ingolfshofdi. Hjorleif went further west along the coast . . . and reached land at Hjorleifshofdi . . ., where he stayed that winter. In the following spring Hjorleif, wanting to sow but having only one ox, had his slaves plough the land. . . . The slaves attacked Hjorleif and his men, murdered them, and carried off the women and moveable goods in Hjorleif's boat to an island offshore, where they stayed. Ingolf was deeply moved when two of his slaves came upon the body of Hjorleif. When he arrived, Ingolf lamented, 'This is a sad end for a brave man that slaves should cause his death. What can be expected of a man who will not sacrifice?' He went after Hjorleif's slaves, found them . . . and slew every last one of them.

The following summer Ingolf travelled along the coast to the west and he stayed this third winter at Ingolfsfell, west of the Olfus River. During this season Vifil and Karli found the high-seat pillars near Arnarhval. In the spring Ingolf crossed the fields and made his home where the high-seat pillars had come ashore. He called it Reykjavik, and the pillars remain there till this day.

Whatever pre-eminence Ingolf might actually have had, this account does reveal some patterns followed by early settlers and raises some issues still troubling historians. At an early date, no doubt in the 870s, Iceland was circumnavigated by intending settlers. Not all perhaps but many of the early settlers undoubtedly cast their high-seat pillars overboard so that providence might indicate where they should settle. These pillars were like a door-frame within which the seat of the paterfamilias would later be located in his house; they represented his authority, familial and priestly. Like Ingolf other settlers came in family groups accompanied by servants and slaves. From other sources we know that each settler could 'stake' out for himself only the area that he and his men could carry fire around in the course of one day. Land distribution to his principal men normally followed and with this the local lordship of the principal settler and his successors.

The mention of Celtic thralls in the service of Hjorleif touches on the larger issue of the Celtic component of the Icelandic settlement. Of the 400 settlers mentioned in *Landnámabók* perhaps 7 per cent came from recognizably Celtic lands, principally Ireland and the Outer Hebrides. Some of the settlers such as Aawang, Thormon, and Cetil are actually called Irish (*Iskr*), and closer analysis shows that some of the wives and concubines of Norse settlers who came from Ireland were, in fact, Irish, as were many of the *thralls*, themselves frequently of noble birth. Among the names of legendary Icelandic figures is the great Njall (i.e., Neil), a Celt about whom a great saga is told. In this much disputed question of the extent of the Celtic factor in the Icelandic settlement two facts remain clear. The first – and its significance needs the boldest underlining – is simply that the settlement of Iceland was a Norwegian settlement: the place-names in the *Landnámabók* exhibit the principal pattern of widescale emigration from southwestern Norway, especially from Sogn, Hōrdaland, and Rogaland, and a minor pattern of some Norse emigrating directly from the western islands (Scotland and the islands to the immediate north and west, the Faroes, and Ireland). No doubt the vast majority of the 7 per cent or so from the Celtic lands were first or second generation Norwegians. Of much less significance is the second fact: among the settlers of Iceland there were Celts. They were not principal landholders, but mainly wives, the result of *connubium* in Ireland, and slaves who had been enslaved in Ireland. Modern Icelandic historians stress – and perhaps overstress – the Irish factor as a means of explaining the differences between Iceland and her

Scandinavian mother, particularly as a partial explanation of the enormous literary achievement of Iceland. *Quaestio stat*!

Easily overlooked in this Celtic dispute is the more basic question of the size of the Icelandic settlement. Our principal source mentions only sixty years of settlement and only 400 settlers: not much to go on. The 400 in question were 400 *settlers*, i.e., men of substance, who with their families, retinues, and slaves peopled the island. Estimates vary from 10,000 to 60,000 and clearly depend on how complete one thinks the *Landnámabók* is and what one concludes about the average size of a *familia*. A figure somewhere between 15,000 and 25,000 might not be too far wrong.

It is very easy – and probably erroneous – to say that the Vikings settled Iceland during this sixty-year period as a result of political conditions in Norway: Harald Finehair had extended his control over a large area of Norway; the battle of Hafrsfjord (probably fought at a date between 885 and 900) ended the rule of many kings and *jarls* in the Vestland. Snorri Sturluson, the thirteenth-century historian, attributed this *Völkerwanderung* to Iceland to the tyranny of King Harald. The *Landnámabók*, in fact, mentions that several of the settlers had actually fought against Harald at Hafrsfjord. Thus, it has been concluded, political émigrés peopled Iceland. The actual picture is much more complex. No doubt political dissidents and the defeated found Iceland an attractive place of exile. Its attraction was no less real to the apolitical, the land-hungry, the younger sons, and the Norse already living in their diaspora among the Celts, far removed from the Vestland and Harald. Evidence even suggests that Harald helped to foster or, at least, control the colonizing of Iceland. At least two of the most noble settlers, Ingimund the Old and Hrollaug, are described as friends of Harald. A thirteenth-century account states that the son of Gardar, one of the island's 'discoverers', was actually sent to Iceland by Harald in an attempt to gain control. Harald tried to control the landtaking not only by limiting the extent of land each settler might take but also by imposing a head tax on émigrés leaving Norway ('land ounces'). Certainly the prospects of new land which was there for the taking would have been enough, in any case, to entice large numbers of ambitious and adventurous men to flee the overpopulated fjord-country of southwestern Norway and begin life anew in a place where, despite its name, one early visitor saw 'blades of grass dripping with butter'.

This new society needed organization, and an aristocratic form of governing based on a Norwegian model became quickly established. Sometime between 927 and 930 the ruling chieftains agreed that a national body should be formed to settle disputes and determine law. In consequence, they sent Ulfljot to Norway to find out what their ancestral laws were. The result was Ulfljot's Law, about which little is known except for its ritual provisions. Regional *things* (assemblies) had existed since the early stages of the settlement, but an *althing* (a general assembly) probably met for the first time in the summer of 930. The place chosen for this assembly, called the *thingvellir* (the assembly plain), remains to this day one of the most impressive sites in Iceland: situated north of the island's largest lake at the end of a vast natural cleavage twenty-five miles long and six miles wide and convenient to the populous areas of the south and west. Here once a year the great landowners would meet for a fortnight; they – and not a king – were to rule this republic: 'The Icelanders', said Adam of Bremen in the 1070s, 'have no other king than the laws.' The secular and the sacred merged in these aristocratic settlers; they were called *godars*, chieftains and priests or, rather, chieftain–priests. Three members came from each of the twelve districts of Iceland, and these thirty-six men chose a Law Speaker, who would, for three years, preside over their meetings at the Law Rock and who, at each meeting, would recite one-third of their laws. Adjustments were made to the *althing*. In 965 Iceland was divided into quarters (north, south, east and west), each having three districts (except the north which had four) which were controlled by a local *thing*. These thirteen districts sent three *godars* each to the *althing* which now comprised thirty-nine members. To describe this remarkable body as Europe's oldest democratic parliament is to misunderstand the essentially aristocratic, non-democratic nature of the *althing*; to describe it as Europe's oldest continuous parliament is to distort historical reality and submerge from view the numerous hiatuses in that body's history. What the *althing* actually was stands out more importantly than its age and alleged continuity: it was the first attempt by Vikings to establish *ex nihilo* a constitution for themselves in a new land; it was based on Scandinavian models, yet tailored to a new experience. Its achievement lies in the fact that it worked, roughly at first and then more smoothly, providing the order and stability which were to make the golden age of Icelandic culture possible: the thirteenth century with its sagas and scalds stands as a legacy of the tenth-century constitution.

The conversion of the Icelanders to Christianity – despite tales of sudden volcanic eruptions thundering God's call to the good news in the year 1000 – was not such a road-to-Damascus experience. There were probably always some Christians among the early Icelanders, converted in the Celtic lands: devout women like Aud the Deepminded, who, unwilling to have her body laid in unhallowed ground, instructed that she be buried in the sands between high and low tidemarks; others, like Helgi the Lean, believed in Christ but prayed to Thor in crises. A few place-names from the settlement period show a Christian connection (for example, Kristnes and Patreksfjord). Whatever element of Christianity existed among the settlers, it was only of minor significance and this early Christianity probably soon disappeared: the sons of Helgi built temples to their gods.

Massive conversion – the conversion of the Icelandic nation – came at the turn of the millenium. It was preceded by several attempts by Christian missionaries to evangelize the heathen Icelanders. As early as the 980s some Icelanders who had been converted abroad returned preaching the new religion, although not with notable success. The crucial point in the Christianization of Iceland took place hundreds of miles to the east, in Norway, where Olaf Tryggvason, a Christian, became king in 995. For this process our closest reliable account is Ari's *Íslendingabók*. Ari's foster father had been baptized by one of King Olaf's early missionaries; Ari's tutor, Teit, was the son of Isleif, first native Bishop of Iceland (1056–80). With a Bede-like zest for citing sources, Ari recounts the successful mission: 'Teit told me that he knew this from a man who was actually present.' What does Ari (and Teit and Teit's eye-witness informant) tell us? After an only partially successful mission by Thangbrand, a mission which made considerable progress but which left most of the island still heathen, King Olaf sent two converted Icelandic chieftains back to Iceland to establish Christianity as the official religion of the land. They sailed from Norway with the priest Thormond, their mission political and his evangelical. In mid June of the year 1000 – some commentators suggest 999 – their boats landed in the Westman Islands off the southwest coast. One of the converted chieftains, Hjalti, had in the previous year been convicted of blasphemy at the *althing*; for this reason, he was left behind on the Westmans while the other converted chieftain, Gizur, pursued his political mission. It was *althing*-time, and Gizur joined his fellow Christian supporters at the *thingvellir* – even the blasphemous Hjalti cast restraint aside and joined them unbidden. The greatest confrontation in Icelandic history then took place: two armed bands faced each other amid the cleft rock. At the Law Rock a stream of Christians and heathens affirmed that they would not live under the same law with the others. They returned to their various booths to await the decision of Thorgeir, the Law Speaker, who then laid himself down at the Law Rock, covered himself over, and remained there all that day and throughout the night. He stirred the following morning and called together the parties. There at the Law Rock he began to speak: divisiveness has cursed the lands of Norway and Denmark; it would destroy this land also; there cannot be two laws, one for the heathen and one for the Christian; each side must give a little and each side win a little; there will be one law and one faith in Iceland. These sentiments appealed to his audience: they agreed that Thorgeir should pronounce the one law. Thorgeir decided that all men should be publicly Christian and, if they wanted, privately heathen. Baptism was to be universal, but the old ways would prevail, although only in private, with regard to the exposing of infants, the eating of horsemeat, and sacrificing. 'But', Ari informs us, 'these forms of paganism were soon abolished.' Ari's account presents a compromise not unfamiliar to Christian evangelization: Constantine, Boniface, Augustine of Canterbury, the Carolingians knew circumstances of new and old coexisting in the transition between paganism and Christianity and in recognition of acculturated religious forms.

The first bishop, Isleif, was appointed in 1056 and he established himself at Skalholt. A second bishopric, at Holar, was established in 1106. Archaeologists have discovered the ruins of the enormous stave-built cathedral of Skalholt and the sarcophagus of Bishop Pal Jonsson (1195–1211). A codification of church law was made in 1123, seventeen years before Gratian the Canonist was to produce his famous *Decretum* at Bologna. The refinements of canonical discipline, however, were not put into practice: priests and bishops had concubines and children, and bishops exercised considerable secular authority. When, in a later age, the Reformation came to Iceland, it came as the religion of a Danish king, and the Bishop of Holar and his two sons died as defenders not only of the old religious order but also as defenders of the national liberties of the Icelandic people.

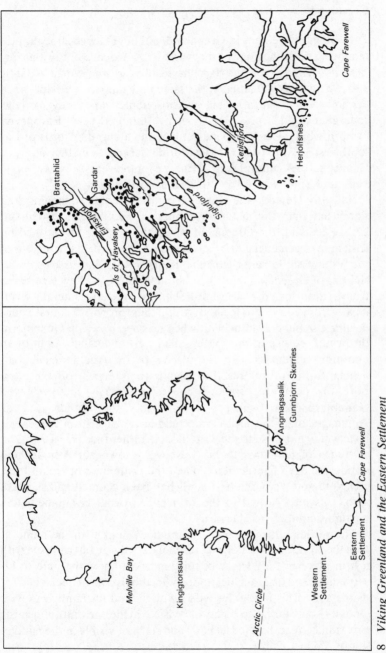

8 *Viking Greenland and the Eastern Settlement*

Greenland

The Viking settlement in Greenland, although never large, at best tenuous, and at the edge of the world, was evidence of the amazing capacity of these seamen–farmers to traverse the North Atlantic and live on marginal land. At the same time it provided evidence of the limits which nature, not always hospitable, imposes even on the courageous and strong. For about five hundred years Europeans lived in what were European settlements along the fjords of the southwest of this island – the world's largest – in the Western Hemisphere. A cultural map of Europe for the years between about 1000 and 1500 would have to include Greenland.

As with Iceland, the 'discovery' of Greenland remains less significant than the actual beginning of a European settlement. Unlike Iceland, the Greenland which the Vikings settled had no Irish monks penancing themselves *pro Christo* and, in the regions of the Viking settlements, no inhabitants at all. The first *recorded* sighting of Greenland took place about 900 and, as elsewhere, came from a storm-tossed, bearings-lost ship, this the ship of Gunnbjorn on its way from Norway to Iceland. A ship thus thrown off course could do little else but sail latitudinally when seas became calm; Gunnbjorn, thrown off course to the south, sailed west and caught sight of an enormous landmass with the glacier of Inolfsfjeld reaching to a height of 1900 metres. The islands (or skerries) off the coast bore his name for some centuries and early maps showed Gunnbjarnarsker, which were probably the islands east of Angmagssalik. The place-name could have come from the legend history that gave rise to the written saga, rather than *vice versa*. The existence of landmass to the west was known about in Iceland during the age of settlement. When the settlement of Iceland was complete and when the best lands had been claimed and secured, ambitious men turned to the west and to what lay immediately beyond Gunnbjorn's skerries.

The settlement of Greenland is synonymous with the name of Eric the Red, who was not a mere legendary figure but a person with a firm place in the history of this land. We know the date of his settlement and its exact location; archaeologists have unearthed for us the site of his house, his wife's church, and his family's graves. Unlike Gunnbjorn who is only half visible in the early morning mist, Eric stands clear, his Nordic body and red hair visible in the midday sun of Viking history.

Precise dates are not easy to come by in this matter. In the early 980s, probably 983 or 984, Eric the Red had his first view of this new land. His story, as told in the sagas, rings true and, at some crucial points, is corroborated by archaeological evidence. Eric and his father Thorvald had been forced to flee their home at Jaeren in southwest Norway near Stavanger about 970. They came to an Iceland already heavily settled, with only marginal lands remaining for latecomers. Feuding with neighbours in these marginal western lands led to bloodshed and the outlawing of Eric for a period of three years. This punishment gave Eric the time to explore the land sighted in the west by Gunnbjorn decades earlier. The distance from Snaefellsnes in Iceland to Angmagssalik, the nearest point in Greenland, is almost 450 miles, a four-day sail in good weather along the 65th parallel, out of sight of land for perhaps a day. Eric saw the formidable and uninviting eastern coast of Greenland and turned his ship southeast following the coast and rounding Cape Farewell. In the very southwest of this landmass – there is no evidence that they knew or even suspected it was an island – he and his men found green, rich-looking land on deep fjords, reaching out towards the mountains, a sight clearly reminiscent of Norway. The three years Eric spent along this southwest coast were years of 'land-development research'. He determined that the land was conducive to two distinct settlements: one in the extreme southwest and the other 400 miles further north along the west coast, to be called respectively the Eastern Settlement and the Western Settlement, for, in fact, they lay southeast–northwest in relation to one another. Although the saga says that Eric named the land 'Greenland' to make it sound more enticing to prospective settlers, a practice still known to land developers, the truth is that the land in the southwest around the cape was verdant, and promised abundance and growth, and that the climate was undoubtedly warmer then than later and, despite moderating trends, somewhat warmer than it is today.

The settlement which Eric founded in 985 or 986 was a response to his salesmanship. To those Vikings living on poor land in Iceland and remembering recent famine, the prospect of settling in a land of long fjords and green pastures must have been alluring. The story of twenty-five ships starting out from Iceland, filled with families and livestock, and only fourteen of them reaching their destination, might be an overdramatization, but surely a significant number of Icelanders sailed with Eric for the purpose of settling in Greenland.

Other settlers were to follow. In subsequent years the links with Iceland were to be maintained and fresh links were to be made directly with Norway. Two fairly large settlements resulted: according to contemporary accounts the Eastern Settlement at its height had 190 farms and the Western Settlement ninety farms. Eric established his farm at Brattahlid, and nearby the *thing*-place was fixed in an area of grassland. Christianity came to Greenland at the same time that it came to Iceland, about the year 1000, but there is no reason to believe that Eric's son Leif was its evangelist. The *Eric Saga* describes part of this Christianizing process in three sentences:

Eric was loath to leave the old religion, but Thjodhild, his wife, was converted at once and had a church built at a distance from the farmstead. It was called Thjodhild's church, and it was there that she and other converts would pray. Thjodhild refused to live with her husband after her conversion, and this greatly displeased him.

His displeasure might have subsided as Eric, in time, probably became a Christian. The Christian church was to prosper in Greenland. A diocese was established at Gardar near Eiriksfjord in 1126; a monastery of Austin canons at Ketilsfjord and a convent of Benedictine nuns at Siglufjord were both founded in the twelfth century; and a total of twelve parish churches in the Eastern Settlement and four parish churches in the Western Settlement are signs of a vital, if small, Christian community.

The families which were to inhabit this land for centuries lived principally by raising cattle and sheep. Their other resources included an abundance of fish and game. The Greenlanders had hunting grounds north of the Western Settlement (Nordseta, they called it), where they sought walrus, seals and white bears. How much further up this western coast did the Viking Greenlander go? A stone with runic inscriptions dating from the early fourteenth century has been found just south of 73°N latitude, and we do know that some Vikings sailed into Melville Bay near the 76°N latitude. Yet, for all that, the Viking settlement remained what it was from the beginning: two farming communities in the southwest, about 400 miles apart, with a population at its zenith of about 4000 persons.

Medieval witnesses to this settlement abound: papal letters, Bishops of Gardar at ecumenical councils, saga literature, tales of ships and polar bears as princely gifts at European courts. There is the vivid description written by the author of *King's Mirror,* a thirteenth-century book of court etiquette written in Old Norse:

The people in Greenland are few in number, since only part of the land is free enough from ice for human habitation. They are a Christian people with their own churches and priests. By comparison to other places it would form probably a third of a diocese; yet the Greenlanders have their own bishop owing to their distance from other Christian people. . . . One learns that the pasturage there is good and that the farms are large and prosperous. The farmers are engaged in raising large numbers of cattle and sheep and in making a great deal of butter and cheese; the people live principally on these products and on beef. In addition, they eat meat from reindeer, whales, seals, and bears.

Literary sources alone could provide the historian with a fairly full picture of the land and its people during this age. But this is only a part – might one rashly say a minor part? – of the evidence.

Nowhere else during the Viking era are we confronted with archaeological evidence which is so full, so precise and so clearly related to written sources as we are in Greenland. Beginning in the late nineteenth century and continuing with significant success in the years between the world wars and in the years since World War II, the excavations, which still go on each summer, have produced finds of a dramatic nature and others of less dramatic nature, but with a cumulative effect of probably greater significance. Archaeologists have revealed the sites of the two settlements. They have uncovered the foundations of hundreds of buildings, which in size, number and arrangement are as the sagas have indicated. The very site of Eric the Red's farm at Brattahlid has been clearly identified. The main part of the farmhouse resembles an Icelandic farmhouse of the same period and had a great hall measuring about 15 metres by 5 metres. Extensions had been added: a sleeping room, store rooms, a fire-house, in front of the hall a well, where today a spring bubbles, and, on the slope towards the sea, cow barns with stalls for twenty-eight cows. The walls were generally of thick turf, although some stone was used. Objects from the Viking period were scattered all over the site. Inside the house were walrus-boned gaming pieces, some knives, and a whetstone, and outside were such items as cooking pots and bowls, stone lamps, and fish and animal bones. In 1961 workmen, cutting a trench for a modern building, unexpectedly came across human skeletons: they had found the site of a Viking cemetery. Archaeologists soon took over, and their labours produced the remains of an early Viking church with its burial ground. The church itself had turf-and-stone walls, a U-shape and a wooden facade; its floor was paved with red sandstone. A small building, about 3.5 metres by 2 metres, it is not unlike contemporary churches in Iceland. The conclusion had to be drawn that this church was, in fact, the church of Thjodhild, Eric's wife, 'built at a distance from the farmstead', which was actually about 185 metres from the farmhouse, just within the limits of the fields in the immediate vicinity of the farmstead. The remains of about 150 people were found in this burial ground – men, women and children – and among them undoubtedly Thjodhild and her son Leif the Lucky and, perhaps, her husband Eric the Red.

The cathedral at Gardar, built in the twelfth century using local sandstone, exists now only in ruins. It was once a splendid building some 28 metres by 17 metres with transepts and choir. Nearby were the bishop's palace, which was 47 metres long and had a large hall, a tithe barn and cow barns which could hold a hundred cows. The site was, once again, littered with Viking-age objects: rings, knives, gaming-pieces, and, in the grave of a bishop, a gold ring and a handsome crozier-head made of walrus ivory.

The ice cover and deep frost of a later period helped to preserve a Viking-age cemetery at Herjolfsnes in the Eastern Settlement, south of Brattahlid, for archaeologists. These peculiar climatic conditions preserved the clothing in which the bodies had been lain: thirty dresses with narrow waists, full skirts, longish sleeves, and low decolletage; seventeen hoods with 'liripipes' (long streamers attached to the peak of the hood and falling down the back); and five hats, two roundish and the others conical in shape. Here, then, was part of the wardrobe of the later period of this settlement.

Less extensive but of no less significance are the eleventh-century church, its wall intact, on the island of Havalsey in the Eastern Settlement, the carved wooden crucifix from Sandnes in the Western Settlement, and the runic stone, already mentioned, at Kingigtorssuaq, an island off the western coast at 72°55'N.

The mounting quantities of archaeological evidence describe two settled communities of Greenlanders carrying on lives in a similar fashion to their Viking cousins in Iceland. Their homes, their farm buildings, the siting of dwelling places, their style of churches, their form of dress and their use of the *thing*, all testify to the presence of Europeans in the southwest of Greenland, a long way from ancestral Scandinavia, their lifestyles modified by their environment, but still Europeans.

The demise of this European settlement in Greenland puzzles all who study it. By the year 1500 or thereabouts it had ceased to exist. The colony established by Eric, which had thrived, become Christian, and for centuries adapted to its northerly location, expired without witnesses, without explanation, and without mourners. If there is any single question that historians of Greenland hope that archaeological excavations will provide an answer to, it must surely be the vexing question of the end of Viking Greenland. Theories abound, yet no observer recorded the last days, the final gasp of this civilization. An explanation that stresses climatic changes and plays down politico-economic factors probably lies as near to the truth as we can get at the moment. In 1261 this small, self-governing land came under the control of the King of Norway, who, it is often said, restricted its trade. Since much of Greenland's livelihood and well-being depended on the export of goods such as homespun cloth, skins of oxen, sheep, and seals, walrus rope, walrus tusks, and polar bears as well as the importation of timber, iron, and grain, in particular, such trade restrictions, it is argued, made life difficult. When the effects of these trade policies were joined to the effects of severe climatic changes, the settlements could not survive. More will be said about the climate later. Something must be said now about the reputed ill-effects of the subjection of Greenland to Norwegian rule in 1261. There was, indeed, an agreement in 1261 between the people of Greenland and the King of Norway; by this agreement Greenland was subject (until 1814, as events would have it) to the authority of the Norwegian monarch: fines were to be paid to him, his ombudsman was to act for him, and there were to be royal lands in the Eastern Settlement. It may be true that Norwegian merchants at Bergen were given a monopoly over trade with Greenland and that, as with Iceland, a specific number of ships (six a year for Iceland in 1262) could sail from Greenland to Norway. Yet, for this argument to have force, one must assume that Greenland was economically dependent on such trade with Norway. The truth seems to be that Greenland was essentially an economically self-sufficient land. Its major import need was timber: but there was no need to sail to Norway when ample supplies were to be found nearer than Norway at Markland – more about its location in the next chapter, but, for the moment, identify it with still wooded Labrador – and ships sailed to Markland as late as 1347. There is no evidence of a large volume of exports: in 1282 the Bishopric of Gardar paid its crusading tithe in goods (ox and seal skin, rope, and ivory from walruses), and their broker had trouble selling them in Norway. Walrus ivory and norwhal tusks probably were the mainstays of what was undoubtedly a small export business. The economy of Greenland was sufficiently independent to sustain the dislocation of its trade link with Norway.

Climatologists have reinforced what the sagas tell us: during the eleventh and twelfth centuries ice was virtually unknown in the waters between Iceland and the two Viking settlements in Greenland, and the temperature in these settled areas was 2°C to 4°C warmer than at present. From the beginning of the thirteenth century a mini ice-age affected the northern hemisphere, plunging the seawater temperature down to between 3°C and 7°C (about 3°C below the present-day temperature). This change was enough to bring the ice further and further south. Seasonal ice floes began to appear in the sailing lanes and near the settlements; their quantity increased; the ice season lengthened; and the ice floes were followed by icebergs. The author of *King's Mirror*, writing in the thirteenth century, described the ice hazards:

When one has sailed over the deepest part of the ocean, he will meet almost at once huge masses of ice in the sea, a phenomenon without parallel anywhere else. . . . There is also ice of a much different shape: the people of Greenland call them icebergs. They look like mountains rising high out of the sea.

In the middle of the following century a writer giving directions for sailing to Greenland warned that the old course could no longer be used: 'from the northeast ice has come down'. The Eskimoes had lived in Greenland long before the Vikings, and newer Eskimoes, probably from Alaska, lived in the northern part of Greenland during the Viking age. As the ice came further south so did these Eskimoes or, more exactly, so did the seal and their hunters, the Eskimoes. The Western Settlement had disappeared by the mid fourteenth century, overrun by the Eskimoes and left or utterly abandoned by the Vikings in the face of the impending peril from ice and man. An Icelandic annal under the year 1379 described how Eskimoes killed eighteen Greenlanders and enslaved two boys. This, however, could have been a hunting party of Europeans which had travelled too far north. Two years before this event Alf, Bishop of Gardar, died; he was never replaced. In 1385 the settlement was visited by Bjorn Jorsalafari, who remained for two years. Some Icelanders driven off course visited the Eastern Settlement in 1406. They stayed for four years and during their stay they attended a wedding preceded by the publication of banns and replete with Nuptial Mass according to proper ritual and solemnity. A hundred years later and, indeed, probably before 1500 the community was no more. In 1492 Pope Alexander VI wrote of a dimly remembered outpost of Christendom:

The diocese of Gardar lies at the bounds of the earth in the land called Greenland. The people there have no bread, wine, or oil; they sustain themselves on dried fish and milk. Very few sailings to Greenland have been possible because of the ice in the seas and these only in the month of August, when the ice has melted. It is reckoned that no ship has sailed there for eighty years and that no bishop or priest has resided there during this period. As a result, many inhabitants have abandoned the faith of their Christian baptism; once a year they exhibit a sacred linen used by the last priest to say Mass there about a hundred years ago.

It was gone, this last western outpost of European Christianity, its expiring unrecorded, its epitaph written by a Borgia pope in the same year that Christopher Columbus sailed west in search of India and 'discovered' instead a new world.

Selected further reading

The relevant sections of Gwyn Jones, *The Norse Atlantic Sagas*, Oxford University Press 1964, are filled with useful information and much good sense. Knowledgeable and eminently readable is Magnus Magnusson, *Viking Expansion Westward*, The Bodley Head 1973. For the Faroes see P. G. Foote, *On the Saga of the Faroe Islanders*, H. K. Lewis 1965; G. J. Marcus, 'The Norse emigration to the Faroe Islands', in *English Historical Review*, vol. 71 (1956), pp. 56–61; Sverri Dahl, 'The Norse settlement of the Faroe Islands', in *Medieval Archaeology*, vol. 14 (1970), pp. 60–73, and 'Recent excavations on Viking age sites in the Faroes', in P. G. Foote and Dag Strömbäck (eds.), *Proceedings of the Sixth Viking Congress*, Viking Society for Northern Research 1971, pp. 45–56. For Iceland Knut Gjerset, *History of Iceland*, Allen & Unwin 1924 is still quite useful. More recent works include Jon Johannesson, *A History of the Old Icelandic Commonwealth*, Winnipeg: University of Manitoba Press 1974, and Dag

Strömbäck, *The Conversion of Iceland: A Survey,* Viking Society for Northern Research 1975. Essential reading on Greenland is the magisterial work by Finn Gad, *The History of Greenland,* vol. I *Earliest Times to 1700,* C. Hurst 1970. For an excellent review of some of the archaeological excavations see Michael Wolfe, 'Norse archaeology in Greenland since World War II', in *American Scandinavian Review*, vol. 49 (1961), pp. 380–92.

4 The Vikings and the New World

The Vikings reached North America. This is an historical fact. The evidence, written and archaeological, allows for no doubt: sometime around the millenium men whose cultural ties reached beyond Greenland and Iceland to Scandinavia arrived on the shores of North America. To deny or even to cast doubt on this would be to fly in the face of overwhelming historical evidence.

The question of the historicity of the Vikings in the New World arises only because it is related to the question of who actually discovered America. The fascination with the discovery of America is really a fascination, not with the discovery of the Western Hemisphere – it was discovered perhaps 30,000 years ago by Asiatics – but with its much later discovery by *Europeans*: who was the first European to sight the New World? A more significant question historically would be: what circumstances, what patterns of human development led to a European presence on the western shores of the Atlantic Ocean? The discoveries in the late fifteenth century led to European settlements and, since then, to a continuous and dominant European presence. If not Christopher Columbus, then surely someone else – perhaps that Anglicized Italian Giovanni Cabotto – would have landed in America during the last decade of the fifteenth century. The person is less important than the historical forces at work which made, at least at that time, such a discovery inevitable. In the Viking age, four centuries earlier, still other forces made a landing in North America a virtual inevitability. The identity of the first Viking to sight America may never be known, perhaps with historical justice, for the first Viking to make landfall there was driven by forces spanning in distance the North Atlantic from the fjords of western and southern Norway and spanning in time several centuries of Viking explorations.

Early discoveries

Before the Vikings did other peoples cross the Atlantic to reach

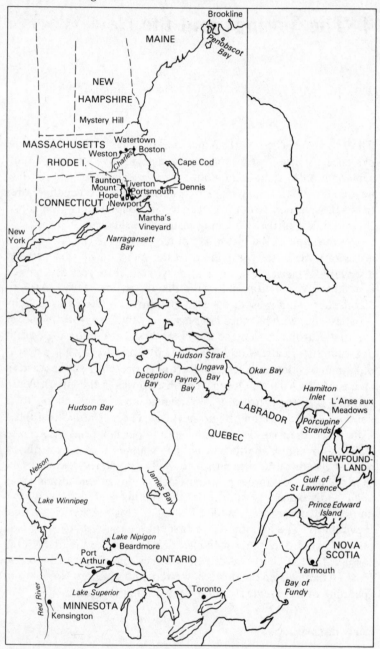

9   *The Vikings and the New World showing New England in inset*

America? The short answer is that they might have but the evidence at this point is non-existent. This whole matter has been bedevilled by frauds and forgeries as well as by well-intentioned enthusiasm. There is always a danger that important data in the hands of amateurs might be disregarded and even discredited by scholars because of the lack of professional presentation. An open mind on this issue allows for the possible emergence of compelling proofs – another Troy or Knossos might arise – but, for the moment, convincing evidence does not exist. What evidence there is should be looked at.

America before the Vikings? The question has the ring of anachronism about it. Better to ask: were there Mediterranean or European people in the Western Hemisphere before the arrival of the Vikings in about the year AD 1000? An affirmative answer can be based only on vague texts and very ambiguous engravings. With engaging enthusiasm the marine biologist Barry Fell, emeritus professor at Harvard University, has discovered, particularly in northern New England, a number of markings on stones which he identifies as from a proto-Ogam alphabet in early Celtic. At Mystery Hill in North Salem, New Hampshire, he read markings on stones associated with a series of underground chambers and interpreted these markings as words referring to Bal, the Celtic sun god. This form of proto-Ogam alphabet, as Fell describes it, only had consonants, which are rendered by straight vertical lines parallel to one another:

$$| = h, \quad || = d, \quad ||| = t, \quad |||| = c, \text{ etc.}$$

No other vowelless Ogam alphabet is known. Lines, such as the ones he describes, could easily have been cut into stone by means other than human beings intent on communication: tree roots, farm tools, glacial scarring, etc. It is intriguing, but we are no closer now than we ever have been to proving the existence of a Celtic community in New England 2500 years ago.

Stone engravings which, on the face of it, are evidence of a Phoenician presence in America have been found in places as far distant as Brazil and Tennessee. The inscription, allegedly discovered in Pouso Alto, Brazil, in 1873, describes its authors as Canaanites swept by storms across the South Atlantic from Africa. Scholars are now virtually unanimous in seeing this inscription as a clever forgery. The same verdict would seem to apply to the stone which was reputedly found about 1890 beneath the skull of a skeleton in Bat Creek, Tennessee, and which contains an Hebraic inscription allegedly of the second century AD.

The tale of Atlantis tells of a vast island west of Gibraltar, eventually swallowed up by the sea; a land whose inhabitants were once wise and mighty but later became corrupt and were defeated by the Athenians. It is just a tale. Plato, in telling it, conflated accounts of the Minoan decline on the island of Crete and Athens's rise to power. The tale was not taken seriously in antiquity nor should it be taken seriously today. Like Plato, the philosopher Plutarch spun the yarn of pilgrim-scholars sailing west from Britain beyond the ice to a great continent on the far fringe of the ocean, where Cronus slept in a shrine in a cave. Another myth, to be sure. These tales, and others like them, helped to keep alive a tradition of mythical lands across the Atlantic.

Saint Brendan – or, more exactly, the author of the *Navigatio sancti Brendani* – perpetuated this tradition of transatlantic islands and lands. Mystery surrounds Saint Brendan, his voyage, and the account of this voyage itself. In the mist of the Brendan story several facts are clearly visible: there was an historical Brendan (*c.* 490–580) who founded monasteries in the west of Ireland, the best known being Clonfert in Galway, and who sailed to Iona, the Western Isles, Wales, and possibly even Brittany. There the light of history fails us and we are back in the mist, with only the *Navigatio* to guide us. The text of the *Navigatio* probably dates from the early tenth century. It exists in over 120 Latin manuscripts, not to mention the manuscript tradition of the later, vernacular versions. An early Latin account probably existed by the year 800. The work, although clearly ecclesiastical, belongs in the tradition not of miracle-recounting hagiography but of *immrama*, Irish and Latin accounts of sea voyages. Briefly, the Brendan story describes a seven-year sea journey by Saint Brendan and his companions in a currach, a leather-sided sailing boat. Their pilgrimage in search of the Promised Land of the Saints took them to many islands, such as the island of sheep, the island of birds, the island of grapes, the island of smiths, the island of the fiery mountain. They encountered monasteries on many of these islands. Strange occurrences befell Brendan and his companions during these seven years. They went ashore on one island and lit a fire on the ground only to discover that the ground was not ground and the island was not an island: they had landed on the back of a whale and their fire had stung the whale.

(A similar incident is described in the second-century Greek bestiary *Physiologus* and, later, in *The Arabian Nights*.) Each year they would return to their whale at Easter time and conduct services on his back. On another occasion they encountered a huge sea monster which spouted foam from its nostrils. They even met a talking bird. One day they saw at a distance, and then went closer to examine, a crystal pillar, higher than the sky, with a meshed net around it where it rose out of the sea. Another day they came upon the apostle Judas sitting on a rock. And so their adventures went.

It is very tempting to try to identify some of these places and to see the island of sheep and the island of birds as two islands in the Faroes (Streymoy and Vagar), the island of the fiery mountain as Iceland, and the island of grapes as the Vinland of the Vikings. These are treacherous waters with uninviting shores: the directions given in the text, the inconsistencies of time durations, and the vagueness of relative locations, all make any precise identifications perilous in the extreme. By the year 800 Irish monks were indeed present in the Faroes and in Iceland, and the general description of these lands was undoubtedly known in Ireland at the time when the *Navigatio* was composed. Not much more can be said; the text speaks of other lands, and, even if these were real lands and not just fanciful, there is no reason to conclude that any one of them is to be located in America. Friendly and curious whales are not unknown in the North Atlantic – whales who, when exhaling, spout spray – nor does it tax the imagination to identify the crystal pillar with its meshed net as an iceberg and apron of surface ice. The currach that leather-sided, wood-framed boat which is still used in a modified form by fishermen in the west of Ireland, could indeed have sailed the Atlantic as Tim Severin proved by his exciting voyages in 1976 and 1977. During the sixth century Saint Brendan could have sailed the Atlantic, could have landed in the Faroes and Iceland, and could even have 'discovered' North America, but the text of the *Navigatio*, our only source, and itself a melange of the fanciful and the verisimilar, of the natural and the preternatural, of old *immrama* material and fresh material peculiar to itself, does not support such propositions. What the text does suggest is the continued existence in the ninth and early tenth centuries of knowledge of lands in the Atlantic and a curiosity about them. Evidence might some day emerge to demonstrate that Irish monks were in America centuries before the Vikings and nearly a millenium before Columbus; that evidence will almost certainly be archaeological. At the moment that evidence is not known to exist. America before the Vikings, for the moment at least, is only a land of fantasies and fairy tales.

The Viking explorations

In about the year 1000 Vikings sighted, landed at, explored, and attempted to settle on the North American littoral. The earliest written source is not, as one might suspect, the saga accounts, which exist in fourteenth- and fifteenth-century manuscripts drawn from twelfth- and thirteenth-century texts. The earliest written source dates from within a few generations of the attempted Viking settlement in America: *The History of the Archbishops of Hamburg*, completed by Adam of Bremen in about 1075. Book four of this history is entitled 'A Description of the Islands of the North', which makes Adam the earliest known German geographer. Sometime during the late 1060s Adam of Bremen visited the Danish court to gather information for his history and, while there, interviewed *inter alios* King Svein Estrithson, nephew of King Cnut the Great.

The king spoke about yet another island which had been discovered by many in that ocean. It is called Vinland because there grow wild in that country vines which produce fine wine. Free-growing crops abound there. I have learned this not from fanciful tales but from the trustworthy reports of the Danes.

Adam of Bremen had gathered this information in the late 1060s. King Svein, at whose court he learned these things, had been born in 1017, about the time when Vikings were attempting to colonize Vinland. It will never be known exactly when Svein learned about this land – as king (1047–74) he seems to have been visited by the Icelander Eadwine bearing the gift of a polar bear from Greenland – but what is certain is that we are dealing here with a nearly contemporary account.

Three other early, non-saga references confirm the continued knowledge of the existence of Vinland in Iceland. A geographical treatise of the twelfth century states:

South from Greenland there lie Helluland and then Markland and, not far beyond, Vinland.

The *Icelandic Annals* under the year 1121 record that 'Bishop Eric of Greenland set out in search of Vinland'. Iceland's first great historian, Ari Thorgilsson, writing in about 1127, indicated that he knew of Vinland and its native inhabitants from his uncle, Thorkell Gellison, who had learned about these things from one of the original settlers of Greenland. And thus, within a hundred years or so of the Vinland settlement Ari wrote about Vinland, almost incidentally, without need of explanation for none was needed.

The sagas, arising out of a different, if kindred, tradition, support this information and add significant facts of an indisputably historical nature. Meant for entertainment, the sagas existed in oral form at first and were written down only much later. The sagas require care in the use made of them by historians: not every detail can be relied on and not every statement rejected. Sagas celebrated the great deeds of the ancestors of later Icelanders, who enhanced their own importance through the flattering descriptions of the heroic men and women from whom they claimed descent. The two sagas which describe at length the Viking experience in the New World derive from this entertainment-giving, ancestor-praising tradition of the sagas. The *Greenlanders' Saga*, the earlier of the two, was committed to writing in the twelfth century and has about it a primitive crudeness which, while not particularly attractive literarily, does add to its historical credibility. The great anthology of Icelandic material, the *Flatey Book*, compiled towards the end of the fourteenth century in northern Iceland, contains the earliest extant text of this saga. The *Eric Saga*, on the other hand, has a more polished appearance and dates, in its earliest written form, from the mid thirteenth century, but exists only in two later medieval versions: the *Hausbók* version of the early fourteenth century and the *Skalholtsbók* version of the late fifteenth century, the latter a more faithful copy of the original. The *Greenlanders' Saga* and the *Eric Saga* tell essentially the same story, yet in some places they complement and in other places they contradict one another. It is now known that the *Greenlanders' Saga* is more reliable and its text more faithful to an oral original. Its story should be related.

The *Greenlanders' Saga* tells the Vinland story in three stages: the sighting, the exploration, and the attempted settlement of Vinland. This land to the south and west of Greenland, according to the saga, was discovered not by Leif Ericsson but by Bjarni Herjolfsson. This Icelander was accustomed to spend alternate winters in Iceland, with his father, and Norway. One winter while Bjarni was in Norway, his father Herjolf moved from Iceland to Greenland with Eric the Red and established a homestead there at Herjolfsnes. Bjarni did not learn about this until the following summer when he arrived in Iceland. Although neither Bjarni nor any of his crew had ever previously sailed to Greenland, they set sail and headed west. Strong north winds and deep fog forced them off course. When the bad weather lifted, they hoisted their sail and headed west once again. One day later they sighted a land, which was thickly forested and had low hills. This did not tally with the description of Greenland Bjarni had been given in Iceland, and, instead of landing, he turned the prow of his ship north. The land ebbed away from his port side. Two days later land was once again sighted. This flat, wooded land was not the Greenland of the glaciers, and, against the advice of his crew, Bjarni ordered his ship to sea once again. Three days later they sighted a land, mountainous, glacier-topped, and, in Bjarni's estimate, worthless. Putting this land astern, Bjarni sailed his ship in front of strong, gale-force winds from the southwest, and four days later they sighted a fourth land. Bjarni judged this to be Greenland and landed at a promontory, which as chance would have it was Herjolfsnes. There he settled and, in time, took his father's farm.

Some years later Eric the Red's son Leif, who, like all Greenlanders, was curious about new lands, decided to explore the places sighted by Bjarni. He bought Bjarni's ship – was there a feeling that the vessel might know its own way? – and enlisted a crew of thirty-five. The sailing plan was simply to retrace Bjarni's route. This they did successfully. They sighted, first, the mountainous, glacier-topped land, which Bjarni had sighted last. Unwilling to bear the same criticism that had been heaped on Bjarni, Leif lowered a boat and went ashore. The land was, indeed, worthless: glaciers inland and, between glaciers and the sea, slabs of rock. He called the place Helluland (i.e., Slab-land). The next land they sighted had white sandy beaches and, beyond these, flat woodlands. Leif landed, called it Markland (i.e., Forest-land), and sailed on. Two days later they caught sight of land again. To the north of this land lay an island and they landed there. They put the dew from the grass to their lips and marvelled at its sweetness. Leif now ordered his ship to go west around the promontory which lay to their south into an open sound. Not waiting for the tide to turn, they rushed ashore. Later they brought the ship up a river and anchored it in a lake at the riverhead, where they set up temporary shelters for themselves. The river had salmon bigger than they had ever seen and the plentiful grass appeared abundant for their livestock. They decided to winter there and so built houses. Leif arranged exploring parties to go out from their camp, but one of his men, a southerner (a German?) called Tyrkir, disappeared and, while Leif was preparing a search, Tyrkir stumbled into the camp, tipsy on the grapes he had found. Leif called the place Vinland (i.e., Wine-land). Night and day in this land were of more equal length than in Greenland. Leif and his crew readied a cargo of vines, grapes and timber and returned to Greenland the following summer. That was the extent of Leif's involvement in the explorations: he had retraced Bjarni's route, landed at three places, named them, and spent a winter at the third (Vinland). Thus ends the story of Leif Ericsson and the New World.

The colonizing expeditions which followed involved other children of Eric the Red: Thorvald, who died in Vinland, Thorstein, who never reached his destination, the latter's widow Gudrid and her then husband Thorfinn Karlsefni, and Eric's murderous daughter Freydis. The boat which had taken Bjarni by accident and Leif by design was sold to Thorvald Ericsson. With a crew of thirty he sailed to Vinland and found Leif's houses, where they wintered. Explorations to the west revealed attractive country of woods and sandy beaches. After another winter at Leif's houses Thorvald and his men sailed, first, eastward along the coastline and then, north, putting in at a thickly wooded promontory between two fjords. It was here that the Vikings made their first recorded contact with the native people of North America. The Vikings noticed what looked like three humps on the beach; closer inspection showed the humps to be skin boats, each covering three men. One man escaped; the other eight were captured and executed. Europe met America in unprovoked violence. Suddenly the fjord was alive with skin boats, and the Europeans fled for their lives, although Thorvald, stung by an arrow, failed to escape with his. The crew returned to Greenland without Thorvald's body but with tales of *skraelings* (uglies) on the beautiful shores of Vinland.

Thorstein, another son of Eric, went with his wife Gudrid and a crew of twenty-five in search of his brother's body so that he might bring it back to Greenland. They set out in the same ship, which had already travelled the route three times, but foul weather tossed them mercilessly until it was almost winter when they were able to land at the Western Settlement of Greenland. During that winter, sickness struck the settlement, killing Thorstein and leaving Gudrid widowed. She returned with her husband's body to Brattahlid, in the Eastern Settlement, where she buried it in consecrated ground. There she met a visiting Icelander, the wealthy Thorfinn Karlsefni, and they married. At Gudrid's urging Karlsefni agreed to undertake a colonizing expedition to Vinland. Together they sailed, taking with them a company of sixty men, five women, and a cargo of livestock of various kinds. The familiar voyage – presumably some of the men had sailed this way before – was easily accomplished. The new settlers quickly adjusted to life at the Leif site: they put their cows out to pasture, lived off the wild fruit and crops as well as the game and fish they caught. The intention was to stay and create a permanent settlement. After the first winter they encountered a large number of *skraelings*, who one day simply came out of the woods at the settlement site. The settlers' bull roared at the *skraelings* and frightened them. Soon, however, the Vikings and *skraelings* were trading: the natives' furs for the colonists' cow's milk. During that summer Gudrid gave birth to a son Snorri, the first European reported born in the Western Hemisphere. Early that next winter the *skraelings* returned to trade and, in a disagreement, a *skraeling* was killed. Battle soon followed, and the Vikings, pushing their bull ahead of them, drove their attackers away. Karlsefni decided, when spring came, to abandon the settlement. After only two winters the colonists returned to Greenland. Karlsefni, Gudrid and the young Snorri eventually settled in Iceland. After her husband's death Gudrid was to travel to Rome and, later, back in Iceland she became a nun. Among her descendants were three twelfth-century Icelandic bishops: small wonder that the twelfth-century *Greenlanders' Saga* sang the praise of this woman and her relations (Eric's family and Karlsefni).

One member of Eric's family, however, is not praised in the *Greenlanders' Saga*, and that is Freydis, Eric's daughter. In partnership with two Icelanders she sailed to Vinland and the Leif site. Disagreements broke out there, and Freydis had her partners and their men killed, she herself slaying their five women with the sharp end of an axe. This tale of the murderous Freydis ends the *Saga's* description of the attempted settlements in Vinland: three in number, all at the same site, two unsuccessful because of hostile encounters with the native people and the third unsuccessful because of a wicked woman. Nine brief chapters and the story of Vinland is told – or, at least, part of the story.

The *Eric Saga* tells a fuller story, repeating some of the details of the earlier saga, omitting some, changing others, and adding still others. This saga makes no mention of Bjarni and attributes the discovery of the New World to Leif Ericsson, now described as a missionary sent by King Olaf of Norway to evangelize Iceland and Greenland. Difficulties at sea threw Leif's ship off course, and he sighted a new land where there grew wild wheat, grapes and mosur (maple?) trees. Nearby he discovered and saved some shipwrecked men, and from this time he was called Leif the Lucky. After one winter there Leif made his way to Greenland to carry out his evangelizing mission. At this point, after less than a chapter, Leif disappears from the *Eric Saga*. The next voyage was led by Karlsefni and his wife Gudrid, widow of Thorstein Ericsson, and contained a company, including Freydis and Thorval, intent upon settlement. They sighted and landed briefly at a place they called Helluland and later at a place they called Markland. Beyond a long stretch of sandy beach – they named it Furdustrand – they found inlets and after some exploration put into a fjord, where there were vines and wild wheat. The first winter proved so severe that they decided to sail further south. After sailing for a long time they came to the estuary of a river that flowed from a lake. Here there were vines and wild wheat and the sea teemed with fish. They settled here; no snow came that winter, but in the spring there came the *skraelings*, first to trade – *skraeling* pelts for Viking cloth – and later to do battle. At this point the *Eric Saga* seeks to rehabilitate the memory of Freydis and portrays her as a valiant woman who, standing her ground while men fled, pulled out one of her breasts and slapped it with a sword as the *skraelings* fled in terror. Despite her heroism the Vikings decided to return to Greenland. On the way they made several stops. At one place they met a uniped, who slew Thorvald with an arrow; at another place, Gudrid gave birth to Snorri. The saga ends by naming the three twelfth-century Icelandic bishops descended from Karlsefni and Gudrid.

What can be concluded from these saga accounts? Three facts stand out above all else as indisputable: the Vikings reached North America; they then attempted to establish a settlement at Vinland; and they abandoned their settlement after hostile encounters with the native people. Minor stories such as the tipsy Tyrkir or the breast-thumping Freydis can be placed to one side: interesting when telling a story, but not necessarily for anything else. Sagas had to be created within an historically and geographically credible context. The heroes had to be real people, their voyages true voyages, the sailing directions believeable to sophisticated seafarers. Some details should be looked at. The omission, for example, of Bjarni as the discoverer of the new lands in the story as told in the *Eric Saga* is quite suspicious. That saga writer, well aware of the account of the *Greenlanders' Saga*, suppressed the Bjarni incident entirely and left it to a sea-tossed Leif to sight the new land. The *Eric Saga* throughout magnifies the families of Eric and his daughter-in-law Gudrid, and, in the case of Leif, this author attributed to him the conversion of Greenland, which we know is untrue. The conscious bypassing of Bjarni in favour of Leif fits into this general pattern. (Consider, too, the turning of the murderous Freydis into the valiant woman!) It is Bjarni Herjolfsson whom we must see in the sagas as the discoverer of North America. The references to the details of the land itself are so insistent and so much in agreement that there can be little doubt that the Vikings found a land where crops and what appeared to be grapes grew wild and where salmon ran in the rivers. This is firm ground for the historian.

Further questions impose themselves: when did these Europeans visit the New World? and where did they land there? The latter question will be dealt with presently; the other, easier question, now. Bjarni made his discovery in the year in which Eric the Red brought settlers back with him from Iceland to Greenland. There is unanimous agreement that this has to be 985 or 986. It was in the late summer that Bjarni failed to find his father in Iceland and sailed on to sight the new land. Dating Leif's voyage of exploration requires some attention. The *Greenlanders Saga*, which generally is preferable, recounts that this voyage occurred while *Jarl* Erik ruled in Norway (1000–14), whereas the *Eric Saga* portrays Leif as a missionary sent by King Olaf Tryggvason of Norway (995–1000). Olaf was killed and *Jarl* Erik became the ruler of much of coastal Norway in September of the year 1000. Bjarni's visit to Eric can be dated as 1001 at the earliest and as 1014 at the latest. Bjarni stayed in Norway a winter and returned to Greenland in the following summer, 1002 at the earliest and 1015 at the latest. It was at this point that Leif then sailed. Greater precision is unnecessary. The only settlement mentioned in both saga accounts was the settlement built by Thorfinn Karlsefni and Gudrid his wife; by each account it lasted three years. When did it take place? At the time of this settlement Snorri was born. We can follow his line. Snorri had a daughter Hallfrid, who gave birth to Thorlak, future Bishop of Skalhold. The Icelandic annals state that Thorlak was born in 1085. If we assume that Snorri was forty years old when he sired Hallfrid and that Hallfrid was twenty years old when she bore Thorlak, this would mean that Snorri was born in 1025. Other assumptions, of course, would lead to other conclusions. Yet it seems fairly safe to say that the Karlsefni settlement, during which Snorri was born, took place some time during the second or third decade of the eleventh century. Where he was born and where this settlement was located remains to be seen.

Location of Vinland

The vexed question concerning the location of Vinland must be faced. One distinction should be made at the outset. The Vikings, in giving names to places, gave names to large regions (for example, Iceland, Greenland) and names to particular places (for example, Breidafjord, Brattahlid). The names Helluland, Markland and Vinland were given to large regions, to areas with hundreds of miles of coastline. Historians are virtually unanimous in locating Helluland at Baffin Island, just two hundred miles across the Davis Strait from Greenland. There the land is much as it was at the turn of the millenium: towering glaciers in the interior and stone-slabs sloping from them to the sea. Markland, that thickly wooded region with miles of sandy beaches, must be seen as Labrador, for, despite intervening climatic changes, the area of Labrador south of Hamilton Inlet is still thickly forested with a strand of sandy beaches, and in Viking times the timber-line might have been as far north as Okak Bay. No mountains are to be found here, just a rolling coastal plain. It was along this coastline that Karlsefni found an extraordinary length of sandy beach, which he named Furdustrand (i.e., marvellous shore). This should be identified, it would seem, with the Porcupine Strands, which are forty-five miles of virtually unbroken beach, at most points about fifty metres wide and backed by dunes.

Vinland, the land to the south of Markland, has been located at scores of places along the eastern coast of North America, as far south even as Florida. Local pride, enthusiastic amateur archaeology, and (alas!) fraud have produced most of these claims. One must begin any inquiry into the location of Vinland with the texts themselves. Adam of Bremen and the two sagas agree not only on the name of this land but the reason for it: Vinland, the land of wine-producing grapes. Ingenious attempts to translate Vinland as grassland are not convincing for they run in the face of the earliest written evidence. What were perceived by the Vikings as grapes were an unmistakable mark of this land. Adam of Bremen and the sagas also agree that the land had fields rich with crops that were self-sown. The sagas marvel at the salmon jumping in the rivers. They describe a promontory with an island to its north and a sound to its west and, along the sound, shallows at the estuary of a river which flows into the sea from a lake: a description applicable to hundreds of places in northeastern North America. Little can be made of the land description by itself.

One way to approach the question is to define the area within which grapes grow and salmon swim, leaving aside the ambiguous reference to the self-sown crops (wheat? rye? grass?). In other words, how far south does one find salmon and how far north does one find grapes? At the present time salmon are found no further south than 41°N and wild grapes no further north than 42°N. This would place Vinland somewhere between New York City and Boston. Such an easy explanation, however, fails to take into account climatic changes which occurred between the Viking period and modern times. If we can believe that a cooling period intervened – and the evidence for this is compelling – then modern references are of no great help. This having been said, it should quickly be added that in the sixteenth century Jacques Cartier found wild grapes growing on Prince Edward Island and along the St Lawrence River. There, with the climatologists, let us leave the literary texts.

If Vinland is to be located with more accuracy than simply 'south of Markland', it will be located by archaeology. With such a long coastline – even if one limits oneself to the region north of Chesapeake Bay – the professional archaeologist is faced with literally hundreds of likely places consonant with the saga descriptions. He must rely to a large extent upon chance finds by fishermen, farmers and amateur archaeologists. A list of sites so far found and alleged to be of Viking origin would fill pages. The discovery in 1824 of an authentic rune stone in Kingigtorssuaq, Greenland, which gave the names of the men and the date at which they reached this northern point, triggered off an interest in discovering Viking remains in Vinland. Alleged runic inscriptions

were found near Taunton, Massachusetts – the Dighton Stone –
inscriptions which, although noted by Cotton Mather and others a
century before, gained considerable attention as Norse runes only in
the nineteenth century. They are now seen clearly not to be Norse at
all but Algonquin Indian in origin, the very conclusion reached by
President Washington in 1789 when he was shown a copy at
Harvard College. Elsewhere in Massachusetts other claims have
since arisen. One enthusiast located Viking traces in the town of
Dennis on Cape Cod: at Follen's Pond at the head of the Bass River
a rock with a mooring hole was found, and nearby was a shoring.
Carbon-14 dating tests show that this is not a Viking site. Likewise,
an eccentric nineteenth-century professor of chemistry, Eben N.
Horsford, saw alleged remains of the Vikings in the Boston area and
located Vinland, as befitted a Harvard man, on the banks of the
Charles River upstream from Cambridge at Watertown. The statue
of Leif Ericsson on the Commonwealth Avenue Mall in Boston's
Back Bay and the Norumbega Monument in Weston are two
reminders of this Viking fever in the Boston area. One further
incident in Massachusetts: in about 1920, at No Man's Land beach
near Martha's Vineyard, a stone was found bearing in runic letters
the name of Leif Ericsson and the date in Roman numerals MI. A
practical joker from nearby New Bedford is suspected here.

The neighbouring state of Rhode Island has made its own claims.
At Mount Hope an inscribed rock was called, variously,
'Northmen's Rock' and 'Leif's Rock'; also, at Portsmouth and at
Tiverton records of other rocks bearing inscriptions have emerged.
The inscriptions on such rocks, used occasionally to authenticate a
Narragansett Bay site for Vinland, have long since been discarded
as either natural markings, Indian words, or schoolboy graffiti.
Taken much more seriously, however, has been the Newport
Tower, a circular stone tower seven and a half metres high, and
located at the top of a rise of land in Newport, Rhode Island. The
claim made for this is simply that it is a fourteenth-century Viking
tower, possibly a baptistry or a church. Visions of Vikings at
Newport inspired Henry Wadsworth Longfellow to write 'The
Skeleton in Armor', a poem about a Viking and his lady:

> Three weeks we westward bore,
> And when the storm was o'er,
> Cloud-like we saw the shore
> > Stretching to leeward;

> There for my lady's bower
> Built I the lofty tower,
> Which, to this very hour,
>   Stands looking seaward. . . .
>
> There lived we many years;
> Time dried the maiden's tears;
> She had forgot her fears,
>   She was a mother;
> Death closed her mild blue eyes,
> Under that tower she lies;
> Ne'er shall the sun arise
>   On such another.

Excavations at the tower site in 1948 and 1949 unearthed not Longfellow's Norse maiden but artefacts no earlier than mid seventeenth-century in origin; principal among these were fragments of clay pipe found in the construction ditch itself. The Newport Round Tower stands on land owned from 1651 to 1677 by Benedict Arnold, Governor of Rhode Island, who referred to this tower in his will as a windmill. Modern debunkers of this alleged Viking tower have described it as virtually identical in design with a stone windmill at Chesterton in Warwickshire, England, near Arnold's family home there, but there is no clear evidence that Arnold had any connection with that part of England. Whatever the source of its design the Newport Round Tower dates from the early colonial period.

Nova Scotia has its claims, chief of which is the Yarmouth Stone. This stone, found on the shore of the Bay of Fundy opposite the town of Yarmouth, contains markings, which, in 1884, were deciphered as 'Hako's son addressed the men'. The conclusion drawn was that Hako was the Haki mentioned in the sagas as a companion of Karlsefni. This fanciful reading is based on markings which bear no resemblance to any known alphabet and are probably nothing more than random scratchings or Indian symbols. Even in upper Canada there have been outbreaks of Viking fever. At Beardmore, Ontario, near Lake Nipigon, a gold miner related that, while blasting for gold, several objects were blown out of the soil. They consisted of a sword, broken in two, an axehead, part of a horse rattle, and three unidentifiable fragments. The iron objects, without any doubt, are Norse and date from the late Viking period. The Royal Ontario Museum in Toronto purchased these artefacts

Overleaf **Top left** *The Kensington Stone, an alleged Viking remain found in 1898 near the village of Kensington in Minnesota*

Right *Two sides of a Norse penny, found at Goddard's farm, near Brookline in Maine*

Bottom *Thingvellir: the site of the Icelandic general assembly, the Althing, which met for the first time probably in the summer of 930*

This page Right *The Jelling stone: the royal memorial erected by Harald Bluetooth in memory of his mother and father*

Below *Part of the Cuerdale Hoard, a hoard of early tenth-century silver, found near the River Ribble in Lancashire*

for five hundred dollars in 1936, not an inconsiderable amount in depression dollars. The son of the alleged finder later swore that he had seen these objects in his father's cellar in Port Arthur, Ontario, at a time before they were 'found' in the earth. These authentic Viking-age pieces appear to have been imported about 1923 from Scandinavia to the Port Arthur area, where there was a Norwegian community. A minor hoax in the history of Viking hoaxes.

The most troublesome and most persistent, the best known, and the seemingly most irrepressible hoax has to be the Kensington rune stone. During the last half of the nineteenth century thousands of Scandinavian immigrants settled in Douglas County in Minnesota, where Kensington is located. They were mainly Swedish and Norwegian, and they began to speak a mixed dialect, known nowhere else in the world. Olof Ohman, an immigrant from Sweden, arrived in Douglas County in 1879. In 1898 he claimed that while clearing farm land he found a stone slab enwrapped, in part, by the roots of a poplar tree. Shaped like a tombstone, the stone he found measured eighty centimetres high, forty centimetres wide, and about thirteen centimetres thick. In November of that year the discovery was announced; the stone had a runic inscription. Its text reads:

Eight Goths [Swedes] and twenty-two Norwegians exploring west from Vinland. One day's journey north of this stone we had our camp near two skerries. One day we went out fishing and found on our return the dead bodies of ten of our men, red with blood. AVM [Ave Maria] preserve us from evil. Fourteen days' journey from this island ten men are looking after our ships.
Year 1362

They had apparently sailed in a westerly direction from Vinland, through the Hudson Strait south of Baffin Island, into Hudson Bay, whence they followed a course up the Nelson River to Lake Winnipeg and then by the Red River into Minnesota. According to the inscription, a group of them on a fishing trip had encountered violence, and the remainder, trying to return to their ship some distance away, left this stone.

The swift reaction of scholars in America and in Scandinavia who studied copies of the inscription was that it was a forgery. And in 1899 the matter rested at that, but, unfortunately, it had a resurrection. In 1909 the writer Hjalmar Rued Holand, a Norwegian by birth but a graduate of the University of Wisconsin, visited Kensington, acquired the stone, and began a crusade, which lasted half a century, to publicize the Kensington rune stone as an authentic fourteenth-century object. At the millenial anniversaries of Normandy in 1911 he exhibited his treasure. Mr Holand's crusade was so successful that in 1948 the Smithsonian Institution in Washington, DC, publicly exhibited the stone. Senior staff members hailed it as authentic, and *Speculum*, the distinguished journal of the Medieval Academy of America, gave an article favourable to these claims prime position in its July 1950 issue. The Kensington stone, in fact, was carved sometime during the 1880s or 1890s – some would suggest between August and November 1898 – by a person (or persons) using a one-inch chisel, available in any turn-of-the-century hardware store in Minnesota, and having some knowledge of the runic alphabet and familiarity with the peculiar local dialect. About one-third of the runes on the stone are either otherwise unknown in the fourteenth century or are in conflict with the usage of that period. In addition, the language resembles no known form of any Norse language except the mixed Norwegian–Swedish of the immediate area. Also, schoolchildren in Sweden in the nineteenth century were taught, in an elementary manner, the runic alphabet of their ancestors. Who actually perpetrated the hoax – the farmer, his neighbour, the local schoolteacher, or someone else – is of no great moment, for the matter might have been intended as a joke which got out of hand. One can only wish the Kensington rune stone, like the fictitious Vikings it describes, a fervent *requiescat*.

During its lifetime the Kensington stone spawned other 'discoveries' in the Minnesota region: one feared for a while that such 'discoveries' might eventually outnumber the lakes of that beautiful state. In the Great Lakes area dozens of objects have been carefully examined and judged to be of recent origin, for instance, the 'Norse halberds', which have now been identified as tobacco cutters distributed by the American Tobacco Company to promote Battle-Ax Plug Tobacco in the late nineteenth century.

It is not clear how the Vikings are supposed to have reached the state of Oklahoma, but a sandstone stone found near Heavener in the Poteau Mountains in eastern Oklahoma is alleged to have a runic inscription: GNOMEDAL (transliterated into Roman letters), which is probably nothing more than the name of Mr G. Nomedal, a Norwegian homesteader. And as for the other fifty runic inscriptions reputed to be in eastern Oklahoma. . . .

Serious attention deserves to be given to two archaeological projects in Canada, one in Quebec and the other in Newfoundland; neither has arisen or taken hold from sentiments of local piety. The first, about which opinion has not yet crystallized, is taking place in northern Quebec along the western shore of Ungava Bay at two sites: Payne Bay and Deception Bay. It would not appear unreasonable that Norse Greenlanders sailed south of Baffin Island through the Hudson Strait into Ungava Bay. At these sites Thomas E. Lee has discovered a number of longhouses as well as stone implements, a piece of bone, and an iron axe-head. It is not in doubt that the material could be as old as the Viking age. What is in doubt is whether these material objects are Norse or Dorset Eskimo. Parallels with known Norse houses, particularly in Iceland and in Scandinavia, have been suggested as having parallels with known Dorset-type houses in the Canadian arctic. Although the iron axe-head was laminated in a way that accords with contemporary European practice, it is unlike any known Viking axe-head. The jury is still out, but one must not rule out the possibility of a Viking presence in Ungava Bay.

Until 1960 L'Anse aux Meadows, Newfoundland, was a tiny, unknown fishing village of about seventy souls, cut off from its neighbours except by the sea. Now a road runs into that village, a national park has been opened there, and its name has been broadcast across lands and seas. L'Anse aux Meadows is the site of the well-publicized excavations which have unearthed ineluctible evidence of an early Norse settlement in the New World. In 1960 Dr Helge Ingstad, former Governor of Greenland, sailed north from Rhode Island along the northeast coast of North America in search of a Vinlandic site. At the village of L'Anse aux Meadows on the northernmost tip of Newfoundland he asked George Decker, a descendant of original English settlers, about any ruins in the vicinity. Dr Ingstad was led a short distance west from the village to the shores of Epaves Bay at Black Duck Brook. Contours on an old beach terrace led him to believe that this might be a site worth further investigation. Behind this beach-side site rise low, rolling hills. The forests are now some distance away. The outstanding feature today is the lushness of its fields, unparalleled at this latitude in North America. Great Sacred Island stands sentry-like to the north of Epaves Bay. Dr Ingstad decided to excavate. Every summer from 1961 to 1968 the archaeologist Anne Stine Ingstad, his wife, directed the operations at the site, and in 1977 she published a scientific report of the excavations.

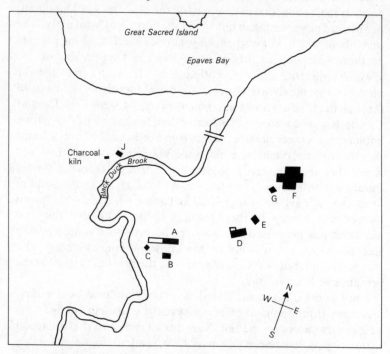

10   *Excavated site at L'Anse aux Meadows, Newfoundland.*
   A–F are buildings and J is a smithy

What did the Ingstads find at L'Anse aux Meadows? Quite simply, they found the remains of a small Norse community of the eleventh century. They discovered to the east of the brook three clusters of houses and to the west of the brook a smithy and a charcoal kiln. The buildings have walls constructed of horizontal layers of turf placed one on top of another. In each cluster there was a longhouse and one or more smaller, satellite houses; they were built on an ancient marine terrace which lies about 4 metres above sea level at high tide. Each of the longhouses (A, D, F) had a side wall facing the sea, and the entrance was through a door on the other, southerly side, facing the sun. House A had curved walls, and its interior measured 24 by 4 metres. In its four rooms were found hearths, cooking pits, and post holes. It resembles the longhouse at Narssaq in the Eastern Settlement of Greenland, which bears a runic inscription dating back to about AD 1000. A wall might have enclosed the area between A, B, and C, thus forming an animal yard. House D had three rooms and seems to have been built by adding an extension to a longhouse along the longitudinal axis and, later, a smaller extension from that. House F, the largest building on the site with an interior area of 14 by 21 metres, had five or possibly six rooms. The largest room, its 'hall', measured 8 by 3.2 metres; in its centre was a long hearth (1.9 by .5 metres), containing a cooking pit (50 centimetres in diameter and 15 centimetres deep), a stone-lined ember pit, and a large, flat stone used for cooking. Near to this longhouse lay building G, which closely resembles Scandinavian steam (or bath) houses, not unlike the sauna houses still used in Finland: a fire in the hearth heated stones, on to which cold water would have been poured. The smithy across the brook had been cut into the terraces, and these formed three of its walls. A hearth for a forge, a stone slab for an anvil, and hundreds of slag and iron fragments were found at the smithy. In general, the buildings at this site represent Scandinavian buildings, and on the basis of the buildings themselves one has sufficient confidence to describe this as a Norse community.

The artefacts found at L'Anse aux Meadows, although not as plentiful as one would have liked, confirm the architectural evidence and point unmistakably to a Norse origin. Near the doorway to longhouse F, a soapstone spindle whorl was found; it resembles very closely a spindle whorl found in Greenland – nothing of this sort can be attributed to aboriginal North Americans at this date – and indicates the presence of sheep at this Norse settlement. A small, rounded stone with a hollow was, no doubt, a lamp used to burn oil; it is very similar to Icelandic lamps of the Viking period and not similar at all to known Eskimo lamps. Near a hearth in house D, the excavators found a fragment of copper which had been produced by smelting, a process not used by natives of the area. A fragment of a bone needle had a drilled eye, a feature impossible for the Dorset Eskimoes. Of greatest significance is the ring-headed bronze pin, undoubtedly of Norse–Celtic origin. This pin, with a ring looped through a hole drilled at the top of the shank, has no ornamentation and measures 10 centimetres, and it bears a very close resemblance to pins found throughout northern Europe. Over a score of such pins from the Viking period have been found in graves in Norway alone, a half dozen or so in Iceland, and one, most recently, has been found at the site of the High Street excavations in

Dublin. Many fragments of iron rivets, now almost completely rust, were also found. In addition, most hearths contained charcoal remains.

The age of this Norse settlement at L'Anse aux Meadows is still to be discussed. The excavators have had some of the material found at this site subjected to radiocarbon testing. This process presumes that the concentration of radioactive carbon 14 in atoms in living organisms has remained constant for thousands of years and that upon the death of a living organism the rate of decay of these atoms takes place at a measurable rate: roughly speaking, the more C^{14} remaining the younger the object, the less C^{14} remaining the older. The carbon-14 test does not permit precise dating; the margin of error is expressed as a plus or minus ($\pm$) factor of a specified number of years. Since 1962 the measurement process has been corrected and further refined.

Sixteen samples from the L'Anse aux Meadows site were subjected to C^{14} analysis. They included thirteen samples of charcoal, two of turf from walls, and one of a whale bone. Table 1 indicates the results.

Table 1   *Results of C^{14} analysis on samples from the L'Anse aux Meadows site*

Sample	Corrected dates
House A – turf	1020 ± 100
– charcoal	670 ± 140
House B – charcoal	760 ± 120
House C – charcoal	740 ± 140
House D – charcoal	920 ± 80
House E – charcoal	850 ± 80
House F – charcoal	900 ± 80
– bone	1040 ± 110
– turf	1020 ± 60
– charcoal	730 ± 80
House G – charcoal	1090 ± 80
Smithy J – charcoal	890 ± 100
– charcoal	1080 ± 80
Kiln – charcoal	850 ± 80
Cooking pit 1 – charcoal	820 ± 100
Cooking pit 2 – charcoal	840 ± 100

What strikes an observer is the closeness in age of the turf and bone samples: all (with plus-or-minus factors) in the first half of the eleventh century. Equally striking is the wide variety in dates attributed to the charcoal samples, one as early as 670 ± 140 and one as late as 1090 ± 80. Charcoal presents a difficulty for the scientist because of the uncertainty of the time elapsed between the death of the tree and its subsequent use by man as fuel. It is reasonable to assume that the charcoal samples at L'Anse aux Meadows derive from driftwood: among the tree sources identified by particle analysis are species of trees which have never been known to grow in this part of Newfoundland and which must have arrived there as driftwood. Every indication of tide and current would suggest that Epaves Bay has long been a driftwood bay. Hundreds of years could have elapsed from the time when a tree died till the time when, as driftwood, it was used as fuel in the fires of this settlement. It is scarcely scientific, however, for the researchers to give us a mean age for all the samples (charcoal and others) in an apparent attempt to discount the very early dating of some charcoal samples; it is given as 920 ± 30 and is clearly meaningless. Setting aside the charcoal samples, however, the remaining samples (two turf and one bone) yield dates (1020 ± 100, 1020 ± 60, and 1040 ± 110) which are quite consistent with the archaeological findings and the evidence of the sagas.

One worrying issue about L'Anse aux Meadows remains: the name Vinland. According to Adam of Bremen and the sagas, the land discovered by the Vikings abounded in wine-yielding grapes. No grapes now grow in this region. Inconveniently, sophisticated pollen analyses of samples taken from the site clearly show that no profound vegetational change has taken place there for the past seven and a half millenia and, hence, it is highly improbable that grapes grew there during the Viking age. The climate at the time of the Viking settlement, despite an intervening cold period, was similar to the climate of today: sharp differences between winter and summer temperatures, which, in both seasons, are moderated by the Labrador Current and the Gulf Stream, thus producing much fog and a short season (about 100 days) for crops. Grapeless though this land was a thousand years ago, it did produce a wide variety of berries, some of which were 'wineberries', particularly the squashberry and both the red and the black currants; these might quite conceivably have been interpreted as grapes. Currants are still used in Scandinavia for making wine and are commonly called 'red and black wineberries' in Sweden, and elsewhere in the north (in parts of Norway and England) the red currant is known as a 'red wineberry'. It should be added that the pollen analysis test also showed that any 'self-sown wheat' in the area must have been *elymus arenarius* (var. *villosus*), a perennial grass growth, belonging to the corn family.

The duration of the Norse settlement at L'Anse aux Meadows in the eleventh century could not have been very long. The middens contain relatively small amounts of waste. Relatively few objects were found at the site, and this suggests a short period of settlement. The turf-walled house had a life expectancy of perhaps twenty years, and all the archaeological signs indicate that the three clusters of houses existed simultaneously and not successively. Twenty years – or, at the outside, thirty years – was probably the lifespan of this Viking-age Norse settlement on the northern shores of Newfoundland. Why did it end? Archaeology provides no answer. Apart from House F having been destroyed by fire – an ever present danger in this kind of house – there is no evidence which can suggest a violent encounter with hostile natives. It ended, for us, in silence.

Is L'Anse aux Meadows, then, Vinland? The answer has to be that L'Anse aux Meadows must have been a Viking settlement in the large region called Vinland. It would be rash, indeed, to identify this settlement with any of the settlements mentioned in the sagas, although the temptation, which must be valiantly resisted, to see this as the colony established by Thorfinn Karlsefni is strong.

It still remains for scholars to determine the extent of Vinland. How far west did it extend? – to Ungava Bay? – to Hudson Bay? And how far south did it extend? – to Nova Scotia? – to the Maine coast? – to Cape Cod? – to Narragansett Bay or beyond? It is only archaeological evidence, perhaps accidentally found by fishermen, beachcombers, or amateur archaeologists, which will determine how far the Vikings went in the New World. The finding of a Viking-age silver coin on a point of land (Goddard's Farm) at the eastern mouth of Penobscot Bay, near Brookline in the state of Maine, raised hopes that the necessary evidence to show that the Vikings had indeed penetrated as far south as the Maine coast was at hand. First found in 1957, it was subsequently wrongly identified as twelfth-century English and only in 1978 recognized for what it is, an authentic Norse coin from the 1070s. The Goddard coin is the only European artefact found at this rich site, one of the richest in northeast North America, which has revealed over 50,000 artefacts. The widespread presence at the site of chert from

Labrador and the discovery of a burin-like tool of the Dorset Eskimoes suggest that this Indian settlement was part of a trading network that extended along the northeast coast of North America and that it was by aboriginal exchange that this coin, probably as a piece of ornamental jewellery, reached the Maine coast in the first half of the second millenium. However far Vinland might have extended – and it remains an open question – there can be no question that the Vikings established a settlement, short-lived though it was, on the marine terraces overlooking Epaves Bay in Newfoundland.

The Vinland Map: the great forgery

Yale University Press, in a mood of what seemed near truculence, published, on the eve of Columbus Day 1965, 'the most exciting cartographic discovery of the century'. With a press agentry unusual for a university press Yale announced publication of the Vinland Map, a pre-Columbian map of the world in which Vinland was shown. Front page articles and headlines appeared in the *New York Times*, the *Chicago Tribune*, and elsewhere. The public relations undertaken to promote the Vinland Map succeeded in drawing the attention of the scholarly world forcefully and quickly to this publication. The results of the scholarly investigations have placed the Vinland Map next to the Piltdown Man among the great forgeries of the twentieth century. Much of the story can now be told, although tantilizing mysteries still remain.

Where the story begins is perhaps the greatest mystery, but 1957 is as good a place as any to start, although it is not the beginning. In that year the bookseller, Enzo Ferrajoli de Ry, an Italian long resident in Barcelona, was seen in various places in Europe (Geneva, Paris, London) displaying manuscripts to local booksellers. In London, the bookseller J. I. Davis of Davis and Orioli Ltd. showed considerable interest in a volume containing what were later to be called the Vinland Map and the Tartar Relation; he even arranged for the volume to be brought to the British Museum, where it was seen by R. A. Skelton, then superintendent of the Map Room, and others. What happened at the British Museum is still shrouded in mystery–doubts? budgetary worries? – at any rate, a sale was not concluded. For his own catalogue Mr Davis did, however, purchase from Ferrajoli a

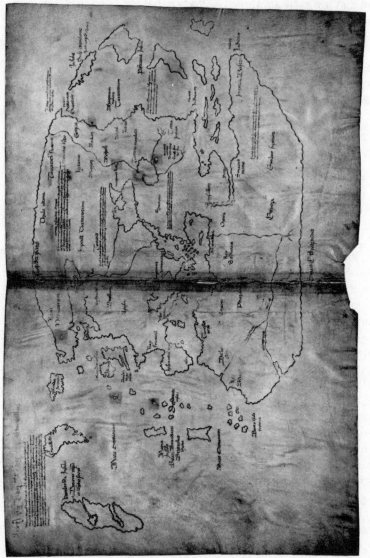

11   *The Vinland Map: the great forgery*

fifteenth-century copy of the *Speculum historiale* of Vincent of Beauvais, which had come from the same library as the 'map'. Ferrajoli went on his way. In September he met, in Geneva, the American bookseller, Laurence Witten of New Haven, Connecticut, who indicated an interest in the 'map', but he was told that it had been returned to the owner. Ferrajoli arranged to take Witten to see the owner. At the owner's home Witten saw the 'map' and decided on the spot to buy it, judging it to be genuinely fifteenth-century. The purchase price was US $3500. Late in September, 1957, Witten returned to New Haven with his newly acquired manuscript. He showed it to Thomas E. Marston, Curator of Medieval and Renaissance Literature at Yale University Library, and to Alexander O. Vietor, Curator of Maps at that library. They showed considerable interest, and Vietor asked for first refusal should the volume be put up for sale. Witten quickly transferred ownership to his wife.

What was this manuscript which came from Europe to America in 1957? Bound in a leather cover of recent origin it contained eighteen folios: the first two folios formed a bifolium (i.e., one large parchment sheet folded in two), whose inner opening contained a map of the world, and the sixteen remaining folios constituted a full quire containing a description of a thirteenth-century Franciscan mission to the land of the Tartars. These two components have become known, respectively, as the Vinland Map and the Tartar Relation. The parchment bifolium had split at the crease but had been repaired; it had four worm-holes at matching points on each folio. The Tartar Relation quire had one worm-hole which went through this quire at a point not matching any of the worm-holes on the Vinland Map. It was clear to Witten that the Vinland Map and the Tartar Relation could not have been bound together in this manner at the time of the worming since their worm-holes did not match. A description of the contents of the Tartar Relation need not detain the Viking student: suffice it to say that this text, written two columns to a side for eleven folios, leaving the last five folios ruled but otherwise blank, calls itself *Hystoria Tartarorum* and is a hitherto unknown description of the mission of the Franciscan friar John of Plano Carpini to the Mongols in 1245–7. The authenticity of this valuable text has not been seriously questioned.

The contents of the Vinland Map deserve a fuller description. On the otherwise blank recto of the first folio appear the following words (incorrectly transcribed by the editor of the Yale edition):

delineatio prima pars secunda pars tertia partis (or *parte*) *speculi.*
What they mean is unclear because of the words *tertia partis* (or
parte), which make no sense. It should perhaps read (translated): 'a
map, the first and second parts of the third part of the Speculum'.
However one might read these words, the final word, *speculi*, had
no meaning in this context and rightly puzzled Witten. Turning the
page, one encounters a mappamundi spreading across the opening.
At the furthest points east lie the Great Sea of the Tartars and a
number of islands. Westward from there are Eurasia in the north
and Africa (*Ethiopia*) in the south. In the *Mare Oceanum* (the
Atlantic Ocean) three islands are drawn in the north. These are
called, east to west, *Isoland Ibernica*, *Grouelanda*, and *Vinilanda* [or
Vimlanda] *Insula a Byarno reperta et leipho sociis* ('Vinland Island
discovered by the companions Bjarni and Leif'). Ironically enough
the Yale edition incorrectly transcribed the names given to the last
two islands. The three names refer, of course, to Iceland,
Greenland, and Vinland: Iceland was given a name otherwise
unknown, Greenland was shown as an island, its delineation in the
north strikingly in agreement with modern maps, and Vinland was
called and shown as an island having three clearly marked land
divisions. In no other source (saga, chronicle, etc.) is mention made
of Vinland as an island. A Latin legend appears above Vinland and
Greenland. It reads:

God willed that after a long journey from Greenland to the farthest
remaining parts of the western ocean sea the companions Bjarni and Leif
Ericsson, sailing south through the ice discovered a new land, which was
very rich and which even had vines; they called it Vinland Island. Eric,
bishop of Greenland and the neighbouring regions and legate of the
apostolic see in this truly vast and rich land, arrived in the name of the
Almighty God in the last year of the reign of Pope Pascal. Eric stayed some
time in summer and in winter before returning to Greenland and later
proceeding southward in obedience to God's will.

Two events are described here; the discovery of Vinland by Bjarni
and Leif and the journey of Bishop Eric to Vinland 1117–18. The
first conflates the two saga accounts, and the second refers to the
event recorded in the *Icelandic Annals* under the year 1121
('Bishop Eric of Greenland set out in search of Vinland').
    This was the book which Witten purchased in 1957. Puzzles
persisted. They centred around the word *speculi* and the

unmatching worm-holes. It was all very strange. Both puzzles were resolved in April of the following year by an extraordinary chance occurrence. Yale University Library acquired at that time, from Davis and Orioli Ltd of London, two manuscripts and Witten was invited to examine their bindings. One of these was a fifteenth-century fragment of the *Speculum historiale* of Vincent of Beauvais, the copy, it will be remembered, purchased by Davis from Ferrajoli. Witten took this volume home with him for examination and made a remarkable discovery: the copy of the *Speculum historiale* had worm-holes front and back and the worm-holes in the front matched precisely the worm-holes of the Vinland Map and the worm-hole at the back matched precisely the worm-hole in the Tartar Relation. He quickly found that each folio in *Speculum historiale* measured 285 by 21 millimetres, the same size as both the Vinland Map and the Tartar Relation. Furthermore, the watermarks in the paper in *Speculum historiale* were identical to the watermarks in the paper in the Tartar Relation. The paper had been produced in the Rhineland in the 1440s. The conclusion was obvious: the missing link had been found. At the time of the worming there was a codex which contained the map at the front, the history of the Tartars at the back, and sandwiched between them the text of Vincent of Beauvais. The worming was now explained; the reference of the word *speculi* was now clear; the argument was clinched. The Vinland Map was an authentic map of the mid fifteenth century.

For the next year (April 1958 to April 1959) Witten researched his find. Yale University, in a calculated gesture, gave to Mrs Witten its *Speculum historiale*, for which it had paid only £75. In the spring of 1959 Witten offered the two manuscripts for sale to the Yale University Library. They were bought instead by a philanthropic friend of the university, reportedly at a price of about a million dollars. The new owner commissioned a book to be produced about this material. In unnatural secrecy the project went forward and, as has been said, the book was published on 11 October 1965. By that time the new owner had donated the manuscript to Yale University.

It was proclaimed the only pre-Columbian map of North America. Scholarly conferences were held to discuss its significance, and at one conference (the Anglo-American Conference of Historians in London in 1966) security measures were taken to keep journalists *out*. Widespread acceptance of the authenticity of the map greeted its announcement. But, reservations were voiced. These concerned the circumstances of its purchase: Witten refused to name the previous owner, and Ferrajoli subsequently served two years in prison in connection with the alleged theft of manuscripts from the Cathedral of Saragossa. Aspects of the map drew attention: the insular nature of Greenland, the conflating of the Bjarni and Leif stories, and the mission of Bishop Eric. A number of Icelandic and Scandinavian scholars were concerned that the self-imposed secrecy precluded the editors from consulting more widely with experts.

These few, lingering doubts would be dismissed, it was said, by subjecting the text of the map to scientific analysis. To this end, the authorities at Yale University, much to their credit, commissioned Walter McCrone Associates of Chicago in 1968 to undertake the tests. It was not until 1972 that the tools and techniques were considered advanced enough to analyse the ink. Very small particles, invisible to the naked eye, were removed from the three texts (Vinland Map, *Speculum historiale*, Tartar Relation). A series of extremely refined tests were employed. The results with respect to *Speculum historiale* and the Tartar Relation showed that the ink used was iron-gallotannate, an ink type consistent with that used in the fifteenth century. The scientists proceeded to the examination of the Vinland Map. They made a microscopic study of every line and letter on the map. This examination revealed that two lines were drawn throughout; the first, a thick yellow-brown line, and over it the second, a shiny black line, most of which was flaked off to reveal the underlying ink as faded. The scientists took a total of twenty-seven samples of the yellow-brown ink from fourteen different areas of the Vinland Map. These samples showed that the ink used in the Vinland Map was not the same kind of ink used in *Speculum historiale* and the Tartar Relation. The ink of the Vinland Map contained, as an integral constituent, significant percentages of the pigment titanium dioxide in the form of anatase. The kind of anatase used in the ink on the map could not have been available before about 1920. The conclusions were unavoidable: the Vinland Map was drawn sometime after 1920, and the method of its production indicates without doubt the intention to pass it off as an original. In a word, it is a forgery.

The story could be pursued. Who was the forger? Was it a central European priest, as the arch anti-clerical Robert S. Lopez suggests? Was the forgery perpetrated, as others suggest, in Spain, to which the circumstances of purchase direct attention? Why would someone go to such extraordinary lengths to execute this forgery in the years between 1920 and 1957? Financial gain? Ideological profit? The mystery continues, but it concerns modern events and not the age of the Vikings.

Selected further reading

A mountain of literature exists on this subject. Of general use are Gwyn Jones, *The Norse Atlantic Sagas*, Oxford University Press 1964; and the old but venerable G. M. Gathorne-Hardy, *The Norse Discoverers of America: The Wineland Sagas*, Clarendon Press 1921, reprinted 1970. See also Halldor Hermannsson, *The Problem of Wineland*, Ithaca, New York: Cornell University Press 1936; and Farley Mowat, *Westviking: The Ancient Norse in Greenland and North America*, Boston: Little, Brown 1965.

Two important works deserve attention: Jon Johannesson's study of the relevant sagas, first published in Icelandic in 1956 and later in an English translation: 'The date and composition of the saga of the Greenlanders', in *Saga Book*, vol. 16, no. 1 (1962), pp. 54–66; and the excavations at L'Anse aux Meadows, reported in scientific form by Anne Stine Ingstad in *The Discovery of a Norse Settlement in America: Excavations at L'Anse aux Meadows, Newfoundland, 1961–1968*, Oslo: Universitetsforlaget 1977.

Many of the essays in G. Ashe (ed.), *The Quest for America*, Pall Mall Press 1971, provide a critical analysis of a number of the issues. Barry Fell's novel views can be found in his *America BC*, New York: New York Times Books 1976 and, more recently, *Saga America*, New York: New York Times Books 1980. The text of the Brendan voyage can be found in J. J. O'Meara (trs.), *The Voyage of St Brendan*, Dublin: Dolmen Press 1978. Tim Severin's transatlantic crossing is described in *The Brendan Voyage*, Hutchinson 1978. A useful translation of Adam of Bremen is that by F. J. Tschan: *History of the Archbishops of Hamburg-Bremen*, New York: Columbia University Press 1959. A modern translation of the pertinent sagas by M. Magnusson and H. Palsson is *The Vinland Sagas: The Norse Discovery of America*, Penguin 1965. S. E. Morison gives an excellent, if salty, review of the relevant primary and secondary source material in *The European Discovery of America: The Northern Voyages, AD 500–1600*, New York: Oxford University Press 1971. On the Kensington stone see Eric Wahlgren, *The Kensington Stone: A Mystery Solved*, Madison, Wisconsin: University of Wisconsin Press 1958. The two essential sources on the forged Vinland Map are R. A. Skelton, T. E. Marston, and G. D. Painter, *The Vinland Map and the Tartar Relation*, New Haven: Yale University Press 1965, and W. C. McCrone and L. B. McCrone, 'The Vinland Map ink', in *Geographical Journal*, vol. 140 (1974), pp. 212–14.

5 The Danes in the south

Pagan ships attacked the coast of Aquitaine in 799. They were repelled, many of the attackers being slain on the shore.

This first reported attack on Frankish lands by the Vikings was noted by Alcuin, the English adviser to Charlemagne. He lamented this attack not with the same passion but with similar perception – God was punishing Christians for their sinfulness – as he had lamented the Viking attack upon Lindisfarne in his native Northumbria six years earlier. With this attack – fleeting, scarcely significant in itself, the subject of a passing moralizing reflection, and then quickly forgotten – a new chapter in Viking history begins. The target of Viking attacks were now the lands to the south, principally the lands controlled by the Franks, which, from the year 800, had been called an 'empire', lands stretching from Saxony to the Pyrenees and central Italy. But some attackers went beyond these lands to others, whose cultural ties were with the Moslem world of Baghdad.

Alcuin died in 804 and his 'David', Charlemagne, in 814. Suspicion about the looming menace of the men from the north may have clouded their dying thoughts. Charlemagne, at least, is said to have been horror-stricken by the harm they might inflict on his descendants and their subjects. One might wonder what judgements they would have made from their graves about the impact of the Vikings on the Frankish empire. Would they have seen the Vikings solely as a destructive force in their national history, as the traditionalists among us do, or would they have taken a longer-term view and stressed the positive effects of these raids on national development? Probably neither. Alcuin would probably have stressed divine retribution, and Charlemagne the primacy of the Frankish state. Mercifully, their judgements have not been disinterred.

The attacks upon western Europe were predominantly Danish. Although occasional raids might have come from Norway or from

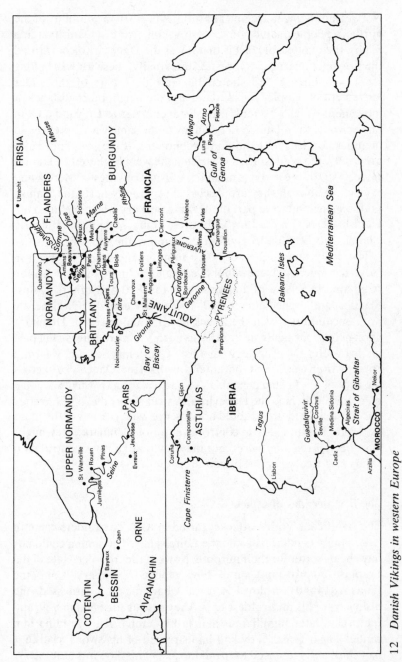

12 *Danish Vikings in western Europe*

Norwegians living in Ireland and although, given the mobility of the northern peoples, some non-Danish Vikings were in Danish raiding bands, the unalterable fact is that it was the Danes who constituted the principal threat to the west. Contextually, these attacks belong to Danish history and should be viewed as part of the wider movement of people from Jutland and the neighbouring islands, a movement which also took Danish adventurers to England and, in one episode, to Ireland. Indeed, many of the same warriors engaged in attacks on England and on the continent. If the sons and, more especially, the grandsons of Charlemagne were bothered by Danish raiders, so too were the sons and grandsons of kings of Mercia and Wessex. Although they are discussed separately here, the Danish raids on England were part of the same tapestry which included the Danish attacks on the Low Countries, France, Spain, the Balearic Islands, Morocco and Italy. Let us examine the tapestry.

The early raids – possibly only some of them are recorded in surviving sources – were minor events and included the attack upon Aquitaine in 799, a raid against Frisia in 810 and others against Flanders and in the Seine in 820. These were casual affairs, merely brief encounters. Even the attack by King Godefred of Denmark upon neighbouring Frisia in 810 was not a Viking raid *per se* but part of his defensive strategy against Charlemagne, as was the construction work done on an earthwork (the Danevirke) across the neck of the Jutland peninsula. No one really knows what was going on politically behind the Danevirke. A struggle for the kingship after the death of Godefred should not obscure what is known: the kings were not able to exercise control over all of Denmark; they might have been *primi inter pares,* but they could not always control rival chiefs and free-wheeling adventurers.

The first decades of attacks

The significant Viking attacks started in 834. The raiders came in large numbers into Frisia and the Loire valley. The timing could not have been better for their purpose. News of the troubled state of the Frankish empire must surely have reached Denmark. Louis the Pious (814–40), a loyal son to Charlemagne, witnessed the disloyalty of his three oldest sons. They rose against him in 829, and four years later humiliated their father–emperor by holding him captive at Soissons. They had him stripped of his sword, clad in a hair shirt, and sentenced to spend the rest of his days in a monastery.

However, the sons argued and in 834 Louis the Pious was restored in a ceremony at the monastery of Saint Denis, where, to the applause of the people, the very bishops who had desecrated his imperial person at Soissons were forced to regird him with his sword and clothe him in his purple mantle. With the Frankish royal family in obvious disarray the major Viking attacks began. The inability of the Franks to deal with these attacks owes much to the unseemly civil strife which bedevilled the empire throughout the rest of the ninth century. The moment could scarcely have been more propitious for the Danes. It has been suggested that Louis's son Lothair invited the Danish attack on Frisia in 834. Whatever the circumstances, the large-scale Viking attacks began in 834 with their raids on Frisia. The contemporary entry in the *Annals of Saint Bertin* observes:

A Danish fleet came to Frisia and laid waste a part of it. They then passed through Utrecht to the *emporium* at Dorestad, where they caused widespread destruction. They slew some people, took others away as captives, and scorched the surrounding area.

This entry would be echoed and re-echoed by other chroniclers and about other places for almost a hundred years, for soon, and not only in Frisia, the Franks would feel the sting of the northmen.

The Viking attacks on the continent followed a simple pattern. At first, there were raids such as the one at Dorestad in 834: their ships would take land, adapt to the feudal structure, intermarry and away what they could in precious metals, slaves (for sale), and captives (for ransom). It is only with difficulty that one can see any positive element in these cruel, destructive raids whose aim was simply pillage and plunder. These raids were followed by larger, more co-ordinated raids, not pele-mele, hit-or-miss actions, but planned attacks: wintering in Francia, the Vikings would systematically attack, conduct campaigns, besiege towns, realize profit from tribute, and become a dreaded factor in the unsettled life of those lands and times. Finally, some Vikings would settle: they would take land, adapt to the feudal structure, intermarry and become absorbed. These phases cannot easily be dated with the precision that would be necessary if they were to be applicable to all of the Frankish empire. Different regions experienced these phases at different times, and there was always the inevitable overlap between one phase and another. Still, allowing for regional variations and twilight zones, four periods do appear in the history of the Viking expeditions to the south. From 834 to about 850 the Vikings attacked, during the raiding season (i.e., spring to autumn), northern Francia as well as along the Loire and Seine Rivers and the coast of Aquitaine. From the mid ninth century, for twenty-five years, they wintered and were frequently seen (and felt) in the river systems of modern France and, on one extended expedition, in the Mediterranean. Intense attacks began in 879 and lasted for thirteen years, in what was, no doubt, the most intense period of Viking onslaught against continental western Europe. When they came again in about 900, it was to settle, and the general lines of their settlements were clearly visible by 940. In all the Viking years in Francia and her neighbours, from the initial attack on Frisia in 834 to the establishment of a principality bearing their name in the western part of the Frankish lands, lasted for about a century.

Frisia, the modern Low Countries, was easily accessible to these Danish raiders. Dorestad, the great entrepôt, was well known to Danish traders. In 836 and again in 838, King Horik of Denmark disclaimed any responsibility for the raids on Frisia. But raids there were, and they were Danish in origin: Horik's ambassadors were slain at Cologne in obvious retaliation. Were the leaders of these raids rival chieftains? independent adventurers? Whoever they were, the raids continued year after year. Dorestad, raided in 834, was attacked again in 835, 836 and 837. Virtually defenceless, this trading centre was easy prey to the surprise attacks of the Vikings, who were to return frequently until, in 864, the shifting waters of the Rhine system, and not the Vikings, destroyed Dorestad by leaving it dry and useless. In 836 Viking ships were in the Scheldt where Antwerp and Witla were fired. The attackers seemed to be everywhere in Frisia. In 842 a raiding band left London and sacked the other great northern emporium, Quentovic (near modern Boulogne), and returned to England. In another campaign a large fleet – are we to believe the report that 600 ships sailed against a town of a few hundred inhabitants? – sailed up the Elbe and violently attacked Hamburg.

At almost the same time as the attacks in the north, other Vikings were striking further down the west coast of France. The monastic island of Noirmoutier near the mouth of the Loire River was first attacked in 834. This centre of the salt trade, like its northern counterparts Dorestad and Quentovic, experienced frequent Viking attacks: it suited the raiders to have an island base for raids up the Loire valley. In 843 Vikings sailed up to Nantes, which they

attacked on the feast of Saint John the Baptist (24 June). They seized
the bishop and slaughtered him at the altar of his cathedral, and, if
we can believe later chronicles, a scene of utter barbarity ensued:
the Vikings killed whom they wished in a butchery of epic
proportions, which ended only when, dripping with blood and laden
with bloodied jewels, they returned to Noirmoutier. There
they wintered with their families, who had been brought there with
the purpose of establishing a quasi-permanent settlement. This is
the first recorded wintering of the Vikings in the land of the Franks.
In due course, other parties of Vikings would stay in island bases,
and the pattern was set.

Meanwhile, Viking raiders had begun the first of countless raids
up the Seine. In 841, while the three surviving sons of Louis the
Pious were involved in civil war, a Viking fleet under Asgeir
attacked Rouen and, a few weeks later, the monastery of Jumièges,
and then held Saint Wandrille to ransom. The *Annals of Fontanelle*
(Saint Wandrille) report these raids:

In 841 AD the northmen arrived on the 12th of May with their chief,
Asgeir. Two days later they burned the town of Rouen and stayed there
two days. On the 24th of May they burned the monastery at Jumièges. On
the following day the monastery of Fontanelle was saved from pillage by
paying six pounds, and on the 28th of May the monks of Saint Denis came
and ransomed 68 captives at the price of twenty-six pounds. On the last day
of May the pagans returned to the sea.

Four years later Ragnar entered the Seine in March and headed for
Paris. Charles the Bald attempted to thwart this attack, and he
arrayed his army on both banks of the river. The Viking leader with
his whole force attacked the smaller band of the Frankish defenders
on one side of the river and, before the eyes of the Franks across the
river, he hanged his prisoners. Paris lay before him, and the
halleluiahs of Easter turned into lamentations as Ragnar attacked
and plundered the town. Most of the western part of the Frankish
empire faced Viking assaults during these decades: not only in the
Seine, but also in the Somme, Gironde, Garonne, Scheldt, Dordogne
and Meuse. The northmen were attacking Chartres, Amiens,
Bordeaux, Toulouse, Tours, Angers, Orléans, Poitiers, Blois and
Paris. Year after year they came, relentless, against a land seemingly
unable to defend itself.

Charles the Bald, King of the West Franks since 843, did not take
these attacks seriously at first, and he was otherwise preoccupied

with the ambitions of his brothers. His defence of Paris in 845 was well intended but extraordinarily inept: not only did he offend sound military tactics by splitting his army in two, but he was unable to motivate his army and had to allow Ragnar to escape downriver after paying the Viking leader 7000 pounds of silver. There was virtually no defence against the Vikings of this period: the only defence was self-defence; every man for himself; in a word, flight. The crude roads of France and the Low Countries knew then, as often again, the bands of refugees fleeing the feared savagery of Viking invaders. Monks from cloisters unprepared for hostile attacks fled from such holy places as Saint Maixent, Charvoux, Saint Maur-sur-Loire, Saint Wandrille, Jumièges, and Saint Martin of Tours, and sought refuge in areas isolated from Viking raiders. For two generations these fleeing monks were to be seen on the roads leading to Burgundy, the Auvergne and Flanders. Even bishops left their sees and their flocks, and for this they are still vilified to this day. (Who knows the rightness or wrongness of this? If Saint Cyprian would not judge such shepherds, then surely a humble historian should not.) As the immediate Viking threat passed – temporarily, as we from our vantage point know – the monks returned, monasteries were rebuilt, relics and other treasures brought back, the archives restored. And under fresh attacks the process would begin again. In all their wanderings the refugees took with them their 'saints', as they called their holy relics. The Canons of Tours took the body of their holy father, Martin, first to Cormery in 853; they returned it to Tours in 854 but seem to have taken it away again in 862 and 869; in the attack of 877 they carried their saint to Chablis, then to Auxerre, and finally back to Tours where Saint Martin rested at last. Likewise, the monks of Saint Philibert from the island of Noirmoutier, a very early object of Viking attacks, moved with their relics progressively further and further away from the sea: to the Déas in 836, Cunauld in 858, Messay in Poitou in 862, Saint Pourcain-sur-Sioule across the Massif Central in 872, and Tournus on the Saône in 875, finding only at this last place security from the almost ubiquitous northmen.

From the mid 850s a new phase in these attacks can be seen. Their purpose was now changing. Seldom were individuals held for ransom, seldom now the haphazard devastation of places. The new attacks resembled campaigns in their planning, strategy and designs. The attackers no longer kept to the waterways: the Vikings had become more mobile by seizing and using horses for attacks on the countryside. For example, in 864 they secured their ships on the Charente and travelled cross-country by horse as far as Clermont in the Auvergne. For long periods Viking bands now remained in the same region. For six years (856–62) the same Vikings were present on the Seine, in 856 lodging themselves on the island of Oscelle, opposite Jeufosse, northwest of Paris, where they remained for four years. The contemporary theologian Paschasius Radbertus, reflecting on the Lamentations of Jeremiah and on an immediate Viking threat to Paris, probably in 856 (but possibly in 845), woefully asked:

Who among us would ever have believed or even imagined that in so short a time we would be overwhelmed with such fearful misfortunes? Today we tremble as we think of these pirates arrayed in raiding bands in the very vicinity of Paris and burning churches along the sides of the Seine. Who would ever have believed, I ask, that thieving gangs would perpetrate such outrages? Who could have thought that a kingdom so glorious, so fortified, so large, so populous, so vigorous would be so humiliated and defiled by such a base and filthy race?

Even a moralizing theologian such as Paschasius must have been preaching within a context of fact and, here, of fear. Attacks were made not only on Paris and laments not only by Paschasius. The increased tempo of Viking attacks – again, even allowing for some licence – appears vividly in the oft quoted but still relevant words of Ermentarius of Noirmoutier:

The fleets grow larger and the Vikings themselves grow and grow in number. On all sides Christian people suffer massacre and burning and plunder. . . . The Vikings crush everything in their path; there is no defence. They capture Bordeaux, Périgueux, Limoges, Angoulême, and Toulouse; they destroy Angers, Tours, and Orléans. . . . Ships beyond counting sail up the Seine, where evil pervades. Rouen is attacked, pillaged, and burnt; Paris, Beauvais, and Meaux are seized; the stronghold of Melun is razed; Chartres is occupied; Evreux and Bayeux are pillaged; and all the other towns are attacked.

Something clearly had to be done. Slowly, if not reluctantly, authorities realized that the Viking menace was not a passing phenomenon: the problem had to be faced.

Defence

The Frankish military set up was not geared to defence. Charles Martel and Charlemagne, its principal architects, constructed an offensive military arm; their need for defence was limited to marcher lands. In the face of Viking attacks this army, no longer unified because it was being used in the civil wars, proved incapable of defeating the northmen, who had the advantages of surprise, speed and offence. After the initial attacks Louis the Pious strengthened his coastal defences. Further defence provisions lay in the hands of Charles the Bald. The fact that he delayed taking serious action until 862 is some measure of his other preoccupations, particularly with the Frankish nobility, and of the underestimating of the Viking menace. He met his advisers at Pîtres in that year and devised some defensive strategy. Fortified bridges were to be built blocking most of the major rivers (Seine, Marne, Oise, and perhaps the Loire). Little is known about the nature of these fortified bridges except that they were to be placed at strategically useful bends in rivers and that they required stone and wood in their construction. No doubt, stone forts stood on the banks on each end of the bridge, and the bridge itself, apparently built like a modern pontoon bridge at river level, created an obstacle to river traffic; attackers would be forced to the banks where the defenders in their forts would have the advantage. Problems arose not merely in the manning of these fortified bridges but also in the slowness of construction.

An excellent example of this is the bridge at Pîtres. Situated on the lower Seine about ten miles above Rouen at a place where the Seine could be easily forded, Pîtres was apparently destined to constitute the first line of defence for the upper Seine and its attendant river systems. Below it lay the town of Rouen, the countryside of the lower Seine valley, and also the islands of Oscelle, a frequent base of the northmen. Were the lands below Pîtres simply abandoned and left defenceless except for whatever a much harried local population could do to protect itself? Who knows? Work began in June 862, but, for whatever reasons, it languished. In 864 Charles the Bald once again ordered its construction. The following year the Vikings had control of Pîtres and were making forays as far as Paris and its suburb, Saint Denis (for this the Vikings were punished by severe dysentery), and even up the Oise and Marne. Work was taken up again on the fortified bridge at Pîtres in June 866. A work-force was clearly a problem for in 869 Charles had to draft labourers from throughout his realm – one able-bodied man per 100 *mansi* and one cart and two oxen per 1000 *mansi* – for its construction. It was completed by autumn 873, over eleven years after its beginning. Hardly the dispatch necessary against the swift-moving Vikings. The Eure and, slightly upstream, the Andelle flow into the Seine at Pîtres. The bridge in question was probably built at the site of the modern Pont de l'Arche. The bridge would have spanned the Seine immediately below the Eure. It is a testimony to the regrettably inadequate state of archaeological research on Viking Francia that this site has not yet been fully examined with professional controls. Fortified areas existed at either end of the bridge; one fort remained on the north bank for centuries, and featured in the Canadian military campaign in 1944. Similar manpower problems arose on the Oise and Marne, tributaries of the upper Seine, where bridges constructed at Auvers and Charenton were falling into disrepair and the local people, who had built them, could not effect their repair because of Viking attacks; in 865 Charles, in order to remedy this situation, drafted workers from other parts of his kingdom on the condition that they would never be so called upon again. These were clearly not sought-after jobs. Fortified bridges were not the answer, at least in the 860s and early 870s, to the Frankish problem of defence. Towns did shore up their defences and rebuild their walls as did some monasteries and new *burhs*. Yet Charles the Bald, ever the Carolingian monarch, insisted that there be no new military construction without his permission. In 864, while the Vikings were traversing his kingdom virtually without obstacle, he condemned fortifications which were built without his permission and, incredible as it must seem to us, ordered them to be taken down by the first of August. Later, in the 880s, as we shall see, local people did what they had to do: they fortified bridges and rebuilt town defences.

To consider tribute a defensive weapon is like considering a ransom payment to be a life insurance premium. The excessive payment of tribute to Viking attackers within the Frankish empire underscores the poor defensive posture of the Carolingians. The term Danegeld was used in the eleventh century in England to refer to the tribute paid to the Vikings, and there is no reason why the same term cannot be appropriately used for an earlier time and another place. Danegeld quite simply was money paid to the Danes to go away. In early raids the Danes would attack towns and bear away loot and captives who were held for ransom. By the mid ninth century they found it more profitable to extend the ransom principle: instead of holding individuals for ransom, they would hold an entire community (a town, a monastery, a *burh*, or even an entire region) for ransom. At least fifteen general Danegelds (i.e., payments made over a wide area) were paid by the Franks. The precise amount paid is not known, but the total for seven of these general Danegelds is 39,700 pounds, as can be seen in Table 2 which lists the general Danegelds from the ninth and tenth centuries.

Table 2   *General Danegelds paid in the ninth and tenth centuries*

Year	Amount in pounds
845	7000
853	
860–1	5000
862	6000
864	
866	4000
877 (Seine)	5000
877 (Loire)	
882	
884	12,000
886	700
889	
897	
923–4	
926	

The events at Melun on the Seine in 866 provide a fairly full picture of this process in operation. In that year the Vikings, with significant strength, were menacing places along the Seine: they besieged Melun and demanded payment. Charles the Bald paid them 4000 pounds of silver and much wine. The Vikings left the area, and the Seine valley experienced ten years of relative peace. Like other general Danegelds, this tribute paid in 866 was to be levied on the whole realm – the *mansus,* the basic unit of tenure, being the principal unit of taxation – and required the following payments: six pence for each free *mansus,* three pence for each servile *mansus,* one penny for each inhabitant, a half-penny for each temporary inhabitant, one-tenth of the value of traders' goods, and a payment by priests according to their wealth. Normally the tax would be expected to be collected within a period of three to seven months. Local Danegelds (i.e., payments made by local communities) must have been numerous: examples are known for Brittany and, at various times, for the area of modern Belgium. How effective, it must be asked, was this Danegeld system? Its effectiveness, in the short term, was generally excellent: the Vikings would sail away and leave the area free from immediate attack. The payment did not ensure against other bands of Vikings appearing on the scene eager for plunder. Nor did it buy permanent immunity: Vikings would and did come again. The Danegeld bought time. Some suggest that it brought a profit to the king, who might levy more than the amount of the Danegeld and keep the difference. The relief, of course, was local or, at best, regional. Vikings receiving Danegeld on the Loire might soon appear on the Seine. The raising of the siege of Paris in 886, as we shall soon see, meant the payment of Danegeld and the unleashing of the Viking fury onto Burgundy. However general a Danegeld might have been in terms of the levying to pay for it, all Danegeld was only particular in its effect and did little to relieve what was obviously a national problem.

The nation perhaps had too many problems: Charles the Bald had to contend with threats from his brothers, the Bretons, the Aquitanians, and the Provençals. His acquisition in 870 of much of the middle kingdom held by his late brother Lothair added further to his burdens. Although he did force the Vikings from Angers on the Loire in 873, he failed to press his advantage. Instead, he was quickly off on the road to Rome and, upon his arrival, made a magnificent entry into the eternal city, where he was crowned emperor on Christmas Day. His empire bore little resemblance to the empire of his grandfather, who, three-quarters of a century earlier on that very day, had been hailed as *Augustus*. It was the strength of Charles the Great to know that his new title was recognition of his power; it was the weakness of Charles the Bald to think that titles confer power. He had little power to control the waterways of his western kingdom, little power to protect his people from plundering invaders. Charles the Great would not have been in Rome seeking empty titles: he would have been striving for the security of his realm. Even while returning north from Rome, Charles the Bald seemed little concerned about the security of his realm: he paid no attention to the appearance of a large Viking fleet (reportedly a hundred ships strong) at the mouth of the Seine, and he proceeded instead to do battle with his nephew, Louis the Younger, on the Rhine. Charles died in 877, the year before the great raids, having failed to stop the breakup of Frankish society. The further dismemberment of the once united empire of Charlemagne and Louis the Pious, by the partition of 876, accelerated the particularizing already well underway earlier in the reign of Charles the Bald. By the 880s, in the face of the massive attacks of that decade, royal permission for local defence was seldom sought or expected. The defence of the realm did not exist; defence was organized locally; castles were built, towns fortified, defensive enclosures constructed, all by local leaders. From this time defence, particularly in the north, lay in the hands of counts and bishops, men with local interests, now left to themselves by the feeble Carolingian monarchs.

Iberia and the Mediterranean

During the ninth century Viking fleets entered the Islamic world of Spain twice and, on one of these occasions, appeared in the western Mediterranean. The meeting of the worlds of Thor and Allah is well recorded, and in a geographical sense appears appropriate. The ninth-century Viking attacks were not designed as attacks specifically upon the Franks: they were, particularly in their earlier stages, unco-ordinated raiding adventures. Once Aquitaine was reached, then why not Spain? And once Spain, why not carry on through the Straits of Gibraltar to the Mediterranean Sea? And so it happened.

The attack in 844 came directly from Aquitaine. The Vikings had penetrated the Garonne 130 miles to Toulouse and without attacking that town retraced their course to the Bay of Biscay. They then turned their ships south. They raided the Christian communities at Gijon and Coruña, along the northern coast of Spain, but the Asturians quickly gathered an armed force and sent the northmen fleeing in disarray to their ships, a number of which were destroyed. The Viking fleet was still strong – numbers are dubious, but the original fleet reportedly numbered 100 ships in Aquitaine – and it regrouped and sailed around Cape Finisterre. Down the western coast of Iberia they sailed, raiding as they went. The Vikings were now in the land of the Moors, the Moslems of Spain, and they were to find the followers of Allah formidable foes.

At Lisbon the Vikings plundered in the region of the mouth of the Tagus for thirteen days, but they left before having any serious encounter with a Moorish armed force. Part of their fleet might have detoured to Arzilla on the Atlantic coast of Morocco, but the main part of the Viking fleet attacked Cadiz and, in the interior, Medina Sidonia with great success. The Guadalquivir leads into the heartland of Moorish Spain with Seville and Cordova on its banks, the latter the capital of this mighty caliphate. Undaunted or, more likely, unaware, the Vikings sailed up its waters. What they could have thought as they came within sight of Seville the historian cannot know, but he does know that they captured the city, except for the citadel, and that for six weeks Seville was a Viking city or, at least, that the Vikings, in control of most of the city, used it as a base for plundering the hinterlands. The Moors, now ready, ambushed a large part of the Viking fleet. The emir, Abd al-Rahman II, took prisoners, some of whom he had hanged in Seville and others from palm trees at Talyata. He then sent the heads of a Viking chief and 200 noble warriors to his allies in Morocco. The Vikings had met their match: they used what captives they had to purchase escape and food and clothing. After a few raids on the west coast they were back in Aquitaine by the following year, bruised, battered, and sadly depleted after their first encounter with Islamic Spain.

A strange sequel occurred the following year. In 845 Abd al-Rahman II sent an embassy under al-Ghazal to the King of the Majus (i.e., fire-worshippers, in this instance the Vikings), who lived on a large island or peninsula – the language allows either translation – which had beautiful gardens and flowing streams. It was three days' journey from the mainland and in its vicinity were other islands inhabited by other Majus. Al-Ghazal, before his audience with the Viking king, insisted that he should not be required to kneel before the king. This was agreed upon, but, when al-Ghazal arrived at the king's dwelling, he found that the king had constructed the entrance so low that he would be forced to enter on his knees. The Arab ambassador met the challenge diplomatically by lying on his back and dragging himself on his bottom, feet first, into the royal presence. During al-Ghazal's visit to this northern court the Viking queen offered him hospitality of an intimate nature, assuring him that northern men knew no jealousy and northern ladies had liberated views. The southern gentleman was understanding. No one knows the purpose of his mission – perhaps it had to do with trade – nor can one be sure whether the land in question was Ireland or Denmark or whether the king was Turgeis or Horik. The identity of the queen remains discreetly veiled as befits a lady of her graciousness.

The second assault of the Vikings on the southern world lasted longer than the expedition of 844 and knew greater success. In the annals of Viking adventures the four-year adventure of Bjorn Ironside and Hasting from 859 to 862 must be considered among the boldest. They were to penetrate the middle sea, *mare nostrum*, and touch on most of its shores and some of its islands, at the very time, it must be remembered, that Viking cousins were settling England, intermarrying in Ireland, circumnavigating Iceland, harassing the Franks, and establishing hegemony in Russia.

These two well-known Viking adventurers, who are still heroes to many, had been raiding in the area of the Seine. They took a fleet – Arab sources say it contained sixty-two vessels – southwards and attacked, as had their predecessors, the Christians of Asturias but with no more success. They pillaged as they sailed along the west coast of Iberia, and two of their ships, cruising ahead of the others, were captured by Moorish coastal guards, who found that the Viking ships were already laden with silver, gold, prisoners and provisions. The main fleet soon arrived at the mouth of the Guadalquivir (intent upon Seville and Cordova?), but the Moors were prepared for them. The new emir, Mohammed II, his army and ships at the ready, drove the attackers away. With the Viking fleet still very much intact, Bjorn and Hasting headed their ships through the Straits of Gibraltar and, taking Algeciras by surprise, burned its great mosque. They soon crossed the short distance to the North African coast, and five Moslem accounts tell of the Viking attack upon Nekor, city of the Rif, in Mauritania (Mazimma in modern Morocco). One account relates that 'they captured the city, plundered it, and took slaves'. Were these the same slaves ('dark men') that an Irish source states were brought to Ireland from Africa at this same time? The notables among those captured by the Vikings were ransomed by the local emir. After spending eight days at Nekor they were off again. Back in Spanish waters the northmen attacked along the eastern coast and then sailed eastward where they engaged in lightning raids upon the Balearic Islands (Formentera, Majorca and Minorca) and, from there they turned upon Rousillon on the southern coast of Francia. Winter was approaching and the island of Camargue, near the mouth of the Rhône, was found to be an ideal place to spend it.

When spring came in 860 the Vikings, using their island base, raided settlements up the river as other Vikings had done from their island bases on the Seine and Loire. They raided the lower Rhône valley, attacking Nîmes, Arles, and even as far up river as Valence. Not every raid was successful, as a contemporary letter, in which Abbot Lupus of Ferrières praises Count Gerard of Provence for defeating the plunderers and driving them away, shows.

As the Vikings were attacking southern France, then why not attack Italy? At least part of the Viking fleet, probably under Hasting, sailed down the western coast of the Italian boot, then up the Arno, devastating Pisa and sacking Fiesole. To these Italian exploits belongs the story of their attack on Rome. According to the story, Hasting, flushed with his triumphs, designed to attack Rome and become master of the world. His band sighted a city, magnificent in its buildings and dazzling to their northern eyes. Under a shameless ruse Hasting sent messengers into the town to say that he, in the last moments of life, desired baptism. The inhabitants allowed the entry of the Vikings into the city for this purpose. After his baptism, Hasting 'died' and during the solemn obsequies the 'dead' Hasting rose from his funeral bier and pierced the officiating bishop with his sword. Concealed weapons appeared and the Viking band laid waste the city. Only as they were leaving, we are told, did they discover that the city which they had seized by deceit was not Rome but the coastal town of Luna, the ancient Roman town at the mouth of the Magra on the Gulf of Genoa, far in both distance and grandeur from Rome. The story is related by Dudo of Saint Quentin, writing in the early eleventh century, and bears some resemblance to other tales, especially tales of entry by using simulated funerals such as the story of Pleskow in Russia and London – and could 'Londonia' and 'Luna' have been confused somehow? – and, in any case, merits no serious consideration. One late Arabic and two late Spanish sources claim that the Vikings reached the eastern Mediterranean (Greece and Alexandria), but the lines are too long and the witnesses too weak for us to explore.

In the summer of 861, after their Mediterranean experience, these Viking raiders sailed again past the Pillars of Hercules into the Atlantic, where they were harassed by gale winds and a Moorish fleet: the former they endured and the latter they defeated. One last raid, however, remained in this southern world. From the Bay of Biscay they descended upon Pamplona and held its prince to ransom. In 862 they were back in the familiar waters at the mouth of the Loire, their great adventure over. Other Viking raids in the south are mentioned in the sources – Compostella in 968, the caliphate of the Umoyyads in 966 and 971, and Asturias in 1013 – but the principal action remained in the lands of the Franks. The Iberian raids, though adventurous and revealing the Vikings' ambitions, were off-shoots of the Danish attacks upon Francia.

The great attacks (879–92)

Thirteen years of the worst devastation wrought by the Vikings was not the result of a strategic plan, a big 'push', an all-out offensive. The Danish Great Army which appeared in the Low Countries in 879 had arrived in England in 878 to join its brothers-in-arms in the wars against the Anglo-Saxons. The new army, learning upon its arrival in the Thames valley that its brothers had indeed been defeated by King Alfred at Edington, stayed the winter at Fulham on the Thames and in the following year sailed for the continent. This army was to range almost freely in the northern part of the Frankish lands – between the Seine and the Rhine – lands which had been largely free from Viking attacks for the previous fifteen years.

The progress of this army can be easily followed. In mid July 879 the Great Army landed on the coast between Calais and Boulogne. By the end of that month they had raided Thérouanne and the abbey of Saint Bertin. Attacking as they went, they visited violence upon the Yser, Lys and Scheldt valleys and encamped for the winter at Ghent. Early in 880 this Viking army left its camp at Ghent and attacked Tournai, Condé, Valenciennes, and even Reims, before returning to Ghent. The next winter (880–1) they camped at Courtrai, from where they attacked Arras, Cambrai and Péronne – all of these raids probably occurred during a one-month period from late December 880 to late January 881. Within a matter of only weeks they were on the move again, harassing Thérouanne, the coastal region between Boulogne and Saint Valéry, and the Somme valley including Amiens and Corbie before returning to Courtrai. The itinerary goes on and on: in 881–2 they were on the Meuse attacking Tongres, Liège and Maastricht; on the Rhine attacking Cologne, Bonn and Koblenz, and on the Moselle attacking Treves, Metz and Remich. Under the year 884 the annalist of Saint Vaast recorded:

Excavation of the Gokstad ship from a burial mound in Vestfold, Norway

Top left *Spindle whorl of soapstone from L'Anse aux Meadows*

Centre left *Stone lamp from the Viking site at L'Anse aux Meadows*

Bottom left *A ring-headed pin of bronze excavated in a house site at L'Anse aux Meadows, and photographed in situ*

Below *Site of the largest house excavated at L'Anse aux Meadows, Newfoundland*

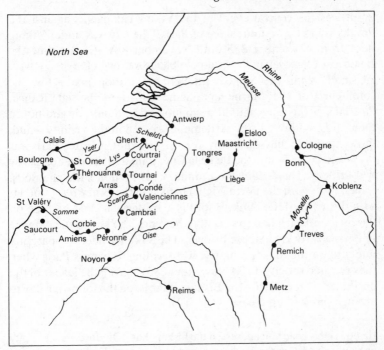

13   *The great attacks (879–92)*

The northmen continue to kill and take Christian people captive; without ceasing they destroy churches and dwellings and burn towns. Along all the roads one sees bodies of the clergy and laity, of nobles and others, of women, children, and infants. There is no road on which the bodies of slain Christians are not strewn. Sorrow and despair fill the hearts of all Christians who witness this.

And the Christians who witnessed this must have despaired of ever finding relief, for the Vikings seemed able to criss-cross these lands almost at will. Some opposition was in fact mounted, and the Vikings lost one battle to Louis III at Saucourt in 881 and were besieged by Charles the Fat at Elsloo on the Meuse, although neither Carolingian chose to press his advantage. By July 885 the invaders, having exhausted the region – but not themselves – headed south for the Seine. They were not to return to these tired lands of the north and northeast for another five years.

The central event of the Great Army's thirteen years – some would say it was the central event of the Viking campaigns against the Franks – was the famous siege of Paris. The city was under Viking siege from November 885 until November 886. At this time the greatness of Paris lay in the future: in 885 it was one of several towns, all small, along the Seine, although its location just below the confluence of the Marne and Seine added to its significance. Parisians at this time should be numbered in hundreds and not in thousands. Although tiny settlements existed in the vicinity – and, thus, suburbs in that sense only, for Paris was not an *urbs* – Paris was the island in the Seine, the Île de la Cité, joined to the river banks by two bridges. The *Grand Pont,* under construction since the 860s, joined Paris with the north (right) bank and the *Petit Pont* joined it with the south (left) bank. Both these bridges blocked passage on the river and each had towers at either end. The key to the defence of Paris clearly lay in these bridges. The Viking leaders, apparently intent upon the Marne country, were willing to bypass Paris when they reached the city on 24 November 885. Sigfrid, the leader of the northmen, met Joscelin, the Bishop of Paris, on the following day to arrange passage upstream.

He bowed his head and addressed the bishop thus: 'Oh, Joscelin, have pity on your self and on the flock entrusted to your care. For your own good listen to what I have to say. We ask only that you let us pass beyond your city; we shall not touch it. We shall strive to safeguard your rights and also those of [count] Odo.' . . . The bishop responded loyally with these words: 'We have been charged with the protection of this city by our king Charles [the Fat], whose kingdom extends almost over the entire earth under the authority of the Lord, King and Master of the powerful. The kingdom must not allow itself to be destroyed; she must be saved by our city. If these walls had been committed to you as they indeed have been committed to us and if you had acted as you have asked us to act, what would you think of yourself?'

Sigfrid answered, 'My sword would be disgraced and unworthy of my command. Nevertheless, if you do not grant my request, I must tell you that our instruments of war will send you poisoned arrows at daybreak, and at day's end there will be hunger. And so it will be; we will not cease.'

And so it was, almost. As Sigfrid had threatened, the attack began at daybreak on 26 November. The northmen launched a full-scale assault on the tower on the right bank of the Seine. All day long stones were hurled and arrows shot against the defenders while burning pitch and boiling oil were poured down upon the attackers.

At the end of that day the tower remained in the hands of the Parisians but much damage had been done to it. The defenders, working by night, added another storey to the height of the tower. When the Vikings returned on the following day, they came equipped with a battering ram to strike at the structure itself and a catapult to send fire into the wooden entrails of the tower. Again, the Parisians prevailed.

The Vikings began their siege. They pitched camp before the city at the Abbey of Saint Germain l'Auxerrois. On the last day of January 886 they began another attack. Dividing themselves into three groups, the attackers sent one band to set upon the tower on the right bank and the other two bands were sent against the bridge. For three days the Vikings fought to capture the tower, trying to fill its ditch with straw, tree branches, animal carcasses, and even with the bodies of dead prisoners, but to no avail. They sent three blazing boats to destroy the bridge but it survived.

The winter weather accomplished what the Danes could not. The Seine flooded on the 6th day of February and the *Petit Pont* was washed away; passage was possible south of the city. The Vikings quickly attacked the tower isolated on the left bank. Some of the Vikings raided overland beyond Paris as far as the Loire, others raided Chartres and Evreux to the south and east, and still others remained at Paris to maintain the siege. The call went forth from Paris for help, and Count Henry of Saxony led an army to lift the siege. His soldiers, weakened by a march in winter, made only one desultory attack on the besiegers before withdrawing. The Danish camp was now on the left bank at Saint Germain-des-Prés. Sigfrid offered to lift the siege for a tribute of a mere sixty pounds of silver, but the Parisians refused and the siege continued. The bishop–leader of the Parisians, Joscelin, died in April. The attackers knew of his death and shouted tauntingly at the gates that the bishop was dead. Odo, Count of Paris, rallied the defenders, overwhelmed by grief and stricken with disease, to continue the defence. Secretly, Odo left Paris to beg his fellow Franks, particularly the Emperor Charles the Fat, to come to the aid of his city. The Danes, who seemed to know a great deal about their enemy, knew Odo was returning and blocked his entry into the city. The great defender of Paris, his horse killed beneath him, fought on foot and, slaying the Danes on the left and right, gained entrance to Paris. Charles did respond to the Parisian plea, and by October his army was at the foot of Montmartre. Instead of attacking with his strong army he made terms with the enemy: if they would lift the siege, Charles would let them pass Paris and follow the Seine into Burgundy where they would be free to spend the winter harassing Charles's Burgundian subjects. The Parisians were enraged by this settlement and refused to allow the enemy to sail past Paris. The ships had to be carried overland to a point beyond the city. The Parisians were even further enraged when in the spring Charles paid the Vikings 700 pounds to leave the Seine. Justice was seen to be done, in the eyes of the Parisians, when, in 888, Charles was deposed and in 889 Odo, saviour of Paris, became King of the West Franks. And from that year Paris was spared any further fúry from Viking attacks.

During these years other Vikings, taking advantage of the weak and fractured condition of Francia, raided on the other rivers. Hasting was active in the Loire. The Oise and the Scheldt were repeatedly visited by Viking bands, who were disciplined and adept in military tactics, and well equipped for the type of war that they were now waging. The attempts by Odo and others to repel these attacks were only partially successful. In 891, at the same time as Hasting with his army was raiding in Picardy, part of the Viking great army in Frisia suffered a defeat at Louvain. Both armies left in 892, not the victims of Frankish military strength – the army of the north could have recovered from the Louvain defeat – but the victims of nature herself. An exceptionally dry summer in 892 had left a parched earth and a very small harvest. The twin devastations of famine and disease struck these lands, and in the face of these the Vikings retreated, to undertake campaigns against the English King Alfred. This provides further evidence of the interrelation between Danish campaigns. The period of the raiding campaigns in Francia was now coming to an end. Yet, the Vikings were to return, and the great principality of Normandy was to be founded.

The settlements: Normandy and elsewhere

Permanent Viking settlements in Francia were the exception rather than the rule. The great success of their settlement in Normandy and the subsequent glory of that principality might give the impression that this was the only Viking settlement in Francia. It was not the only settlement, but it was the only successful settlement. In about the year 840 two Vikings became vassals of Louis the Pious, and they and their successors held the territory around Dorestad until

885, when Charles the Fat ended their rule and also ended what Marc Bloch calls 'this Netherlandish Normandy'. The Vikings on the Loire seemed intent on settling or, at least, on establishing a colony. In 869 Salomon, Duke of Brittany, made peace with the mighty Hasting and his raiders, and after three years these Vikings sailed up the Loire and its tributary the Marne as far as Angers, where they established themselves, perhaps with their wives and children. Charles the Bald was disturbed by the thought of a permanent Viking settlement within striking distance of Tours and successfully besieged Angers by diverting the waters of the Marne, leaving the Viking ships high and dry. An agreement was quickly reached and the Vikings went back down the Loire, remaining in its basin until 882. This early attempt to establish a 'Loire Normandy' in the 870s was a precedent, if not an exact model, for the attempt to establish a settlement in the area of the Loire around Nantes in the early tenth century, at about the same time that Rollo and the Seine Vikings were settling the area of the lower Seine around Rouen. In fact, in 921 Count Robert, son of Robert the Strong, recognized the rule of the Vikings in the county of Nantes; later, in 927, Raoul, King of the West Franks, also recognized them. Their power probably extended into the romance-speaking eastern borders of Brittany. The Loire Vikings were finally driven from their nascent settlement by Alan Crooked-Beard in 937, their attempt at colonization having lasted for, perhaps, a quarter of a century. One can only imagine how different French and, indeed, European history would have been had there been successful Viking settlements on both the Loire and Seine.

Normandy, the Viking settlement on the Seine, its future brilliant with accomplishments, had its beginnings shrouded in the darkness of morning before first light. To say that Normandy was established in 911 as a result of an agreement between Charles the Simple and Rollo is to say too much and too little. The two great chroniclers of this period – Flodoard and a monk of Saint Vaast – both miss the crucial years. Much national pride has been involved in trying to determine, without complete success, the origin of Rollo himself – was he Danish? or Norwegian? or possibly Swedish? No document of the settlement survives, and its terms can be inferred only from later documents. What is known is – and has to be – enough for us to gain a general outline of the process. When Charles the Simple became King of the West Franks in 893, he appeared intent on ridding his kingdom of the Viking menace. He did reach an agreement with the leader of the Seine Vikings in 897: the latter was baptized, with Charles acting as godfather. (Are we to believe that Charles led him physically to the baptismal font?) This plan failed. Fourteen years later – it is one of the dates we do have – in 911 Rollo, whose place of origin is not really of consequence, led a *Danish* army to the town of Chartres, which he besieged. The siege proved unsuccessful, and Rollo's army suffered a major defeat. In 913 and 918 Rollo, acting as a Christian leader with full authority over Rouen, apparently issued charters, which have, unhappily, been lost. In 918 Charles the Simple referred, in a royal charter, to an agreement which had been made with Rollo. This agreement, then, must have been concluded sometime between 911 and 918, and probably between 911 and 913, established Normandy. Rollo was probably baptized at this time, since it is assumed that Rollo was not a Christian at the time of the siege of Chartres and that Charles demanded his baptism, as he had demanded the baptism of the leader of the Seine Vikings in 897. Rollo also undertook to defend the lower Seine from further attack, thus providing a buffer against both the Bretons and other Vikings. Charles the Simple, for his part, allowed the Vikings to settle in that region; this is clearly implied in the royal charter of 14 March 918, in which Charles the Simple stated that he had given land to Rollo and his companions *pro tutela regni* ('for the defence of the kingdom'). It is not known exactly what lurks behind these words, but the obvious explanation is that sometime, soon after his defeat at Chartres, Rollo became a vassal of the French king: he received the lands around the lower Seine in return for swearing fealty to Charles. The story that Charles and the Viking leader met at Saint Claire-sur-Epte in the late autumn of 911 and that, in paying obeisance to Charles, the Viking Rollo tripped him, has no better foundation in fact than the fertile and impish imaginations of later historians.

What were these lands conceded to the Vikings *pro tutela regni*? The charter of 918 does not itemize them. Even if originally – as seems to have been the case – these lands extended only to the area of Upper Normandy, the lands of the Normans grew to include Bessin and, temporarily, Maine in 924, and also Cotentin (i.e., the peninsula) and Avranchin in 933; these additions no doubt legally recognizing *de facto* Viking occupation.

The lands which the Vikings settled were probably

underpopulated at this time due to the generations of Viking activity in the area and the apparent abandonment of the Seine defences below Pîtres. The bulk of the settlers were men. They came principally from Denmark, although some came from the northeast of England and others from Ireland, a conclusion suggested by a sophisticated analysis of known names. How long did the colonizing take? The main lines of the settlement would have been completed in the period of two generations. Intermarriage between newly baptized Viking men and Christian Frankish women – even if one does not accept that Rollo married Gisèle, the daughter of Charles the Simple – must have occurred from the very beginning. The process of assimilation was well underway and is captured at this dynamic stage in the practice, which was more than symbolic, of Vikings having two names, one pagan and Norse, the other Christian and French. Rollo was Robert; his daughter Gerloc was Adèle; Thurstein of Cotentin was Richard; Stigand of Mezidon was Odo. If Rollo was responsible for winning a permanent home for the Vikings on the Seine, it was his son, William Longsword, who was responsible for the integration of Viking and Frank. A pious Christian, at one time restrained from entering a monastery, William married a Frankish princess, Liégeard, the daughter of Herbert of Vermandois. William's sister married William of Poitiers. Assimilation was taking place. Duke William's son Richard, in order to be brought up a Viking, had to be sent to Bayeux from Rouen for the Viking capital was by then a French-speaking city, a transformation that had taken less than twenty-five years. Of course, new settlers were still coming in the 930s, some of them still pagan, and at one moment in the early 940s Normandy almost reverted to paganism, but the danger quickly passed. The future course of Normandy was now set. Duke Richard became espoused to a Carolingian princess and was known to contemporaries by the Frankish title of count: *comes piratarum* (not 'count of the pirates' but rather 'count of the Vikings'). The Normans quickly adopted Frankish institutions. By mid century Normandy was not a Viking colony; it was a region of France, distinct, indeed, from other provinces (as they were distinct from one another) but unquestionably French.

If change and continuity are the two themes of history and if it is up to the historian to judge which needs emphasis, then an easy generalization to make is that *continuity* is the theme to be stressed in the establishment of Normandy. After all, the Norse language died quickly – first in Upper Normandy and later in Lower Normandy and there is no sign of its use after 940. It has left few traces in the French language except for nautical words (for example, *bâbord, tribord, quille, havre*) and place-names (for example, those ending *-bec, -bu, -dique, -tot*). Their religion did not survive into the second generation and left no permanent mark. The *thing*, the assembly used by Vikings in the north, is not known at all in Normandy. The political and social structure was feudal: the dukes were vassals of the French king and their men linked to them by feudal tenure. The Normans did more than merely tolerate a change of religion and, with the fervor of the newly converted, championed the Christian cause. They were soon patronizing monasteries and, a century later, leading a reform movement and, soon after that, taking the cross. The younger sons of Norman lords who landed in southern Italy in the decades after 1016 were *French*, and the Norman duke who landed at Pevensey in 1066 was French *tout à fait*. And so the argument for continuity runs. What emerged in Normandy, it is argued, was a feudal, Christian, French society. This view understandably looks to specific, concrete historical phenomena: laws, language, religious practice, societal structure, etc. More elusive, since it is less specific and not at all concrete, is the spiritual dimension brought by the invaders, the Viking qualities which enabled them to adapt to their new conditions and to create their principality. Daring, vigour, drive, vitality, organizational and administrative ability – one resists the temptation to add *élan* – are not so susceptible to measurement and cannot be placed on a scale against the weighty factors arguing for continuity. Yet, the very question concerning continuity and change in this context reflects a Franco-centric view of history: Neustria became Normandy and this process belongs to French history. The Viking historian merely notes that only one successful Viking settlement was established in the south and that, by measurable criteria, the Vikings became quickly assimilated.

The settlement of the Loire – unsuccessful – and the settlement on the Seine – successful – came during the final phase of the Vikings in Francia. Other raids were made in the tenth century, but by then the Viking force was spent. What began in the 830s was by the 930s virtually exhausted, its momentum gone or, rather, directed elsewhere. The Danes, no longer active in France, continued their activity in England, but that belongs to another chapter.

Selected further reading

The most important works are, of course, in French and in this generation have been written by Albert d'Haenens and Lucien Musset. The reader will find Marc Bloch, *Feudal Society,* Routledge & Kegan Paul 1961, book 1, chapter 2 useful. Among the more general books (see above, Chapter 1) Kendrick, Shetelig, Brøndsted, and Jones are in varying degrees helpful. An important interpretive essay is J. M. Wallace-Hadrill's *The Vikings in Francia,* University of Reading Press 1975, reprinted in *Early Medieval History,* Blackwell 1975. For a discussion of the Danegeld, see Einar Joranson, *The Danegeld in France,* Rock Island, Illinois: Augustana Library Publications, no. 10, 1923. The Iberian adventures can be studied in W. E. D. Allen, 'The Poet and the Spae-Wife: An Attempt to Reconstruct al-Ghazal's Embassy to the Vikings'. in *Saga Book of the Viking Club,* vol. 15, part 3, 1960, and Jon Stefansson, 'The Vikings in Spain from Arabic (Moorish) and Spanish sources', in *Saga Book of the Viking Club,* vol. 6 (1908–9), pp. 30–46. Although it is old, much of interest can still be found in C. H. Haskins, *The Normans in European History,* Boston: Houghton, Mifflin 1915. For a reconsideration of Charles the Bald see Margaret Gibson and Janet Nelson (eds.), *Charles the Bald: Court and Kingdom,* British Archaeological Reports, International series, vol. 101, 1981.

6   The Danes in England

Heroes abound (Alfred, Athelstan, Cnut) as do saints (Edmund, Alphege, Oswald) and villains, (Eric Bloodaxe, Ethelred the Unready) and famous places (Edington, Maldon, York). It is the world of Viking-age England. It is the period when Danes attacked, invaded and settled, when they brought England out of its insularity into the wider life of northern Europe. For 200 years the Vikings from Denmark dominated English history, attacking her shores, traversing her roads, and permanently changing her landscape and language. Fortifications were built; new towns came into being; new markets were opened at home and abroad. England was never to be the same again.

The story of the Vikings in the land of the English is at once blessed and bedevilled by the account in the *Anglo-Saxon Chronicle* and by the towering figure of King Alfred.

Overshadowed as an early vernacular history only by the contemporary Irish annals, the Old English chronicles, known collectively as the *Anglo-Saxon Chronicle* (and, familiarly, as the *Chronicle*), reveal such a wealth of information about the Viking invasions that, were we forced to rely solely on other sources, we would be left historically poverty-stricken. Yet the *Anglo-Saxon Chronicle* is, at best, a partial, prejudiced account of these years. Its manifest emphasis on the south and, in particular, on the fortunes of the kingdom of Wessex for much of its account of the Viking age leaves vast areas of the country virtually unchronicled over long periods. Paying only occasional attention to events of the northeast and almost no attention to events of the northwest, the *Chronicle* cannot be considered an English *national* history for the period of the Vikings. That was never its intention and that was never the historical reality.

Alfred's great fame owes much to his good fortune in having the deeds of his reign so fully reported – and so favourably – in the *Anglo-Saxon Chronicle* and his life so eloquently hagiographed by the fawning Asser. Also, since nothing succeeds like success and since the house of Wessex was successful in uniting the English into one kingdom, the Whig and neo-Whig historians have turned to Alfred as the founder of the English state, the greatest monarch before the Norman Conquest, in a word 'the Great'. In truth, the success of the house of Wessex was far from certain at the death of Alfred and the unity of England had been far from Alfred's mind. As a king of Wessex, Alfred was an able monarch, equal but, arguably, not superior to Edward the Elder and Athelstan. The triple tyrannies of the *Chronicle,* Asser and traditional historiography leave us with the fame of a good local king inflated into majestic national greatness. If the Viking age produced a monarch of greatness, then one need look no farther than the foreign-born Cnut, whose legacy to Edward the Confessor and William the Conqueror provided a substantial base for the successes of post-Cnutian England.

Definitions are not easy in all this. Words like 'king', 'England' and 'Denmark' roll very easily from one's pen, but what do they mean? Does 'England' mean anything more than the place where the Anglo-Saxons lived and 'Denmark' the place where the Danes lived? We may be tempted to attribute a political organization and unity to these places which they did not in fact possess. Neither for England nor for Denmark in the beginning of the Viking age should one assume 'one nation, one king' or, even less, 'one state, one king'. The overlay of subsequent centuries can disguise the fact that, at this time, 'king' among the Danes referred to a powerful regional leader with some hereditary claim to rule and that in England a 'king' was ruler of a regional kingdom, again with an hereditary element of some sort. There might have been three such kings ruling in different parts of Denmark and possibly as many as five kings in contemporary England. Kingship was about power, and power was about men – particularly warriors – and wealth. A powerful leader could by force of arms intimidate weaker leaders and demand from the latter military and financial support. Almost like a chant historians must repeat to themselves (and to the world) 'titles do not confer power'. Alfred might have been called 'king of all the English save those captive to the Danes' and Athelstan 'king of all Britain', but the claim and the reality are scarcely the same. Power is not conferred; it is held. Some semblance of unity came to England when Edgar became sole monarch in 959 and to Denmark about the same time under the rule of Harald Bluetooth. In neither case was regionalism stamped out nor was there anything more than the primitive apparatus of a national state, although England was further advanced in this process than Denmark.

To mention England and Denmark in the same breath helps to emphasize the point that from the 850s to the 1060s England and Denmark belonged to the same northern world. The Danish connection dominated English history during this period. Greater Scandinavia included England, and it took a Norman invasion to break the connection and to draw England into the world of France, the empire, and the reformed papacy.

14   *Early Viking raids on England (835–65)*

The first Viking wave (835–954)

In 835 the Danes came to England. The same impetus which had moved them to attack Frisia and Francia the previous year moved them to attack England. What released the fury of the Danes at that particular time may never be known: dynastic struggles, population stress, a climate which was growing cold, and restricted crops may all have contributed. The raids upon England from 835 to 865 were surprise raids, in-and-out raids of a seasonal nature, as were the early raids by the Danes – at times the same Danes – on the Continent. Between 865 and 954 the attacks were by large armies and settlement followed. The seasonal raids and the colonizing attacks combined to form the first wave of Danes to come to England.

Table 3 *Early Viking raids on England*

Year	Place
835	Sheppey
836	Carhampton
838	Cornwall (Hingston Down)
840	Southampton
	Portland (Dorset)
841	Romney Marsh
	Lindsey
	East Anglia
	Kent
842	London
	Rochester
843	Carhampton
848	Somerset (mouth of Parret River)
850	Devon
	Sandwich
	Thanet
851	Canterbury
	London
	Surrey
853	Thanet
855	Sheppey
860 x 865	Winchester

An analysis of these early, seasonal raids in England – or, rather, an analysis of the reports of these raids – is instructive. The *Anglo-Saxon Chronicle* mentions raids in only thirteen of the years during this period and indicates only twenty-two places which the Vikings visited (Table 3).

The first point to be made from Table 3 is a geographical one. These were obviously coastal raids against *southern* England, seldom penetrating more than fifteen miles inland. With the exception of 841, where the chronicler simply says that 'in Lindsey and in East Anglia and in Kent many men were slain', the raids mentioned in our chief source were southern raids, none of them north of London and the Thames. It should not be overlooked that the south coast and not east Kent, as one might expect, were particularly favoured by the Viking attackers for the raids during the years up to 850. All of the raids chronicled here, except those against Lindsey and East Anglia in 841 and against London in 842, were of immediate concern to the kingdom of Wessex; its principal seat, Winchester, was itself attacked sometime during the reign of Ethelbert (860–5).

Are we to conclude from this evidence that the raids during the period 835 to 865 were in fact mainly raids against Wessex? that the rest of England remained virtually untouched? that there were no Viking raids on England between 843 and 848? It would be fool-hardy for us to rush to these conclusions in the face of such a paucity of surviving sources. It would be historically naive to believe that what is recorded – or, rather, what survives of what was recorded – constitutes the principal events of English history. The so-called 'national chronicle' is, for these years, a chronicle chiefly concerned with Wessex. The fact that the chronicler could dismiss the events in Lindsey and East Anglia in 841 so briefly suggests the narrowness of his interests and perhaps, too, the extent of his information. The *Chronicle* itself has no entry at all for many years during this period. The *Parker Chronicle* (the A version of the *Anglo-Saxon Chronicle*) does not list events for sixteen of these thirty years, although the annals for 855 and 860 are terse quinquennial summaries and might be amended to read, 855–9 and 860–4 respectively; still, that leaves at least eight years totally unrecorded: 837, 844–7, 849, 852 and 854. The *Annals of Saint Bertin*, concerned with events in contemporary Francia, state under the year 844 that 'the northmen began a major attack on that part of the island of Britain where the Anglo-Saxons live and after a three-day battle the northmen emerged victors: plundering, looting, slaying, they wielded power over the land at will'. For the year 844 the English chronicle records no Viking attack. In view of such a patently incomplete record, whose focus effectively excludes large regions of England, we can only wonder about the extent of the unrecorded Viking activity outside Wessex. What hides behind the words 'in Lindsey and in East Anglia . . . many men were slain'?

The period of the Vikings' first major attacks on England was marked by alternating victories and defeats. These attacks began in 865: 'in this same year there came a great army to England and it established winter quarters in East Anglia'. And so the *Chronicle* begins its account, and from this time until the year 954, when peace came, its pages are concerned with the Viking invasions and little else. During these years settlements took root; Viking kingdoms were established; the political map of England took on new shapes and these were fluid. The story is not the accepted one of King Alfred defeating the Vikings and his son and grandson mopping up afterwards. On the English side – and here we have names and, behind them, at least faint outlines of people – heroes of equal accomplishment do appear and include Alfred, Edward the Elder, and Athelstan. 'And there came a great army.'

The 'army' which came to East Anglia in 865 numbered somewhere – and the estimates vary widely – between about 500 and 2000 Vikings. They formed a fairly cohesive group, probably led by the brothers Ivar and Halfdan, sons of the legendary Ragnar Lothbrok. Their intention was different from their predecessors' for theirs was not meant to be a summer's raiding; these Vikings came prepared for a sustained campaign, intent upon winning English land for themselves. The unified action of this army suggests a unified leadership: the army moved as an army, although it contained petty kings and *jarls*, who might have been allowed occasional tangents from the general line of attack. It was this army, added to on occasion, which harassed Northumbria, Mercia, East Anglia and Wessex; it was this army which gave the first outlines to Danish settlement; and it was a remnant of this army that Alfred defeated at Edington in 878. All the evidence invites the conclusion that this was an army whose ultimate purpose was to take land and settle.

The progress of the Viking army from 865 to 886 can be followed without interruption. The East Anglians, faced with this invasion in 865, quickly made peace and provided the invaders with horses, which were to make their rapid advances possible. In the autumn of 866 the Vikings crossed the Humber and entered into a

Northumbria riven by dissension. Rival kings were competing for authority. On All Saints' Day 866, the Danes captured York, having encountered no opposition. York was to be their capital in the north, a Viking city to rival Dublin, Hedeby and Birka, but that lay in the future. For the moment the Vikings had to contend with a gradually uniting Northumbrian response to their presence in York. On 21 March 867, the Northumbrians, their differences put aside for the moment, tried to regain their city. A battle was fought inside and outside the remaining Roman walls, and, in the words of the chronicler, 'A great slaughter was made of the Northumbrians, including both kings.' Again, peace was made. From York the Viking army, mobile on their East Anglian and, perhaps, now Yorkshire horses, turned south towards the enticing land of the Mercians. They seemed to have no trouble in seizing Nottingham, where they spent the winter of 867–8. The King of Mercia, aided by his brothers-in-law, Ethelred, King of Wessex, and the young Alfred, advanced on the Vikings in Nottingham, but the Vikings knew the danger of leaving their fortifications to engage in open battle and so declined. Again, a peace was made. At what price to the Mercians, the suing party? Whatever the price – and the sources are mute – the Mercians were spared further Danish attacks for over three years. The following year, 869, the Danes left Mercia and returned to York, where they had presumably kept some military force to maintain their authority. Later that same year their army was permitted to pass through Mercia on their way back to East Anglia, where they made winter quarters at Thetford. During that winter of 869–70, the East Anglians attempted a stand against the Danes. Like the Northumbrians at York, they failed; their King, Edmund, was slain in the process. There seemed no power in England capable of stopping this disciplined, mobile, well-led Viking army.

There remained Wessex – that is, if one believes that the intention of these Vikings was a conquest of England, and the evidence for this view is not compellingly clear. The scenario that has Alfred saving Wessex and, hence, England depends on a presumed Viking policy of total conquest. If conquest was their intention, why only England? Why not the whole island? How precisely could the invaders distinguish the political units then existing in Britain? What sense could they have had of the movements of political power in Britain? Nevertheless Wessex and its rich lands remained as yet untouched by their fiercely successful army.

York

Humber

Torksey

Nottingham

Repton

Watling Street

Welland

Thetford

Bedford

Cambridge

Cirencester

Ashdown

Shoebury

Mersea

Chippenham

Reading

London

Benfleet

Wedmore

Basing

Edington

Rochester

Athelvey

Aller

Exeter

Wareham

━━━
Boundary between Alfred's Kingdom
and Guthrum's Kingdom, 886

15   *England in the time of King Alfred*

The defence of Wessex lay principally in the hands of Alfred. His eldest brother Ethelred only fought the campaigns of the first season. Not a military genius, Alfred responded to the Viking attacks with tactics of passing adequacy. His defence of *England* did not exist: Wessex alone concerned him. At first, each side tested the strength of the other. In 870 the Danes seized Reading, situated at the junction of the River Kennet and the Thames, without difficulty; like York, Nottingham and Thetford it was to serve as a regional headquarters, because it was an easily defended location, and a base for action in the general area. Almost immediately (three days after their arrival, according to the *Chronicle*) the Danes were tested.

Local levies from Berkshire skirmished with them. Four days later (i.e., one week after the Danes seized Reading) the brothers Ethelred and Alfred brought up their army. Major engagements followed at Reading, Ashdown (i.e., the Berkshire Downs), Basing and *Merantūn* (not now identifiable). Despite a victory by the West Saxons at Ashdown the Vikings held the advantage. Ethelred's death left Alfred with the task of facing his opponents on his own; this he did at Wilton but without success. The chronicler sums up the year 871 (i.e., September 870 to September 871):

In the course of the year nine general engagements were fought against the Danish army in the kingdom south of the Thames in addition to the countless skirmishes which Alfred, the king's brother, and a single ealdorman and king's thane engaged in.

Wessex was not ready, and Alfred wisely sued for peace. Whatever the price – and it need not have involved silver – it removed the Danish menace from Wessex for four years.

The Viking horde left Wessex and wintered (871–2) at the Mercian market town of London. In 872 they travelled from London to Torksey in Lindsey. The Mercians were not able to successfully oppose the seasoned Viking army at either London or in Lindsey, and, in both places, made peace. These must have been local peaces for, after wintering in Torksey, the Viking army proceeded to Repton in Mercia in 873, where they spent the following winter. The occupation of Repton was accomplished only by the slaughter of more than 150 Mercian warriors, whose disarticulated bones were discovered in excavations undertaken during the years 1974 to 1982. The kingdom of Mercia was at an end: the Vikings forced King Burhred into exile and set the subservient Ceolwulf on the throne. Bristling with confidence – in less than ten years they had been victorious in East Anglia, Northumbria and Mercia – the Vikings reached a major decision in 874. The army which had stayed together since its landing in East Anglia in the autumn of 865 now divided. Halfdan took his army north from Repton and, in 876, after a year spent establishing firm border areas against the Picts to the north and the Strathclyde Britons to the west, he began the process of settlement. The *Chronicle* records that 'he shared out Northumbria between himself and his men, and his army was soon ploughing land and living off it'. The other part of the Viking army also left Repton in 874 and went south, its purpose to gain the coveted lands of the West Saxons. From Cambridge, where they wintered in 874–5, this remnant of the Great Army 865, now led by Guthrum, Oscytel and Anund, attacked Wessex. Whatever might have pre-occupied Alfred during the four-year lull, it certainly had not been the defence of his kingdom. The fact that the Danes moved without interference from Cambridge to Wareham in 875 testifies to the weak state of West Saxon security. Attempts at peace at Wareham and, in the next year, at Exeter led eventually, but not till 877, to the return of the Danes to Mercia. The confident Danes further diminished the size of their army by dividing Mercia in two – West (or English) Mercia and East (or Danish) Mercia – and sharing out the latter for settlement.

The peace was only temporary: the Vikings re-entered Wessex in January 878, determined to acquire land. They used Chippenham as their base and were so successful in occupying large parts of Wessex that the chronicler laments that 'they drove many of the inhabitants overseas'. During his four-year respite, Alfred had not established an adequate defence against the heathen invaders. He had no alternative, short of surrender, but to make a strategic retreat, and this he did. The Danes did not pursue him into the useless wastes of Athelney; they were too busy reducing the land to submission. Alfred engaged in lightning attacks upon the invaders. These were only small skirmishes, but gave combat experience to the local men who joined his small force in the marshes of Somerset in the spring of 878. He then called up what men he could from Somerset, Wiltshire and the nearest part of Hampshire.

And they saw Alfred vigorous and full of vitality despite his misfortunes, and they were overjoyed. (*Chronicle*)

While Alfred was preparing for a spring offensive, his kingdom received yet another blow – an unco-ordinated Viking raid from South Wales upon Devon – and it was the men of Devon who repelled it. The victory won by Alfred's army at Edington in Wiltshire in the spring of 878 was not a total victory nor was it followed by the total surrender of the Viking Danes. The Danish 'army' represented only a fraction, perhaps a small fraction, of the Great Army that had landed in East Anglia in 865, parts of which had already settled in Northumbria and East Mercia. Peace came after Alfred's two-week seige of the Danes in their fortifications at

Chippenham, to which they had fled from the battlefield. The *Chronicle* relates:

The Danes gave him hostages and took a solemn oath that they would quit his kingdom and that their king would be baptized.

The baptism of Guthrum (now known as Athelstan) followed at Aller and his confirmation at Wedmore.

The Danish army, still strong, still a potential menace, did not quit Wessex at once. They remained at Chippenham for the summer and only at the summer's end did they move to nearby Cirencester in West Mercia. It was not until the spring of 879, one full year after the events at Edington, Aller and Wedmore, that they moved to East Anglia, where they shared out and settled the land. There is no evidence to link the Chippenham agreement to the settling of East Anglia. The Danes fulfilled their oath to Alfred by simply moving into English Mercia, i.e., out of Wessex. Why they moved from Mercia into East Anglia is a separate issue, about which our sources are silent. Neither side was to consider this peace as final. In 884 the East Anglian Vikings rose to support their kinsmen who had crossed the English Channel from the Somme and who attacked Rochester in Kent and raided in the lands south of the lower Thames. In response Alfred sent ships to attack East Anglia, where, after an initial victory, they were defeated by the Danes. The partisan West Saxon chronicler charges that the Danes broke the peace when they retaliated by attacking Alfred later that year; the peace, in fact, had been broken many months earlier. Surely, it was in reply to these provocations that Alfred seized London by military force in 886 and placed it under the Mercian ealdorman Ethelred, who seems to have succeeded to the position formerly held by Ceolwulf II.

The claim made by Alfred's chronicler at this juncture – 'and all the English, except those subject to the Danes, submitted to him' – needs closer examination. Certainly a new arrangement existed. The events of the period 878 to 886 had led to a realignment of the power structure and the political geography of England. Alfred was uncontested ruler of Wessex, which was now more secure in its boundaries than it had been since 870; he exercised some power over English Mercia including London, but Mercia remained Mercia and was not annexed to form a Greater Wessex. What about the English outside Wessex and Mercia? It is not clear which of these English were not subject to the rule of Danish kings in 866; perhaps none. The claim of the chronicler, even if taken at face value, may perhaps be a summing up of the obvious consequences of the taking of London: Alfred ruled Wessex without fear and enjoyed hegemony over parts of Mercia. The Guthrum–Alfred agreement (878–86) drew a boundary line between their territories. The southern boundary of Guthrum's kingdom can be traced along the Thames from its estuary west to the River Lea, up the Lea to its source, then to Bedford and up the Ouse to Watling Street, which formed the western boundary. The northern boundary of his kingdom allows no such clear delineation, but it probably reached as far as the Welland and the upper Avon. Beyond that boundary were other Viking kingdoms at York and elsewhere in the north. The situation was at best fluid and the lines were to change frequently before the Viking age in England came to an end.

Six years of peace followed the taking of London. Then in 892, the Great Army of the Danes which had been harassing the Low Countries, and which was now unwilling to bear the consequences of a bad harvest on the Continent, turned their Frisian-made ships towards England. Their campaign in England, lasting four years, proved unsuccessful. During the years of peace before 892, Alfred had set in motion plans for the defence of the realm. The method of raising a West Saxon military force was being adapted to meet late ninth-century needs. Defensive fortifications had probably been under construction for some years and were almost completed by the time of the new Danish attacks. Alfred also attempted to provide naval defences, but English shipbuilding could in no way compete with either Viking or Frisian techniques. It is a sign of the self-confidence of a man successful in so much else, as indeed Alfred was, to think his talents boundless. The *Chronicle* again:

King Alfred ordered ships to be built in order to oppose the Danish ships: twice as long as the Viking ships, some with sixty oars, some with even more. They were to be faster, safer, and with more deck space. They were not built according to Frisian or Danish design but as the king thought it best.

Of course, bigger-is-better is a heresy which is not peculiar to the twentieth century. Alfred's ships proved difficult to navigate in tight places: defeat after defeat showed their inadequacy against the best ships and seamen of the time.

Horses, wives and children accompanied this new invasion; the horses at the very beginning and the women and children at least by 893. These Vikings intended to settle. A narrative of their campaign would show their armies criss-crossing England, taking bases among fellow countrymen in Mercia and Essex, never inflicting a serious defeat on the West Saxons, and yet remaining a threat, and never being seriously defeated. This stalemate ended in 896 when the Vikings split up: those who could afford it settled in Northumbria and East Anglia, those who could not looked for further adventure on the Seine.

Hasting and the other leaders of these Viking attacks were, to some extent, aided by their fellow Danes, at times perhaps unwittingly. For example, when, in 893, a Danish band was trapped on an island in the River Colne in Buckinghamshire, Alfred and his advancing army, poised to inflict a crushing blow, were forced to march to Exeter, instead, to confront the 'peaceful' Danes who were besieging the place. That same year the Viking army, on its great trek from Wessex to the then deserted town of Chester, was joined by an army from Northumbria and East Anglia. Their main bases were in Danish Essex (at Benfleet and Mersea), and they seemed to have free passage across these Danish lands. It is difficult to imagine the relative success of the raids of 892–4 without acknowledging the active and passive support of the 'Old Danes'.

This is not the place to assess the reign of Alfred: much transpired during his twenty-eight year reign other than the two periods of Viking attacks (871–9, 892–6). Much of Alfred's posthumous reputation, however, derives from his handling of the Viking menace. It is frequently said that he saved England and, also, that he was a military genius. Whatever else Alfred did, he did not save England; and, whatever else he may have been, he was not a military genius. In 871, at the beginning of his reign, the Vikings had a firm hold only in Northumbria, where they were centred at York. In 899, at Alfred's death, they controlled not only Northumbria but also East Anglia and East Mercia and they still posed a threat to Wessex. At best, Alfred 'saved' Wessex and saved it only temporarily. For the time being he succeeded in securing the territorial integrity of his own kingdom. In 873–4, when the Vikings attacked Mercia, Alfred did not move a finger to help. When Alfred made peace with Guthrum in 878 and 886, it was a peace between equals, and he implicitly acknowledged the Danish right to settle large regions of England.

Alfred's fame as a military leader is even more difficult to understand. Against the first major Viking attacks in 871 he distinguished himself by suing for peace and, despite four years untroubled by the Danes, he was still unprepared for their renewed attacks in 875 and had to sue for peace again. In 878 he was still unready and had to seek refuge in the marshes of Somerset. (Alfred the Unready?) Of his victory at Edington nothing is known about field tactics, the size of opposing armies, positions held, etc. Like most battles of the time, victory was achieved as much by the weight of numbers as by superior generalship.

The Alfredian defences did not exist *in vacuo* but existed only in the context of the type of attack which his enemy used in England. Nothing could be further from the truth than a picture of Viking ships appearing in the elaborate waterways of England, cruising through the river systems of the Thames, Trent, Ouse, Severn, Humber, Ribble, etc., penetrating deep into the heartland, attacking from their ships as they went, and striking terror into the souls of the English, most of whom lived near waterways. Such a picture overlooks the crucial fact that it was not by ship that the Vikings conducted their major campaigns (866–86, 892–6). With a few notable exceptions the Vikings, once they had landed in England, penetrated the coastal defences, and established bases, undertook an attack on England over land. The key to their attacks and, indeed, to their successes was not the English waterways but the Roman roads. Without the Roman roads the Viking attacks on England as they happened would be unimaginable. To reach their inland destinations the Danish Vikings used the road system left by the Romans as their most enduring legacy to Britain. Prehistoric trackways and Anglo-Saxon tracks also were used, but it was over the roads laid out by Roman engineers, which can be measured in the thousands of miles, that the Vikings travelled by horse. They did not need roads in full repair or at full width, merely roads good enough for horses to pass. These roads provided a context and dictated a shape for the Viking inland attacks on England. They either got horses from the English, as in East Anglia in 865–6, or brought the animals with them, as when they landed in Kent in 892. The Viking warriors did not fight on horseback – a mode of warfare which was to be perfected in time by the medieval knight – but used horses merely as a means of transport from one place to another: combat was on foot.

When the Vikings landed in East Anglia in 865 – we are not told

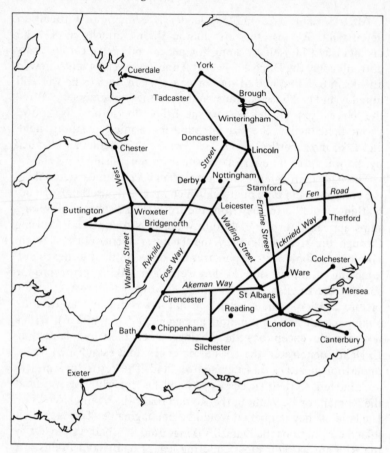

16   *Romans roads used by the Vikings*

where – they acquired horses and captured York the following year. How did they get to York? They took the Fen Road west to Ermine Street, where they turned north. They forded the Welland at what was to become Stamford and continued in a straight line north to the Humber, where they crossed from Winteringham to Brough. And thence to York. In all, it was a journey of about 150 miles, about a week's travelling, not allowing, as one perhaps should, for sorties into the countryside, a journey simply described in the *Chronicle* with the words, 'The army went from East Anglia over the mouth of the Humber to York in Northumbria.' In spring 867 they invaded Mercia and spent the following winter at Nottingham. Again they almost certainly travelled by land. Although one could work out a water-route via the Ouse, Humber and Trent, this route is very unlikely. The Vikings who were *invading* Mercia were well equipped with horses, and in York they stood at the top of a road which reached deep into Mercia. They undoubtedly rode down Ryknild Street as far as the site of a Roman camp, which was later called Derby. From there a spur road took them to the Trent, a few miles from the royal vill at Nottingham. The distance between York and Nottingham was about a hundred miles by this route. When they returned to York in 869, they would have returned by the same route. Later that year the Danes 'rode across Mercia' (*Chronicle*) to East Anglia where they stayed at Thetford for the winter of 869–70. How did they get to Thetford from York? They simply retraced their journey of 866, passing through East Mercia on Ermine Street and taking the Fen Road east as far as the prehistoric Icknield Way, which led to Thetford. How did they attack Reading from Thetford in 871? They rode along the Icknield Way into Wessex, again, no doubt, raiding as they went, until they reached the River Kennet at a point which was only a short distance from the royal vill at Reading. Later, in 878, after the rituals at Wedmore, the Vikings must have returned along the Foss Way to Chippenham, which lies at a point only a short distance west of this great Roman road. When they left Chippenham for Cirencester, they merely rejoined the Foss Way, and headed north for about twenty miles, an easy day's journey. The journey from Cirencester to East Anglia could scarcely have been simpler for them. Cirencester was the hub of a network of Roman roads. To get to East Anglia Guthrum would have led his army east along Akeman Street to the Icknield Way, thence to Thetford and the rich fields of East Anglia, a journey of about 150 miles.

The major campaigns of 890s, when the Vikings came with their horses from the Continent were similar. At the beginning, while they were in Kent (at Appledore and Milton Regis), they were moving by ship, although it should be said in passing that Milton Regis lay on the Roman road from Canterbury to London. When they moved their base into Essex, across the mouth of the Thames, they moved by sea to Benfleet and, later, to Shoebury and Mersea. In 893 they began to use overland routes and for the next three years continued to do so almost exclusively. For example, in 893 a Danish army crossed England and was finally met by a large army of English and Welsh at Buttington on the Severn. How did they get there? They crossed the Midlands using Watling Street and travelled to its western terminus at Wroxeter, from where they took a continuation of that Street which runs across the Welsh Marches. They followed this Roman road along the ridge of Long Mountain to the stronghold at Buttington on the upper part of the Severn. The *Anglo-Saxon Chronicle* leaves us in no doubt that they travelled by horse: while under siege 'they despaired for lack of food and ate most of their horses'. A remnant of these Danes managed to return to their base in Essex. Reinforced, they rode up Watling Street again later in 893, and at Wroxeter took not the Buttington road – too many bad memories there? – but Watling Street West in a northerly direction. It is conceivable that they used the Wroxeter 'bypass' from Stretton to Watling Street West. They found at the road's end a deserted Roman fortress, which was the once impressive Chester. On their return from Wales later in 893 they would have used the now familiar Watling Street route. When, in the following year, the Danes moved base, they sailed up the Thames and then up the Lea, which, it will be recalled, was the boundary between Wessex and Guthrum's lands. They built a fort at a place probably just below Ware. Alfred blockaded the River Lea below them, and the Vikings – they would certainly have carried their horses as cargo up the Lea – travelled cross-country as far as Bridgnorth on the Severn, which was situated on a Roman road which crossed Watling Street West. The impetus of the Viking attacks of the 890s ended with this last long cross-country campaign. It should be remembered that for much of this time their Essex headquarters was at Mersea, close to Colchester, itself the hub of a network of Roman roads.

What kind of defensive strategy did Alfred employ against the predominantly overland attacks via the networks of Roman roads and ancient trackways? Alfred had no obvious strategic defence – as distinct from tactical defence – against the attacks spanning the years 866–86. His strategic defences were probably only in place by the time the Viking Danes attacked in 892. The Burghal Hidage, although dated from the reign of his son, probably represents the defensive position of Alfred in 892, and strong arguments have urged that conclusion. The Burghal Hidage is not a single document; it exists in several but by no means identical documents. It provided for the financing of the construction and maintenance of *burhs* (i.e., fortified places). Thirty places in Wessex were included in these arrangements, and it can be shown that this is the total number – or very close to it – and not a fragment. If, then, the Burghal Hidage was largely completed by 892 and if it represents the sum and total of the Alfredian defensive scheme, it obviously

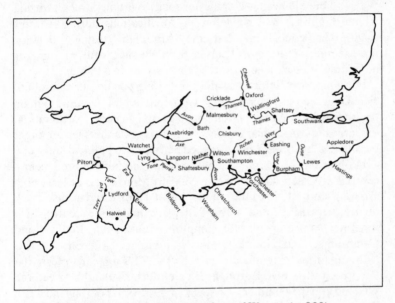

17 *Burghal Hidage defences for Kingdom of Wessex (c. 900)*

merits attention. One feature, above all others, stands out. These fortifications were designed, in general, to oppose water-borne attackers. All but three of these *burhs* were located along the coast or on the inland waterways of Wessex. Of the three that were not – Shaftesbury (Dorset), Chisbury (Wiltshire) and Halwell (Devon) – Shaftesbury stood overlooking the western end of the Nather River valley and Halwell was, in time, abandoned in favour of Totnes on the River Dart. The coastal defences, the primary line of defence, were situated along the south coast and along the Bristol Channel and were, by and large, successful to the extent, at least, that the major Viking penetration was in the area of the Thames estuary. The secondary line of defence – the inland line – was drawn along the northern border of Wessex (i.e., the Bristol Avon-Thames) and also located at strategic places on other Wessex rivers. This secondary line was particularly ill-suited to oppose attacks by land, and, in general, it was by land that the Vikings came. If the Maginot Line was facing the wrong way in 1940, the secondary

Wessex line was in the wrong place in the 890s. An ideal site for defence which was not used would have been Streately (Berkshire), located on the Thames at the junction of two major roads (the Icknield Way and the Silchester–Dorchester road). Watling Street, a virtual Viking highway, had no defensive fortifications during Alfred's reign. The conclusion that the Alfredian strategic defence represented, at the most, only a partially successful strategy for defending Wessex against the Vikings seems inevitable.

For a moment, let us consider the Viking position in about 900. The Danelaw was splintered into a number of separate Viking territories, having in common language and custom. Northumbria, the largest of these, had its focal point at York and its leader might be called 'king'. East Anglia formed perhaps two political units, one – an older one – centred at Thetford and another – more recent – centred at Colchester. East (or Danish) Mercia had at least nine separate and, at this time, independent Danish territories. Each territory focused upon a fortified place under the control of a separate Danish army: Northampton, Huntingdon, Bedford and Cambridge, and, to their north, Leicester, Lincoln, Derby, Nottingham and Stamford, which by the 920s appear to form the Territory of the Five Boroughs (i.e., eastern England between the Welland and the Humber). To speak of the division of England into a Danelaw and an Englishlaw is inaccurate – since there was also a Mercialaw – and does not do justice to the complexity of the political situation in the parts of England under Danish rule at this time. The first four decades of the tenth century witnessed the attempt of the West Saxon kings to gain control over some of these territories as direct rulers and others as overkings.

Reconquest is not the correct word – itself so redolent with meaning for other countries and other times – to describe the process by which West Saxon kings conquered the Midlands and the north of England during the first half of the tenth century. Three major figures stand out in this achievement: Edward the Elder (899–924), his sister Ethelfled, Lady of the Mercians (911–18), and his son Athelstan (924–39). Alfred's two children and his grandson made the Wessex kings rulers in fact – and not merely in self-description – of a very large part of England.

During the second decade of the century it was Edward and Ethelfled acting in tandem who pushed back Danish rule. Were it not for the brief *Mercian Register,* we would scarcely know anything about the Lady of the Mercians and her defence of Mercia. Before

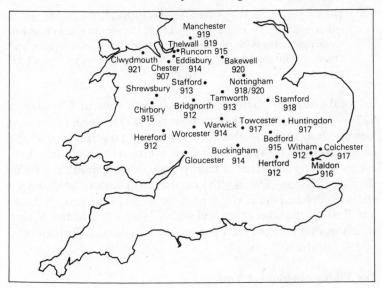

18   *Fortifications by Edward the Elder and Ethelfled, 907–23*

the death of her husband, King Ethelred of Mercia in 911, they had fortified Worcester, Hereford, Shrewsbury, Chester and probably Gloucester. The *Mercian Register* describes the incredible feat of fortress-building under her direction during the years 912 to 915: *Scergeat* (location unknown), Bridgnorth, Tamworth, Stafford, Eddisbury, Warwick, Chirbury, *Weadburh* (location unknown), and Runcorn. Her territory thus protected, she was able to take Derby and Leicester. Her brother, meanwhile, concentrated his attention upon the Vikings at Colchester, then those at Hertford, and in 914 captured Bedford. In the year 917 he defeated the armies of Towcester, Cambridge, Huntingdon and Northampton. Thus, by 917 Ethelfled and Edward controlled England south of the Welland. Soon after Ethelfled's death in 918, Edward reached the Humber, and thus everything south of this natural boundary was in his control. Forty years before, his father had retreated to the worthless swamps in west Somerset. Now the separate Viking armies were no match for the synchronized efforts of Edward and Ethelfled. To dramatize the extent of Edward's power at this time the Wessex chronicler boasted with understandable satisfaction:

920   The king of the Scots and the whole Scottish nation accepted him as father and lord. So, too, did Ragnald and the sons of Eadwulf and all the people living in Northumbria – English, Danes, Norwegians, and others – and also the king of the Strathclyde Britons and all his people.

Such submissions – there was a similar submission to Athelstan in 927 – meant perhaps that there was a vague recognition that Edward and, later, Athelstan were the most powerful men on the island. Neither Edward nor his son were unrealistic enough to misunderstand the limits of their power. When Edward the Elder died in 924, many Danes – the numbers will have to be discussed shortly – dwelled in his kingdom in the areas of the east Midlands and East Anglia where they had settled. The only effective Viking state was that north of the Humber, the kingdom of Northumbria, with its centre at York.

The Viking kingdom of York

On the eve of the Viking raids of the mid ninth century northern England had four principal political units. The Pennines divided northern England effectively between east and west, although Roman roads through the passes allowed some communication. East of the Pennines, between the Humber and the Tyne, was the kingdom of Northumbria and north of it, between the Tyne and the Tweed, the kingdom of Bernicia. West of the Pennines a less clear situation prevailed. A British (i.e., Welsh) kingdom existed in Strathclyde, stretching from the Clyde to the Solway, and to its south an English principality, about which little is known, existed in Westmorland and Cumberland. The kingdom of Northumbria exercised a political hegemony over the entire north, its actual power varying from situation to situation. The coming of the Vikings produced three major effects on the north. First and foremost, they established a kingdom at York, which, in effect, replaced the English kingdom of Northumbria. Second, the English kingdom of Bernicia remained Christian and English and, for a while at least, accepted the overlordship of the kings of Wessex. Third, in the northwest, Strathclyde was to be recognized as separate and independent – not losing its independence until the eleventh century – and between the Wirral and the Solway a number of northmen settled, dependent, at first, on Dublin and, later, on Dublin–York, and later still, on York.

The 'Viking kingdom of York' is the name given to the Scandinavian kingdom north of the Humber, its centre at York, its western limits at times the Pennines and at times the Irish Sea and, for a very brief period, some point west of Dublin. The Vikings held sway over Northumbria from 876 to 954 with some interruptions. When they marched on York in 867, took it unopposed, and defeated in the following spring the Northumbrians who tried to recapture the city, the Vikings made York a Viking city. In 876 a large number of Viking warriors returned to Northumbria from southern campaigns and partitioned the land. Either 867 or 876 can be used as the date of origin of this kingdom. Between these dates they had appointed an English king as their puppet in Northumbria. Halfdan took control in 876, and for much of the next seventy-eight years the north was ruled by Viking kings.

It is one thing to say that Viking kings ruled in the north, but it is quite another to list these Viking rulers in sequence. Gaps, ambiguities, conflicting evidence render this impossible. The tentative list of the Kings of York in Table 4 will illustrate this point.

Table 4 *The Viking Kings of York*

Halfdan	876–877 (expelled and killed in Ireland)
Guthfrith	c.883–c.895
Sigfrid	c.919–c.921
Cnut	c.900–c.902
Ethelwald	902
Halfdan	
Eowils	joint(?) kings c.902–910
Ivar	
Ragnald	c.919–c.921
Sihtric	921–927
Guthfrith	927 (expelled same year)
(Athelstan, king of England, ruled directly, 927–939)	
Olaf Guthfrithson	c.939–941
Olaf Sihtricson	941–943, 949–952
Ragnald Guthfrithson	943–944
Eric Bloodaxe	948, 952–954

Table 4 shows major lacunae in our knowledge. It would be exceedingly rash to assert that there was no Scandinavian king for the years 877–c.883, or to state with certainty the precise sequence of succession from *c.*895 to *c.*902, or to attribute a fully simultaneous reign to the allegedly joint kings Halfdan, Eowils, and Ivar. And should one date the beginning of Ragnald's reign from 912, when he invaded Northumbria, or from 919, when he took York?

Two kings, Sigfrid and Cnut, are known to us only by way of coins found among a hoard discovered at Cuerdale on the River Ribble in Lancashire. The historian here, as in so many other places in Viking history, owes a great debt to the careful, disciplined investigations of numismatists. Discovered as long ago as 1840, these coins, now unfortunately scattered in more than half a dozen places, have yielded rich historical information under the scrutiny of generations of numismatic scholars. Although the Cuerdale coins have introduced two Kings of York to our list – Sigfrid and Cnut – the dates of the reigns of these two kings can only be approximations. The doubts raised at one time about whether they were two persons or only one have now been settled, but the presence of both their names on some coins suggests a period of joint-kingship. That the Sigfrid and Cnut coins were minted at York within twenty years of the Viking settlement in York and that Christian symbols were used on these coins testify to the rapid seizure of real power and an early Christianizing of these Danes. The size of this hoard (more than 7000 coins) is simply staggering: it is more than all the coins known in Norway before the 1060s. Why were there so many coins in one place? Why were they hidden? No coins in this hoard can be dated after 903. All the circumstances suggest that they were buried about 903: the size of the hoard and the number of coins from the very late ninth century and opening years of the tenth century – over 3000 from Sigfrid and Cnut alone – make an almost contemporary burial a certainty. The location of Cuerdale on the Dublin-to-York route argues for the relationship of this hoard to the Dublin–York connection. Attempts have been made to show a continuing connection between the Northumbrian Vikings and the Dublin Vikings from 860s. There were, indeed, connections: Halfdan, who had shared out Northumbria, died in battle in Ireland and Sigfrid – an unusual name – might have been the same Sigfrid who was involved in Dublin affairs in the 880s. In the opening years of the tenth century the Norse Vikings crossed the Irish Sea from Dublin to the Wirral and to the littoral to its north. The fortifications built in that region by Ethelfled and her brother Edward were aimed at repelling attacks from Ireland. In 902

Hingamund had led a band of Norse Dubliners, who had been defeated by the Irish, to the Wirral. It is surely more than a coincidence that a hoard of enormous size was hidden in the very years of these Hiberno-Norse attacks and buried on the very route from Dublin to York, a route which went up the River Ribble and via a Roman road through the Pennines to York. What would one like to see here? Were a Viking King of York (perhaps Cnut) and his army, who were encamped – the royal treasure with them – to oppose a Norse attack, caught by surprise and forced to bury their silver? Perhaps. Or were Hiberno-Norse warriors, having captured a Danish treasure, themselves attacked by surprise on their return? Or was it treasure brought by refugees driven from Dublin in 902 by the Irish from Meath? Other explanations are indeed possible. But the essential point to grasp here is the fact that from the early days of the tenth century the Dublin factor existed in York history and remained for half a century.

The Dublin kings enjoyed considerable success in Northumbria largely because of the costly defeat of the Northumbrian Danes at Tettenhall in 910, where at battle's end three Danish Kings of Northumbria – Halfdan, Eowils and Ivar – lay dead on the field of battle. Ethelweard, the Wessex nobleman and chronicler, tells us:

They joined battle without protracted delay on the field of Wednesfield; the English enjoyed the blessing of victory; the army of Danes fled, overcome by armed force. These events are recounted as done on the fifth day of the month of August. There fell three of their kings in that same storm . . . Halfdan, Eowils, and Ivar were hurried to the hall of hell as also their jarls and nobles.

Never again were the Northumbrians to attack to their south. More importantly, a leadership vacuum must surely have followed in the north as a consequence of Tettenhall, and the threatening Vikings from Dublin were able to exert their power in Northumbria. In 912, the Dublin Viking Ragnald was active with his army in Northumbria and before the decade's end became undisputed king.

And so the Dubliners came. Some of the English who could flee from the northwest did so. In 910 the Abbot of Heversham and the son of the English 'prince' of Cumbria fled to safety east of the Pennines in the Wear Valley. In about 911 Ragnald captured York temporarily, and coins were issued at the mint in his name. By 913 he had asserted his authority north of the Tyne, and in the following year he crossed lowland Scotland, inflicting defeats on the King of Bernicia and the King of the Scots. In 919 he recaptured York, and it is from this time that it is usual to date the rule of the Irish-Norse in York. The recognition of Edward the Elder as overlord of Northumbria in 920 was not a surrender by Ragnald but merely the realistic recognition of his own limited manpower and of the power of his English neighbours to the south. The meaning of overlordship is far from clear, but it is clear that a virtually independent kingdom existed in Northumbria with its capital at York and that at its head was an Irish-Scandinavian king.

During this period (919–54), although it was interrupted by twelve years of English rule (927–39), Norse kings ruled York. Although Dublin and York were both ruled by Norse kings and, at times, by the same kings, a joint kingdom of Dublin and York did not exist. What did exist was a Dublin–York axis, in which political control permitted a remarkable flourishing of trade, the extent of which is being revealed by the excavations under the streets and buildings of modern Dublin and York. An important factor in this axis was the Irish Sea–River Ribble–Roman road route that took warriors and traders across the waters and through the mountains joining the two cities, who rivalled in significance the great towns of Scandinavia.

The fate of this northern kingdom was inextricably bound up with the ambitions of the West Saxon dynasty to extend active control north of the Humber and west of the Pennines. Contemporaries stressed the importance of Athelstan, son of Edward the Elder, standing on the banks of the River Eamont in 927 and accepting the submission of the King of Scotland, the King of Strathclyde, and the ruler of that part of Northumbria north of the Tees. Ten years later these kings, Olaf Sihtricson and a Norse force from Dublin attempted to undo the Eamont settlement. Their hopes were dashed, at least temporarily, when Athelstan inflicted so serious a defeat on his challengers that the compiler of the *Anglo-Saxon Chronicle* inserted a verse commemorating this English victory.

> In this year king Athelstan, lord of warriors,
> Ring-giver of men, with his brother prince Edmund,
> Won undying glory with the edges of swords,
> In warfare around Brunanburh.
> With their hammered blades, the sons of Edward
> Clove the shield-wall and hacked the linden bucklers,

As was instinctive in them, from their ancestry,
To defend their land, their treasures and their homes,
In frequent battle against each enemy.
The foemen were laid low: the Scots
And the host from the ships fell doomed. The field
Grew dark with the blood of men after the sun,
That glorious luminary, God's bright candle,
Rose high in the morning above the horizon,
Until the noble being of the Lord Eternal
Sank to its rest. There lay many a warrior
Of the men of the North, torn by spears,
Shot o'er his shield; likewise many a Scot
Sated with battle, lay lifeless. . . .

The victory, we know, was less permanent than the Anglo-Saxon poet believed. Two years later, Athelstan having died, the Norse once again ruled the kingdom of Northumbria. But, they never fully re-established their power. Eric Bloodaxe, son of the King of Norway – his nickname unfortunately gives this noble warrior an undeserved posthumous reputation – failed in a last attempt to assert Viking control in the north of England; his dead body lay at day's end on Stainmore in 954 as a symbol and more than a symbol of the end of the first Viking wave against England. Henceforward, English earls ruled the region.

Excavations at York, particularly since 1972, underline the significance of this Viking capital. A peaty layer of subsoil has created very favourable circumstances for the survival of material. At the Lloyd's Bank site, Pavement, striking evidence of leather manufacture was found: leather-stretching frames, animal hairs, beetles used in tanning, and thousands of pieces of cut leather. Its companion industry, shoemaking, left signs of activity at the same site: lasts, tools, soles, etc. The Church of St Mary, Castlegate, was the site where archaeologists found fragments of crosses decorated in the Danish style of the last half of the tenth century. In 1976, the city of York aided archaeologists considerably by acquiring four pieces of property in Coppergate and turning them over to the York Archaeological Trust for investigation. On this archaeologically rich site stood four eighteenth-century buildings. Excavations showed that these buildings were built on the very same lines as Viking-age buildings constructed there, probably as part of urban renewal, between about 950 and 960. These tenth-century structures were long buildings, rectangular in shape and extending from Coppergate along their long-side down a then existing slope towards the River Foss. Behind each of these houses was another building, probably used as a workshop. The material remains clearly show that Coppergate came by its name appropriately ('the street of the coopers'), for the wide variety of finds at this site indicate that it was used primarily by woodworkers. One of the workshops, however, contained beads and amber pieces, evidence of jewellery-making.

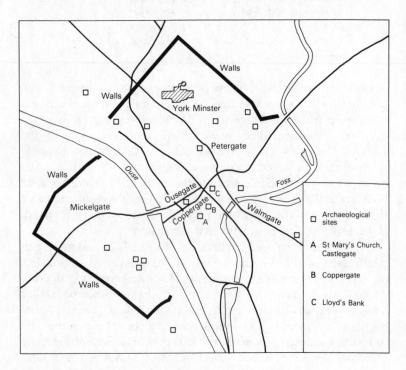

19   *Viking-age York*

In general, the evidence from the various archaeological sites in York indicates a variety of manufacture: textiles, combs, different sorts of metalwork (in bronze, gold, silver and lead alloy), woodwork and leather products. The presence of goods manufactured abroad – silk probably from the East, wine jars from the Rhineland, honing stones from Norway, etc. – argues strongly for a significant mercantile component in the economy of Scandinavian York. The goods manufactured at York and those from its hinterland (for example, pottery from Lincolnshire) provided the exports necessary to balance this trade. Writing about the year 1000, the anonymous author of the *Life of Saint Oswald* described York as:

the metropolitan city of the whole Northumbrian people, nobly built and surrounded by firm walls, yet now become old with age, although still enjoying a large population, numbering now more than 30,000 adults, a city amply fed and greatly enriched by the wealth of merchants, who come from everywhere but especially from the Danish people.

The very size of York signifies its importance. Roman York measured about fifty acres. A short time after the beginning of the Viking settlement, the enclosed area was extended towards the Foss, thus increasing the size of York to nearly ninety acres. Soon the pressures of population and commerce forced the development of the Micklegate area across the Ouse. By the early tenth century York covered an area close to a hundred acres and by the end of that century had perhaps ten churches. At their height the other great northern trading centres were not so large: Hedeby had sixty acres within its ramparts and a total of about eight-three acres over all, Birka had perhaps fifty acres. The population of pre-conquest York, although placed by Saint Oswald's hagiographer at 30,000, was probably between about 5000 and 10,000, making it one of the great Viking cities, comparable in many ways to tenth-century Kiev.

All disciplines have their limitations, and one must not demand more from archaeologists than they can tell us. We should like to know what were the *immediate* places with which York conducted trade. Obviously, the presence of silk from the East cannot be used to argue that there was a direct link between York and the East. What were the trading centres favoured by York merchants? Certainly, Dublin; but where else? There remains the question that is most difficult to answer: given that there was a variety of manufactured and trading commodities, how extensive was that manufacture and trade, and how intensive was the economy of Viking York?

The settlement process

With and after the warring there was landtaking, a great landtaking.

And with the great landtaking came a great migration.

Danes came in very large numbers to work the land, their migration exceeding in size even the migration that settled Normandy. There were no immigration officers to check their papers; no ships' passenger lists with names and places of origin; no accounts written by immigrants of successes in their new world. They sailed to East Anglia and Northumbria, went inland and established farmsteads virtually without recorded notice. They were to create an Anglo-Scandinavian society that survived the political demise of their kings at York in 954, a society which was severely disturbed by the destruction inflicted on the north by William the Conqueror in 1069, and a society that still lived on in the regional peculiarities existing in the twelfth and thirteenth centuries. The word Danelaw itself was first used in the eleventh century and continued in official use well after the Norman Conquest.

The widely accepted 'two-step' theory argues that the Danes migrated to England in two stages: first as warrior–settlers and then as settlers who came later, protected by the military shield. According to this theory, the colonizing took no more than about seventy-five years, probably less, and was a period of settlement comparable to the Norwegian settlement of Iceland. The Viking warriors, whatever their initial intention – they were capable, as are we, of multiple intention – settled in England. The *Chronicle* in a number of laconic but revealing passages tells us of the first step in the settlement by these warriors-become-farmers:

876   In this year Halfdan divided out the lands of Northumbria, and they began ploughing and supporting themselves.

877   In harvest time the Danish army went into Mercia, and a part of it they shared out.

879   In this year the Danish army left Cirencester and went into East Anglia, which they occupied and shared out.

892   In this year the great Danish army . . . crossed the sea, horses and all.

893   The English army attacked the [Danish] fortifications [at Benfleet, Essex] and seized everything, personal property as well as women and children.

895   The Danes had sent their women to safety in East Anglia before setting out from the fort [on the Lea].

896   In the summer the Danish army dispersed, some to East Anglia, some to Northumbria, and those without land to the Seine.

And from a northern source we are told that sometime between 912 and 915

[Ragnald] divided out the villages of St Cuthbert. He gave to his mighty soldier Scula one part, extending from the village called Eden as far as Billingham. He gave to someone called Onalafball another part, from Eden as far as the River Wear.

The pattern is fairly clear. In 876 the portioning of modern Yorkshire occurred and, in the following year, the portioning of East Mercia, centred around the Five Boroughs. East Anglia was divided by Guthrum in 879. Both Northumbria and East Anglia received warrior–settlers in 896. In the second decade of the tenth century Hiberno-Norse settlers colonized parts of County Durham. None of these Viking armies was enormous: the so-called Great Army that was active from 892 to 896 could scarcely have exceeded a few thousand, and the others probably considerably less.

The second step in the 'two-step' theory is known only by way of inference. The argument runs that the place-name and personal-name evidence as well as the linguistic evidence suggest a very considerable Scandinavian colonization, and, since the relatively small armies cannot explain a settlement of such a great size, another immigration, an immigration behind the shield of the warrior, must have occurred. The inference merits elaboration.

Place-names in this context refer to places recorded principally in Domesday Book (1086). Map 20 (p. 169) demonstrates vividly the magnitude of the Scandinavian influence on the names of the Danelaw. A few places with Scandinavian names exist in Warwickshire and Northamptonshire south of the boundary, but, these apart, the south and west are devoid of parish names of Danish origin. Fewer are found in Suffolk than in Norfolk. The densest concentration is clearly in the territory of the Five Boroughs, with the exception of Derby, and in the North and East Ridings of Yorkshire. In Lincolnshire, for example, almost 50 per cent of the still existing names of villages are of Danish origin and, in some parts of Lincolnshire, the density reaches nearly 75 per cent. Domesday Book contains over 500 place-names of Danish origin from the territory of the Five Boroughs. A thick belt of place-names of Scandinavian origin can be traced westward from the North Sea, beginning on the Lincolnshire coast between Grimsby and Saltfleet and extending as far as Leicester. Yet, in all this one must bear in mind the incompleteness of the places recorded in the Domesday survey, the purpose of which was to provide lists of estates as sources of income to the crown and not to provide a full list of settlements. Still, it is our major source.

In general, three forms of place-names of Danish origin appear, and they seem to indicate three phases in the settlement process. A group of place-names called 'Grimston-hybrids' are names with an English suffix such as *-tūn* (a village, a farmstead) but with a Danish personal or appellative name preceding it. Examples abound: Grimston (Leicestershire, Norfolk, Nottinghamshire, Suffolk, Yorkshire), Barkston (Lincolnshire), Thurvaston (Derbyshire), and Colston (Nottinghamshire). A strong case can be made for the argument that these names represent previously existing English villages taken over at the beginning of the Danish colonization, the individual colonizer replacing an English name with his own. The second general category of place-names with a Scandinavian element comprises the names ending in *-by* (a village, a farmstead) and preceded by a Danish word, which is often a personal name (e.g., Derby, Selby, Danby, Thoresby). Such places are common: there are nearly 800 in all, and over 200 in Lincolnshire alone. These names seem to indicate a phase when hitherto unused land was being colonized, and when still desirable land was settled: the in-fill phase. The places whose names end in *-thorp* (a secondary settlement, an outlying hamlet) – for example, Scunthorpe, Mablethorpe, Weaverthorpe, Swainsthorpe – form a third group of places, less suitable for farming and settled last. The Kesteven region of Lincolnshire has twenty-eight such places, and Leicestershire eighteen. The northern part of the Yorkshire Wolds has a concentration of places ending in *-thorp*, but otherwise these places are scattered about other parts of Yorkshire where there is poorer land. A map of the north and east of England which did not contain places with names of Danish origin would be a map of a sparsely settled, underdeveloped area. The wealth of such place-names cannot be explained by the settling of soldiers, whose numbers were never extremely large, but – the theory runs – by a migration of their kinsmen and other fellow countrymen. The assumption in this use of the place-name evidence is that there existed in the Danelaw much unused but usable land at the time of the settlement; thus, the conclusion that the *-by* and *-thorp* places indicate new settlements. No one knows the pattern of land use on the eve of the Viking settlement; indeed, no one knows the

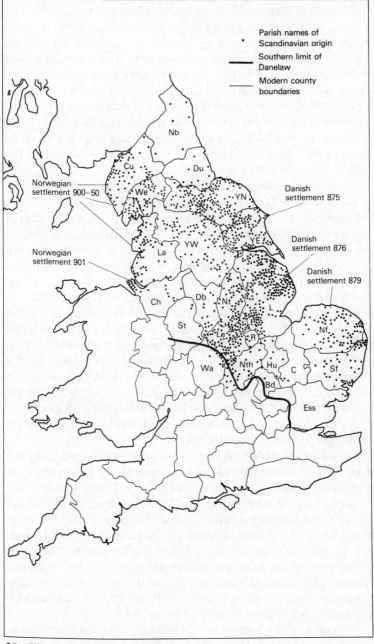

20 *The Scandinavian settlement*

topography of these areas. Broad generalizations about forests and clearings can be made, but particularizations are difficult to come by. A commonsense view suggests that a conquering army would seize, by the right of might, whatever land they wanted and not merely the lands that the vanquished were not using. Otherwise, we would be required to attribute to the Danes a massive restraint, which neither they nor most conquering armies have shown. This does not mean that the Vikings did not use marginal lands – the *-thorp* names probably refer to this kind of land – but it does mean that they must have seized land from the English, particularly in the early days of the settlement.

No other single outside force has influenced the English language to the extent the Danes did. The number of loan-words would fill columns, not words for unusual concrete objects – as was the case in Normandy – but common words such as *happy, ugly, call, fellow, loose, ill, law,* not the sort of words imposed on an English peasantry by a Danish ruling elite. Contemporary English had words which were quite simply replaced by Danish words. Furthermore, there was not merely wholesale borrowing of Danish words: there were substantial changes in the structure of the language, particularly in the development of clear pronoun forms for the third-person plural. Also, pronominal adverbs such as *thence, hence,* and *whence* were introduced into English by the Danes as were prepositions such as *fro* and *till.* Changes of such significance argue to the *dönsk tunga* persisting during a bilingual period, after which it became conflated with Old English to such an extent that the term 'Anglo-Scandinavian' can be used to describe the language during this later period.

No one can provide numbers for the settlers who gave names to places and who changed the English language, but thousands upon thousands of them must have entered the Danelaw under the protection of the warrior–settlers. If one accepts the 'two-step' theory of settlement between 876 and 954, then it would be clear that such a major settlement of Danes in England overlapped, towards the end, with a similar settlement in Normandy. These two settlements, which were almost contemporary, raise for us the veil obscuring Denmark at this time and reveal a nation with an excess population in the century between 850 and 950, an excess which reached a crucial point between 890 and 940.

Without a rapid conversion to Christianity the Danish settlement would have been a much more difficult process than it was.

Connubium between Danish men and English women became easier after conversion. Even marital arrangements below the level of the Christian ideal no doubt existed. The Danes were indeed alien and conquering, but no longer heathen and no longer separated from the English by this one unbridgeable chasm. The speed of this process of conversion is still astounding. Until 878 the Vikings in England were pagan. Then Guthrum, who was to settle East Anglia, was washed with the waters of baptism. Another Viking leader, Guthfrith, was buried with Christian rites beneath York Minster in about the year 895. Not only two individual Viking leaders but undoubtedly the bulk of their followers also took the Christian name and followed their kings to the font and tomb. In 875 the monks of Lindisfarne fled with the bones of St Cuthbert westward to the Irish Sea, but by 883 they could return across the Pennines and establish themselves peacefully at Chester-le-Street, where they soon received a suitable patrimony. The coins of York attest these changes. The Sigfrid/Cnut coins, which were issued at the turn of the ninth into the tenth century, contain Christian crosses; some even contain Christian inscriptions: *Mirabilia fecit* (He has done marvellous things), *Dominus deus omnipotens rex* (Lord God, almighty King). From 905 a series of coins was issued by the mint at York Minster (the Church of St Peter), and they bore the legend *Sancti Petri moneti* (Saint Peter's money).

The coming of Ragnald to York as king in about 919 meant the coming of a pagan. No sign of any general reversion to paganism exists, but there are indications of the coexistence of paganism and Christianity during the early decades of the tenth century. Ragnald's coins seem to have had the hammer of Thor and a Viking sword, while coins issued during the reign of Sihtric carry on their reverse side either Thor's hammer or a Christian cross. On the reverse of some coins dating, it would appear, from the reign of Sihtric one can see the hammer of Thor below the name of Saint Peter. Some archaeologists see in the Middleton Cross an early stage in the conversion process because, it is said, an Anglo-Saxon craftsman tried to incorporate Scandinavian motifs in this Christian high cross. This identification, however, is based on the assumption that Jelling-style decorative elements occur here, an assumption not, on the face of it, fully imperative. Residual acculturated pagan practices were not simply washed away by the cleansing waters of baptism, as was clear from the experience of Saint Augustine in England, Saint Boniface in Germany, and many other missionaries.

Professor Dolley sensibly sees a Viking good-luck symbol as no more offensive to the Christian than the horseshoe on a modern wedding cake! Soon the Danish settlers were as fully Christianized as their English neighbours. Oda, Archbishop of Canterbury from 941 to 958, had a Danish father, and it was this Archbishop who was responsible for re-establishing a diocese at Elmham in Danish East Anglia. The great Saint Oswald, Oda's nephew, then, was the grandson of a pagan Viking. Two or three generations from hammer to cross; by any measure a rapid assimilation.

The second Viking wave (980–1035)

Two stones stand between two burial mounds in Jelling in the central part of the Jutland peninsula in Denmark. The larger of the two – in fact, the largest runestone in Denmark – holds the key to the second period of Danish attacks upon England. It reads:

King Harald ordered this monument to be erected in memory of his father Gorm and his mother Thyra, the same Harald who gained control over all Denmark and also over Norway and who brought the Danes to Christianity.

The King Harald mentioned on the stone (*c.*960) is known to history as Harald Bluetooth, and his son and grandson are known as two conquerors and, indeed, kings of England. The runestone is at once a memorial and a claim of inheritance. Harald succeeded Gorm. Yet Harald not only succeeded Gorm but held control over a Danish state coming of age, his control extending to the limits of medieval Denmark. Jelling, his stronghold, was located near the centre of this state, with the emerging towns almost all equidistant (Arhus, Viborg, Odense and Ribe). The major expeditions to England were led by members of a royal Danish family – the Jelling dynasty – and their lieutenants, and they came as leaders of *national* armies in campaigns undertaken for *national* reasons. They were the political and economic extension of Danish power. There is no need to attribute imperial designs to either Svein or Cnut: the effect of their deeds was the creation of a virtual Danish empire in northern Europe. It failed to last, and the later attempt of a Norwegian king to claim it fell with him at Stamford Bridge in 1066.

Silver, movable wealth, and possibly more land were the goals of the second wave of the Vikings. The payment in the form of

Danegeld is almost totally unknown in the first period of Viking attacks on England, but it became a hallmark of these later attacks. From the 990s such payments, which were astonishingly large, reflect not only the designs of the new Vikings but also the wealth of England. A vast amount of silver was paid to the attacking Vikings from 992 until 1012, when Danegeld became part of the tax structure. The measure of the failure of the English policy of paying Danegeld to the Danes is simply that the English continued to pay it, that a stable peace was not purchased by it, that the Danes came back for more, and that the English ended up with a Danish king. One commentator has observed that England paid for its own conquest. Table 5 lists their payments.

Table 5   *Danegelds paid by the English*

Year	Amount in pounds of silver
991	22,000
994	16,000
1002	24,000
1007	36,000
1009	3,000

More than 100,000 pounds of silver – coins, armlets, etc. – went to Scandinavia, much of it to appear in silver hoards there, including tens of thousands of Ethelred coins. Vast amounts continued to be exacted under the title of Danegeld after 1012. For example, in 1018 the English raised a sum in excess of 82,000 pounds of silver to pay Cnut. Danegeld remained throughout this period – at first, random, then, institutionalized – an instrument of Viking policy against England.

The principal actors were kings and future kings: on the Viking side, Olaf Tryggvason, Svein and Cnut and, on the English side, the long-reigning Ethelred. The English sources blame their defeat on the inefficiency of their leaders and on the weakness and failure to lead on the part of their king. There is no understanding Asser, no fawning chronicler, no successful posthumous rehabilitation for King Ethelred. He stands as the cause and symbol of English defeat. Few Kings of England have a soubriquet which is so easily remembered and so damning – Ethelred the Unready, Noble

Counsel No Counsel – and the misfortune is not merely Ethelred's: it is at the expense of a proper historical focus. This preoccupation with Ethelred emphasizes the English defeat, the failure of the English to defend themselves successfully – as they had done under Alfred – against Viking attack. The spotlight belongs not on this lingering licking of wounds, but on the great victory of the Vikings. They won England. They gained control of one of the wealthiest parts of Europe. They placed their king upon the throne of England. It is Svein and Cnut – not the hapless, defeated Ethelred – who stood in the centre of the stage, triumphant and victorious. Could any of the great Wessex kings – Alfred, Edward the Elder, Athelstan – have withstood this Danish army, which came in organized force under leaders of the blood royal? Would Alfred have been any more successful than Ethelred? Does one hear, even if unspoken, the assumption from insular sources that English defeat can only be the result of English weakness?

The Danish army – well equipped, tightly disciplined, highly motivated and brilliantly led – gained the victory. Although mainly Danish in composition, the invading army had in its number Vikings from elsewhere in Scandinavia: five stones in Sweden commemorate such warriors and the thousands of English coins found in Gotland, mainland Sweden and Norway are evidence of their presence. The legend of the Jomsvikings, a community of Viking warriors whose services were for hire, belongs to a later age, and there is no need to attribute the Viking victory in England to these legendary men trained in the strict and celibate atmosphere of Jomsborg. Three late tenth-century fortresses in Denmark – at Trelleborg, Fyrkat and Aggersborg – were not used as military training camps for the invasion of England, as was once believed, but they stand for us as signs of an organized society capable of garrisoning strategic places for the purposes of defence and toll-collecting. This organized society bred the army that went with Svein and Cnut and their military commanders to conquer England.

These invading Danish armies are not to be numbered in the hundreds, at least not the army of Olaf and Svein in 994 nor, especially, the army of Thorkell and his associates in 1009 – described as 'immense' by the chronicler – nor the victorious armies of Svein in 1013 and Cnut in 1015, when on both occasions the full military force of the Danes was used. These were large armies ready for long, protracted periods in the field, capable of bearing reverses, and ultimately of defeating an English army not as ill-prepared as apologists might have it. No wonder that in 1009, faced with the extraordinary army of Svein's man Thorkell, King Ethelred ordered prayers to be said after Mass beginning with the third psalm, 'O Lord, how they are multiplied that trouble me'. It may not be much of an exaggeration to compare the size of the army Cnut brought to Sandwich in 1015 with the size of the Norman army landed by Duke William at Pevensey in 1066.

The events can be quickly recounted. England lived from 954 to 980 in peace: a hiatus between the first and second wave, a pause not unlike the forty years' rest in Ireland. The early attacks – those of the 980s – were small in size and fairly infrequent; they were only minor raids. But they were indicative of renewed unrest in Denmark. Although the Old English poem about the Battle of Maldon has made famous the defeat of an English army in Essex in 991, the significance of the battle lies not so much in the gallant code of conduct on both sides and the foolhardy courage of the English under Byrhtnoth, as in the English defeat, which was a sign of things to come.

The first major invasion in half a century came in 994, led by Svein, King of Denmark (987–1014), and Olaf Tryggvason, later King of Norway (995–1000), who had recently returned, it seems, from adventures among kinsmen in Russia. Olaf's conversion to Christianity at Ethelred's court in the aftermath of peacemaking in 994 was to have profound consequences in Norway and in the Norse lands of the North Atlantic. The Danish army which came to England in 997 remained until 1000 and probably limited its raids to the south coast of England and to Wales. They returned in 1001, using the Isle of Wight as a base for actions, particularly in the southwest, and peace came only in 1002 with the payment of 24,000 pounds of silver to the Danes. The rehabilitators of Ethelred would have trouble explaining his order to massacre the Danes on 13 November of that year. The *Anglo-Saxon Chronicle* simply states:

The king ordered that all the Danes in England be killed on St Brice's Day because he had learned that they conspired to kill him and his counsellors and then take possession of his kingdom.

The king in a nearly contemporary charter describes the fearsome events of the Saint Brice's Day Massacre at Oxford:

With the counsel of the leading men and magnates I issued a decree that all

Danes who had sprung up in this island, like chaff amidst the wheat, were rightly to be exterminated. All the Danes living in Oxford, fearing for their lives, sought sanctuary at the monastery of St Frideswide, from which they were forced to leave when their pursuers set fire to the monastery.

A massacre of all the Danes living in the Danelaw defies imagination: tens of thousands would have had to have fallen under the English sword without a murmur in contemporary records. Reliable tradition tells us that the sister of King Svein was among those murdered. Vengeance, a potent stimulant, would be enough to explain the way in which Svein descended on England in the campaigns of 1003, 1004, 1006 and 1007 – wisely leaving England during the famine year of 1005. They came relentless, intent on punishing Ethelred. And always the Viking at heart, Svein had an eye for silver, 36,000 pounds of which he and his army took back with them to Scandinavia in 1007. It bought two years of peace.

A large Danish army under the command of Thorkell the Tall came in 1009. It moved, attacked and ravaged at will. There seemed to be no power in England to stay the Viking warriors. The chronicler, under the year 1011, merely said of Thorkell's successes:

They had by this time overrun (i) East Anglia, (ii) Essex, (iii) Middlesex, (iv) Oxfordshire, (v) Cambridgeshire, (vi) Hertfordshire, (vii) Buckinghamshire, (viii) Bedfordshire, (ix) half of Huntingdonshire, and (x) a large part of Northamptonshire as well as, to the south of the Thames, all Kent and Sussex and the district around Hastings and Surrey and Berkshire and Hampshire and a large part of Wiltshire.

This army ceased its attacks only when 48,000 pounds of silver was paid to them. Still greedy for a ransom for Alfheah (Alphege), Archbishop of Canterbury, and more than a little drunk with southern wine, a group of Thorkell's men pelted the Archbishop with bones and ox-heads and split his skull with an axe on the Saturday after Easter. Another Christian to add to the lists of martyrs and saints. The kingdom, its defences almost non-existent after three years of campaigning by Thorkell, was ripe for taking, and that is what Svein did. In 1013 Svein gained the support of the English Danelaw, marched south, and by year's end was sole ruler of England. He enjoyed this triumph for only a matter of weeks, because on 3 February 1014 he was dead. Ethelred revived his kingdom, but only briefly, because Svein's son, the 18-year-old Cnut, at the head of a great army, regained Danish control of England by 1016.

Cnut's reign (1016–35) belongs more to English than to Viking history, yet the fact that a great Viking warrior–king ruled England for nearly twenty years cannot be overlooked. England remained a separate kingdom; it did not become a province of the Danish kingdom, when Cnut became King of Denmark in 1019 nor a part of a Scandinavian empire when Cnut became King of Norway in 1028. Yet, there was a Greater Scandinavia under Cnut. In a proclamation of 1027 he could style himself 'king of all England, Denmark, and Norway, and part of Sweden'. Was it modesty, a most unViking-virtue, that led him to omit 'lord of Orkney and Shetland, overlord of the kings of Scotland and Dublin'? The Viking world had changed since captains of ships had led raiding attacks on the English coast in the 830s. Cnut attended the coronation of Emperor Conrad II in Rome in 1027; nine years later, his daughter married the Emperor's eldest son. Cnut stood with the mighty, and had every right to do so. No previous king in England had cut such an important figure on the European scene. He could

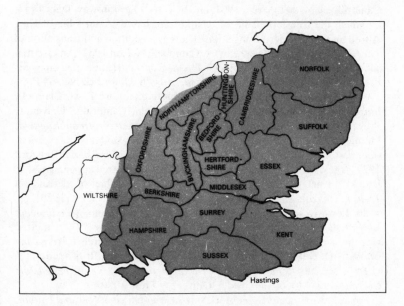

21   *Extent of attacks by the army of Thorkell the Tall, 1009–11*

afford to be magnanimous and honour the cult of King Edmund of East Anglia, slain by fellow Danes in 869, and to help bear the remains of Archbishop Alphege to Canterbury.

The second Viking wave against England came to an end with Cnut's death in 1035. Attempts made by other Scandinavian kings to add England to their diadems failed. Harald Hardrada, the Varangian from the Court of Constantinople and King of Norway (1046–66), failed at Stamford Bridge in 1066, and the attempt of a later Danish king called Cnut was aborted in 1085 before the ships sailed. And with these vain efforts to reassert Viking power in England, the force, first felt at Lindisfarne in 793 and which had dominated English history for much of the interval, was spent. Great forces have struck this island in its recorded history: to the name of Roman, Anglo-Saxon and Norman must surely be added Viking.

Selected further reading

An enormous volume of literature exists on the subject of the Danes in England, and it grows before one's eyes. The *Anglo-Saxon Chronicle,* the principal source, exists in translations by Dorothy Whitelock *et al.,* Cambridge University Press 1961, and by G. N. Garmonsway, Dent 1953, on which the translations in this chapter are based. Asser's life of King Alfred awaits a modern translation. There is an edition and translation of *The Chronicle of Aethelweard* by A. Campbell, Nelson 1962. An essential source in the study of this subject is the magisterial treatment given by Sir Frank Stenton in *Anglo-Saxon England,* 3rd edn, Oxford University Press 1971. More recent studies of considerable interest are P. H. Blair, *An Introduction to Anglo-Saxon England,* 2nd edn, Cambridge University Press 1977; P. H. Sawyer, *From Roman Britain to Norman England,* Methuen 1978; and H. R. Loyn, *Anglo-Saxon England and the Norman Conquest,* 2nd edn, Longman 1970, and *The Vikings in Britain,* Batsford 1977. A revised view of the military threat to King Alfred appears in N. P. Brooks, 'England in the ninth century: the crucible of defeat', in *Transactions of the Royal Historical Society,* 5th series, vol. 29 (1979), pp. 1–20. For a fresh reading of old sources see A. P. Smyth, *Scandinavian Kings in the British Isles, 850–880,* Oxford University Press 1977. Ethelred was the subject of a symposium published under the title *Ethelred the Unready,* D. Hill (ed.), in British Archaeological Reports, British series, 59, (1978); see also Simon Keynes, *The Diplomas of King Æthelred 'the Unready', 978–1016,* Cambridge University Press 1980.

For a study of the north see A. P. Smyth, *Scandinavian York and Dublin,* 2 vols., Dublin: Templekieran Press, 1975–78. A popular summary of the

York excavations by P. V. Addyman is entitled 'Excavating Viking age York', in *Archaeology*, vol. 33, no. 3 (May/June 1980), pp. 14–22.

The key titles in the settlement controversy are P. H. Sawyer, *The Age of the Vikings,* 2nd edn, Arnold 1971; Kenneth Cameron, *Scandinavian Settlement in the Territory of the Five Boroughs,* University of Nottingham Press 1966; and G. Fellows Jensen, 'The Vikings in England: a review', in *Anglo-Saxon England,* vol. 4 (1975), pp. 181–206. For a discussion of the archaeology, see D. M. Wilson (ed.), *The Archaeology of Anglo-Saxon England,* Methuen 1976, and Richard N. Bailey, *Viking Age Sculpture in Northern England,* Collins 1980; for numismatics see R. H. M. Dolley (ed.), *Anglo-Saxon Coins,* Methuen 1961; and for a discussion of towns see Susan Reynolds, *An Introduction to the History of English Medieval Towns,* Clarendon Press 1977.

Lists of new titles appear annually in the journal *Anglo-Saxon England.*

7   The Swedes and the East

And a road led to the East. The Vikings who left Uppland and the island of Gotland followed this road by river and portage deep into the interior of eastern Europe and beyond to the capitals of Byzantium and, perhaps, Islam. A Viking guard was even established by the Emperor in Constantinople. Towns such as Novgorod and Kiev were ruled by Vikings. Lines were kept open with the old country. Coin hoards were deposited decade after decade in Scandinavia. The perils encountered were not perils of the open sea – except the occasional storm in the eastern Baltic – but the physical obstacles of rapids and overland hauling and the human obstacles of fellow trader-pirates and unfriendly tribes.

The modern historian of the Vikings in Russia also faces perils. The outrageous claims and the just as outrageous denials owe much to nationalism, chauvinism and political ideology. Decades before the Russian Revolution of 1917, historians fell into either a Scandinavian camp or into a Slavic camp. And in terminology, which deserves a quiet burial, the camps have been described as Normanist and anti-Normanist, despite the fact that the general convention in English for over a century has been to use the word 'Norman' and its forms to refer to the province of Normandy in France. The Revolution of 1917 has injected a political dimension into this debate as well as a doctrine of historical determinism. In 1949 the Soviet historical establishment proscribed the view that the Russian state derives from Scandinavians. Two books by one author on the question of the Vikings in Russia contain 4500 items of bibliography, a monument, not to an intractable historical problem, but to the conditioning, by environmental factors, of the very process of historical writing itself. For historians, it has not been our finest hour.

For the Vikings their experience in eastern Europe might indeed have been their finest hour. The Baltic Sea at this time was a Swedish lake. Later it was to be called by the Greeks and others the

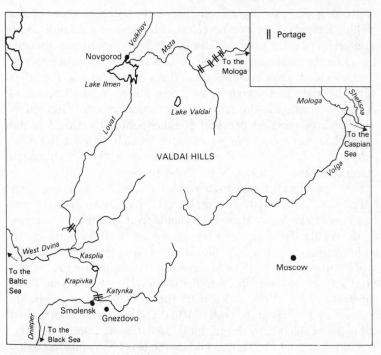

22   *Valdai Hills and river systems*

Varangian (i.e., Scandinavian) Sea. Uppland Sweden held political
sway over the islands of Gotland and Åland. Although Gotland was
unable to exercise political power abroad, its strategic location at
the crossroads of the Baltic Sea insured it a prominent place in
relations with the East. More than half the coins in Scandinavia from
the Viking age have been found in Gotland, among them
thirty-two hoards buried before *c.* 890 and containing more than
4000 coins, mostly Kufic (i.e., Arabic). Eighty per cent of the coins
from Byzantium, which are fairly rare in Scandinavia, have been
found in Gotland. And scattered throughout that island are
memorial stones, some to the memory of Viking Gotlanders who
died on the road to the East; for example, one bearing the epitaph
'Greece, Jerusalem, Iceland, Serkland [Saracenland]'. Wulfstan,
whose descriptions were included in King Alfred's *Orosius*, sailed
through these eastern waters and noted Gotland to port, a land, he
told us, belonging to Sweden. Before the Viking age the Swedes and

Gotlanders had established colonies on the southern shore of the Baltic. Excavations have revealed two important Scandinavian cemeteries near the town of Grobin, which is situated near modern Libau on the Latvian coast. One of these, unmistakably military in character, contains clear signs of central Sweden about it. The other contains male and female graves, jewellery, and indications of domesticity; this was the cemetery for a community of Gotlanders who were carrying on peaceful pursuits behind the shield of the Swedish military. Grobin's two cemeteries can be dated to the years *c.* 650 to *c.* 800 and bear clear witness to pre-Viking Scandinavian colonies on the southern shore of the Baltic Sea.

East from the Baltic the road was not a 'road' but waterways that led into lands inhabited by Finns, Bulgars, Slavs and others. Central to an understanding of these remarkable river systems is the region of the Valdai Hills, an area measuring about 100 square miles, which is situated about 100 miles south of Novgorod and about 200 miles northwest of modern Moscow. In these hills rise four of the most important rivers in eastern Europe. The West Dvina flows westward and northwestward from the Valdai Hills to the Baltic Sea, which it enters at the Gulf of Riga. The Lovat flows northward from the Valdais and drains into Lake Ilmen, from which the Volkhov leads to Lake Ladoga and via the River Neva into the Baltic Sea at the Gulf of Finland. The third river rising in these hills is the Dnieper, which flows south via the town of Kiev to the Black Sea. And, finally, Europe's longest river, the Volga. It, too, has its origin in the Valdai Hills, from which it flows in an easterly direction to modern Kazan, where it bends – the so-called Volga Bend – and then flows south into the Caspian Sea. The Valdai Hills from this perspective are clearly one of Europe's great watersheds. The significance of these hills for the Vikings was that it was possible, via portages in the Valdais, to link these rivers, and thus enable passage from the tributaries of one great river to the tributaries of another great river. The portages of the Valdais gave the Swedes access to the southern and eastern regions of this part of Europe.

Two entrances lay before the Vikings in Scandinavia as they faced eastern Europe. First, they could gain entrance by the Gulf of Riga and the West Dvina, which led them via Polotsk to the Valdai area, from where at least eight different routes, each requiring only one portage, took them to the Dnieper and all that this river opened up to them. The best known route to the Dnieper from the West Dvina followed the River Kasplia, then the River Vydra into Lake

Kuprino, and from there the River Krapivka; whence, after a short portage to the River Katynka, it continued on to reach the Dnieper near Gnezdovo. Second, they could enter eastern Europe through the Gulf of Finland and the River Neva into Lake Ladoga. From this lake they could go either south or east. If they went south, they would sail along the River Volkhov past Novgorod into Lake Ilmen, and from there along the Lovat to the Valdai Hills. There convenient routes joined the Lovat to the Dvina and, of course, via the Dvina to the Dnieper. If they went east from Lake Ladoga, they would sail along the River Svir to Lake Onega, then by river south to White Lake and Beloozero, from where the River Sheksna led into the Volga. This route required only one portage of less than five miles. Alternatively, the Swedish Vikings could reach the Volga from Lake Ilmen by way of the River Msta and the fur markets at Mologa. Again, these were only short portages. The word 'portage' might create the false impression that these Viking ships were carried overland. The Russian word for portage (*volok*) implies the dragging of ships. Such an exercise was necessary not merely to connect the tributaries of great rivers; it was also required to pass some of the great rapids, particularly in the lower Dnieper. At times the ships had to empty their goods, which slaves would carry, in order to make passage through the rapids easier. Thus, these great river systems presented the Vikings from Sweden and Gotland with a highway network comparable to the highway the Roman roads provided for their Danish cousins in England. And along these rivers came the Vikings.

In their travels along these rivers the Vikings encountered a variety of people. To the east, on the banks of the Volga, lived Finno-Ugric tribes and, to their east, the Bulgars or, rather, the East Bulgars – the West Bulgars had moved to the lower Danube – who were centred at Bulgar near the Volga Bend. To the south of the Bulgars they came in contact with the Khazars, who held sway on the lower Volga, on the northern shores of the Caspian Sea, where their capital stood at Itil, and west as far as the Sea of Azov and the Crimea north of the Caucasus Mountains. Various Slavic tribes lived in the lands on the road to Constantinople, notably the Krivichi, the Dregovichi, the Drevljane and the Radimichi in the region of the upper Dnieper. To their south lived a fierce tribe of Turkish origin, the Pechenegs. It was to these regions and to these peoples that Swedes called 'Rus' came in the ninth century.

23   *Viking Russia*

The first coming of the Vikings

Early in the ninth century Vikings from eastern Scandinavia
entered what was to become known as Russia. Their entry is not
fully recorded, but enough literary and archaeological evidence
does exist to provide us with the broad outline. *The Russian Primary
Chronicle* (once known as *Nestor's Chronicle*) is the central written
record. This annalistic chronicle was drawn together in about 1113
at a monastery at Kiev by a single compiler, who used some known
Greek and Russian sources as well as early Russian traditions.
Among these traditions is the calling of the Varangians.

859 The Varangians from beyond the sea imposed tribute upon the Chuds, the Slavs, the Merians, the Ves, and the Krivichians.

860– The tributaries of the Varangians drove them back beyond the sea
862 and, refusing them further tribute, set out to govern themselves. There was no law among them, and they began to war one against another. They said to themselves, 'Let us seek a prince who may rule over us and judge us according to the law.' They, accordingly, went overseas to the Varangian Rus. These particular Varangians were known as Rus just as others are called Swedes, others Norse, others Angles, and others Goths, for they were thus named. The Chuds, the Slavs, the Krivichians, and the Ves then said to the people of the Rus, 'Our land is great and rich, but there is no order in it. Come to rule and reign over us.' They thus selected three brothers, with their kinsfolk, who took with them all the Rus and migrated. The oldest, Rurik, located himself in Novgorod; the second, Sineus, at Beloozero; and the third, Truvor, in Izborsk. On account of these Varangians the district of Novgorod became known as the land of Rus. The present inhabitants of Novgorod are descended from the Varangian race, but aforetime they were Slavs.

Within a few years, the chronicle story continues, Rurik's brothers died and he became master of northwest Russia and ruler over the people already living there (Slavs, Krivichians, Ves, Merians and Muromians). Two Varangians from Novgorod, called Askold and Dir, not kinsmen of Rurik, set sail through the rivers intent on reaching Constantinople. On their way down the Dnieper they noticed a town set on a hill and inquired what it was. They were told that three brothers had founded the town and that it was now a tributary of the Khazars. Askold and Dir, the story continues, gathered a Varangian force and seized the place. Thus began the long history of the Rus in Kiev.

The story related in the chronicle merits general acceptance. The author is clearly making the point that the Rus first took control of the merchant towns and hinterlands of the northwest and then of Kiev and its environs. Once having set this out, he can – as he does – go on to relate the subsequent history of the Rus. Novgorod and Kiev stood as rival Viking centres only for a short time. In about 880 Oleg, ruler of Novgorod, captured Kiev with an army of Vikings, Finns, Slavs and others. 'Oleg', we are told, 'set himself up as prince in Kiev and said that it should be the mother of Russian cities.' And so it became.

The chronology, here as elsewhere in the chronicle, is unreliable.

The coming of the Rus can be placed with some certainty to early in the ninth century: by 860 they were organized in their new country and were attacking Constantinople. Chronology apart, this account from the Russian *Chronicle* has generated some of the most heated discussion in modern historical writing, and at the heart of the controversy is the meaning of two words: 'Rus' and 'Varangian'. The latter should be understood loosely to mean Scandinavian. The five peoples to whom the term is applied by the twelfth-century compiler – himself a Slav, it must be remembered – are Swedes, Norse, Angles (i.e., inhabitants of Denmark near Hedeby), Goths (i.e., inhabitants of Gotland) and, lastly, Rus.. It is clear that, according to the chronicle, the Rus are Varangian (i.e., a kind of Scandinavian) and that Russia had its origin in the Rus who were Scandinavians.

Fortunately other, more contemporary sources exist which explain who the Rus were in the ninth and tenth centuries. The *Annals of Saint Bertin*, a principal source for the Vikings in Francia and, at this point, a contemporary court chronicle, contains under the year 839 an incident relating to the Vikings in eastern Europe. In that year an embassy came from Constantinople to Emperor Louis the Pious, who was at Ingelheim near Mainz. These Greek ambassadors had with them two men 'who said that they call themselves "Rhos" '. They had come as ambassadors from their king (*chaganus*) to the imperial court at Constantinople but were afraid to return the way they had come because of hostile peoples. Would Louis grant them safe passage through his kingdom so that they might return home that way? Who are these people, Louis inquired. They are Swedes, he was informed. Having experienced the menace of their Danish cousins and fearing they might be spies, Louis ordered them to be detained until he could decide if their story was true. Thus, because the 'Rhos' were Vikings, they were detained. Other sources could be adduced – they will appear in due course – but that the Rus in the chronicle were Swedes should be clear enough as it is.

Archaeological digs at various sites have in part corroborated this picture of Vikings coming from across the sea to these merchant towns. At Staraja Ladoga, a place situated about seven miles south of Lake Ladoga on the River Volkhov and known in later Norse accounts as Aldeigjuborg, many items of Scandinavian origin have been found at ninth-century levels as have materials of Finnish origin. A wooden stick bearing a runic inscription, possibly a curse, is so often brought forward, particularly by Swedish archaeologists, that one might think it the only object of Scandinavian origin from that level; it is not. A small, oval brooch made of bronze, four bone gaming-pieces, and a bronze needle case are representative of Swedish design and decoration. Leather shoes which have a heel that tapers to a triangle, a form used in southern Sweden, have appeared at Staraja Ladoga and have been dated as coming from the period that the Scandinavians are known to have first appeared. Brooches and combs resembling only Scandinavian types appear at the next youngest level. These finds are consistent with a view that Staraja Ladoga was a stopping-off point on the way to other places, especially Novgorod.

Novgorod lies on the River Volkhov about three miles north of Lake Ilmen and 115 miles south of Staraja Ladoga: the river, in fact, divides the city. The west side contains the eleventh-century Cathedral of St Sophia and the citadel (kremlin), the site of a fortress since the eleventh century. The east side is the market side. Extensive excavations on the west side have revealed no evidence of a town before the mid tenth century despite ideal conditions (i.e., waterlogging) for preservation. Negative conclusions should not be reached: the Viking site could logically have been on the market (east) side of the Volkhov as would befit traders. A spade a hundred yards away from the boundary of an excavation might uncover significant finds. It is salutary to remember that, if we were limited to archaeological evidence for England and Ireland, virtually the only Viking-age towns of which we would have any knowledge would be York and Dublin. The vast cemetery at Gnezdovo near Smolensk contains 3000 grave mounds – a necropolis – and, although the majority of the mounds are unstudied, reveals a population which was very mixed in character, but which contained a notable portion of Scandinavians. Smolensk, only six miles away, apparently replaced Gnezdovo in the eleventh century, and this helps to explain the absence of materials of Scandinavian origin at the excavation at Smolensk.

The Rus and Byzantium

The connection between Kiev and Constantinople, between Rus and Greek, between Viking and Byzantine, was formed quickly upon the taking of Kiev. At first the connection had trading and political elements, but in time, religion and, to some extent, culture became involved. Although the Kievan Rus posed a serious threat to Constantinople more than once, they were the inferiors in this relationship, at times even the pawns of the experienced Greeks. The presence of two ambassadors from the Rus at the emperor's court in 839 is evidence of the early contacts: in fact, it is the earliest known literary reference to the Vikings in the East. That these Rus were Swedes is not in question, but what their mission was and, more importantly, where they came from are questions which remain subject to argument. They probably acted as ambassadors for trader Rus who had recently settled in Staraja Ladoga or in Novgorod or, as many believe, in Kiev itself. It is, of course, possible that these Rus came from Sweden and had travelled to Constantinople by way of the Dnieper. But this appears unlikely in view of the events of the year 860, merely twenty years later, which seem to require the organization and planning of at least an incipient state.

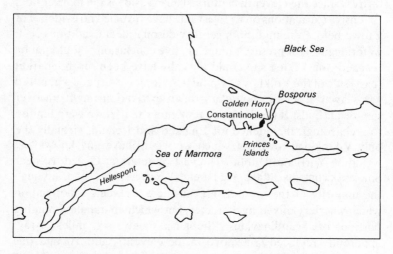

24   *Constantinople and environs*

On 18 June 860 a fleet of Viking ships appeared at Constantinople. The new Rome, hitherto impregnable against assaults, now felt the sting of a massive sea attack from the Scandinavian Rus. The attackers had sailed down the Dnieper from Kiev and from its mouth had navigated the Black Sea to the Bosporus, probably hugging the shore. The fleet was 200 ships strong – *The Russian Primary Chronicle* says 2000 and gives the date as 865, but neither numbers nor chronology are the chronicler's strong points. Allowing for a crew of forty men for each ship – some estimates run as high as a hundred – then, in June 860, a Viking army of some 8000 warrior–seamen faced Constantinople. The city was unprepared: its fleet and its emperor were engaged elsewhere in a campaign against the Arabs. No advance warning had reached the city: the ships simply appeared and, at once, monasteries along the Bosporus were being pillaged. The attackers sailed to the Golden Horn, and the inhabitants could see them as they raised their swords over their heads like the figures in a stone-picture. On a Sunday during the attack the patriarch Photius preached a homily which, even when pruned of its rhetorical flourishes and homiletic commonplaces, endures as the most vivid, absolutely contemporary account of a Viking raid in all the literature, surpassing accounts of the siege of Paris in 885.

What is this? This grievous and heavy blow and wrath? Why has this dreadful bolt fallen on us out of the farthest north? What clouds compacted of woes and condemnation have violently collided to force out this irresistible lightning upon us? Why has this sudden hail-storm of barbarians burst forth, not one that merely hews down the stalks of wheat and beats down the ears of corn or lashes the vine-twigs and dashes to pieces the unripe fruit or strikes the stems of plants and tears the branches apart . . . but miserably grinding up men's very bodies and bitterly destroying the whole nation? . . . Is it not for our sins?

There are echoes here of Alcuin bemoaning the attack on Lindisfarne in 793, but Constantinople was not a crude monastery on an island at the edge of the civilized world: this was the world's greatest city, the heir to Rome, the very centre of civilization. Photius had warned his flock – thieves, fornicators, adulterers and perpetrators of other unspeakable sins – but, he reminded them, while the Viking ships menaced not far from Saint Sophia, they had refused to listen: 'I have not been heard because I can see a cloud of barbarians deluging with blood our city which has been parched by sins.' The invaders came from far off, from land separated from the city by other lands and peoples and 'by navigable rivers and harbourless seas'. Describing the immediate devastations, Photius lamented:

Woe is me that I see a fierce and savage tribe fearlessly poured round the city, ravaging the suburbs, destroying everything, ruining everything –

fields, houses, herds, beasts of burden, women, old men, youths – thrusting their swords through everything, taking pity on nothing, sparing nothing. The destruction is universal. Like a locust in a cornfield, like mildew in a vineyard, or rather like a whirlwind or a typhoon or a torrent or I know not what to say, it fell upon our land and has annihilated whole generations of inhabitants. I consider them happy who have fallen prey at the hands of the murderous barbarians because, having died, they are unaware of the disaster that has befallen us.

The patriarch added that the suburbs were under attack. There the barbarous attackers were setting fire to homes, throwing their victims into the sea or thrusting them through with their swords. No use to bewail this tragedy, no use even to repent unless the contrition was sincere and would not sail away with the attackers.

Finally, beloved ones, the time has come to have recourse to the Mother of the Word, our only hope and refuge. Imploring, let us cry out to her: 'Save thy city, as thou knowest how.'

The Viking attackers, beyond the persuasions of the homelist, passed from the suburbs into the Sea of Marmora and attacked the Islands of the Princes. The old patriarch, Ignatius, who was in exile there, witnessed the overturning of his altar, the stealing of sacred vessels, and the taking of twenty-two of his servants aboard ship where they were cut to pieces by axes.

Why the Vikings finally left no one knows. Photius organized a procession and carried the cloak of the Virgin around the perimeter of the city. The Emperor was returning with his force. The lightning raid had accomplished its aim: booty and, perhaps, a view of 'the great city' (*Michelgard*, as the Rus called it). Whether it was because of the Emperor Michael, the Virgin, or storms experienced on the Black Sea on the way home, the *Chronicle* did not consider the attack a success. Constantinople, which had been brought to its knees for ten days or so, which had feared for its survival, was now safe. But Photius, fearing that time would erode bad memories and good resolutions, preached again:

All of you must know that the perils we have experienced and the sudden assault of this tribe came upon us from no other source than the wrath and anger of the Lord almighty. . . . It did not resemble other raids of barbarians, but the unexpected nature of the attack, its strange swiftness, the inhumanity of the barbarous tribe, the harshness of its manners and the savagery of its character proclaim the blow to have been discharged like a thunderbolt from heaven. . . . The more strange and terrible and extraordinary the assault of the invading nation, the more clear is the proof of the abundance of sins; and again, to the extent that it was an obscure nation, insignificant and not even known until the attack against us, so much the more is the enormity of our shame set down and the parading of our disgrace proclaimed and so much the more bitter is the pain caused by the lash. . . . They have ravaged [the city's] environs, they have laid waste the approaches to the town, they have harshly destroyed those who fell into their hands, they have poured round about it with all impunity. . . .

An obscure nation, a nation of no account, a nation ranked among slaves, unknown, but which has won a name from the expedition against us – once insignificant but now famous, once humble and destitute but now splendid and wealthy – a nation dwelling somewhere far from our country, barbarous, nomadic, armed with arrogance, unwatched, unchallenged, leaderless, has suddenly, in the twinkling of an eye, like a wave of the sea, poured over our frontiers, and as a wild boar has devoured the inhabitants of the land like grass or straw or a crop . . . sparing nothing from man to beast, not respecting female weakness, not pitying tender infants, not reverencing the hoary hairs of old men, softened by nothing that is wont to move human nature to pity, even when it has sunk to that of wild beasts, but boldly thrusting their sword through persons of every age and sex. Infants were torn away from breast and milk and life itself and their bodies were dashed against the rocks which became their graves. Their mothers were slaughtered and thrown upon the still convulsing bodies of their infants. . . . Nor did their savagery stop with human beings but was extended to dumb animals – oxen, horses, fowl, and others. There lay an ox and a man by its side, a child and a horse found a common grave, women and fowl stained each other with their blood. Everywhere dead bodies. The flow of rivers was turned into blood; some of the fountains and reservoirs could not be distinguished because they were level with corpses. . . . Corn-land was rotting with dead bodies, roads were obstructed, forests looked wild and desolate not because of bushes and solitude but because of bodies; caverns were filled up and mountains, hills, ravines, and gullies differed in no way from city cemeteries.

A supporter of the Vikings-as-peaceful-traders view of Viking history would be hard put to explain the extent of cruelty and gratuitous violence that Photius saw and described in vivid word-pictures, even if he were to allow for the excesses of a moralizing preacher using a language well suited for his purpose. His audience had also seen the attack, and his description could not challenge their experience. Thus, five years before Vikings attacked England *en masse* and twenty-five years before Vikings besieged Paris,

Vikings had visited upon Constantinople the most extensive barbarities of which we have record in their adventures. More peaceful relations were to follow later and a Kiev–Constantinople axis was created, encouraging trade between the two peoples and, in time, bringing Christianity to the Rus.

This trading connection received formal terms in 907 and 911 when treaties between the Rus and the Greeks were entered into. An account of a Rus attack on Constantinople was inserted in the Russian chronicle – it is mentioned nowhere else – probably to explain these treaties. Oleg the Wise ruled Kiev at this time. His reign has given rise to significant legends. Among the undeniable events was the entering into treaties by his ambassadors with the Greek Emperor at Constantinople: the fifteen Rus ambassadors all bear unmistakably Scandinavian names. The terms were beneficial to the Rus merchants and must have brought benefits to the Greeks, who wished to encourage business. The Rus traders were to receive as much grain as they needed: bread, wine, meat, fish and other supplies for a period of six months. Baths in any number necessary were to be prepared for them. And for their homeward journey the Emperor would give them what they needed. The Greeks made it quite clear that they wanted no Rus in their capital unless they were merchants. Even then, they were required to live outside the city and could only enter it through one gate and then only if they were unarmed and if there were no more than fifty at a time. They were permitted to conduct business without taxes on their goods. These treaties established the rules – a criminal code – for behaviour between Rus and Greeks.

The peace achieved through these treaties lasted for forty years, and it was, one assumes, a period of peaceful commerce. What led to the breaking of the peace, and what motivated Igor, Oleg's successor, to lead a fleet of 1000 vessels on Constantinople in 941 one can only guess. The time was opportune, for the Greek fleet was engaged abroad. If the size of the fleet sounds exaggerated, we should remember that the Russian *Chronicle* gives it as 10,000 and the Greek sources as 10,000 and, indeed, 15,000. The Italian diplomat, Liudprand of Cremona, who gives the number as 1000, was not present in Constantinople until 949, but his step-father had been an envoy at Constantinople during the great attack of 941: 'I have often heard him speak about the emperor's courtesy and wisdom and of the way in which he defeated the Rus.' In case his reader did not know who the Rus were, Liudprand identified them as the *Nordmanni*, the men of the north, so-called because of the location of their homeland. The Emperor improvised a defence by having his shipbuilders outfit fifteen old ships, which had been retired from service, with fire-throwers fore and aft. Igor, wishing to capture these Greek vessels and their crews but unaware of the fire-throwers, had his fleet surround them. Then, at an instant, the Greek-fire was hurled through tubes upon the Rus and their allies: 'The Rus, seeing the flames, jumped overboard, preferring water to fire. Some sank, weighed down by the weight of their breastplates and helmets; others caught fire.' Liudprand's step-father witnessed the beheading of those captured. The Greek-fire – Arnold Toynbee calls it 'napalm' – which was petroleum probably thickened with resin and fired by smith's bellows, had proved astonishingly effective in the calm waters and was responsible for the fact that only a part of the fleet returned home with Igor, although not before they had ravaged the southern coastal areas of the Black Sea. Three years later, Igor, keen to revenge this humiliation, gathered a large force together, enlisted neighbours as allies, and sailed towards the Bosporus. This time Emperor Romanus Lecapenus was ready with a strategy: his envoys, bearing tribute and gifts, sailed out to meet the formidable Rus fleet. Igor returned to Kiev and in the following year a peace treaty, similar to the previous treaties, was arranged. Of the fifty Russian delegates only nineteen have names of identifiable forms, and, of these, sixteen are Scandinavian and three Slavic.

The Byzantine authorities understood the situation of the Rus well: their needs, their strengths and their limitations. They followed a centuries-old policy of controlling neighbours and of using neighbour to police neighbour. Sometime between 948 and 952 the Emperor Constantine VII Porphyrogenitus prepared a secret document for his son, which, although written in Greek, is generally known by the Latin title, *De administrando imperio*, later given to it. Sir Steven Runciman describes this treatise as 'one of the most important books in the whole history of the early Middle Ages'. It is a manual on foreign policy, in which was distilled the Byzantine experience in diplomacy. If its interest here is confined to the Rus, the nature of the book and its broader scope should not be forgotten. The Rus, it explained, needed to maintain good relations with their neighbours the Pechenegs, from whom they imported cattle, horses and sheep and through whose lands the Rus had to travel to reach Constantinople, since the Pechenegs controlled the lower Dnieper. Obviously it was a cardinal point of Byzantine foreign policy to be at peace with the Pechenegs, who could control both the Rus and the Turks. In order for the Rus to reach Constantinople, they had to pass through the hazardous rapids of the lower Dnieper, the danger there enhanced by the possibility of attack by hostile Pechenegs, hiding in the background, waiting for an opportunity for attack. The Emperor not only listed the seven rapids and gave them Scandinavian names, but he also described the hazards of each one of them. The Rus pass the first rapids by disembarking the crew, who walk along the bank, except for a few who 'walk the ship' through the rocks. At the fourth rapids the crew, the contents of the ship and slaves, and even the ships themselves must go overland for six miles, the ships being dragged and carried on shoulders. During the winter, Constantine told his son, these Rus make their rounds among weaker peoples, collecting tribute from them.

Along the Dnieper and through these rapids, there came, in 957, the great Olga, widow of Igor, on her way to Constantinople to meet the same Emperor, Constantine Porphyrogenitus. The meeting of this princess from Kiev, a Swedish-born Viking, and the Emperor of the East, the successor to Augustus and Justinian, was accompanied by great grandeur, an indication of the importance attached to her visit by the imperial authorities: there were banquets, gifts of gold, and pageants of colour and sound as bright banners fluttered and the voices of two church choirs sang. At the moment when she was presented to the Emperor, 'the princess of Russia', as the Greeks described her, did not bend a knee or bow from the waist to the new Constantine in the new Rome: she simply bowed her head – nodded? – and sat with the ladies. If the Russian *Chronicle* can be believed at this point, we must accept that it was during her visit to Constantinople that Olga was converted to Christianity. The details are indeed arguable, but there can be little doubt that Olga returned to Kiev a Christian. Some commentators suggest that she had been a Christian even before her visit to the imperial court. At any rate, she was soon to write to the western Emperor, the German Otto I, to send missionaries. Thus, a monk from Trier, named Adalbert, became the first Bishop of Kiev. How different the history of Russia would have been if Adalbert's mission had proved successful and if Christianity had come to Russia from the Latin West. His mission did not prosper, and, when Christianity came to Russia, it came from a different source.

Olga's son, Svyatoslav (962–72), had no interest in Christianity – he is said to have told his mother that his soldiers would mock him were he to become a Christian – but he was restless to extend the sway of the Rus, particularly in the land of the west Bulgars on the Danube. In the dizzying double- and triple-cross scheming of the Byzantine Greeks, perhaps there is room to think that they schemed to encourage Svyatoslav to embark on these futile Balkan campaigns. Although the first of the rulers of Kiev to bear a Slavic name, Svyatoslav acted with the ruthless adventurousness of his Viking ancestors and always with an eye for business. Where better to establish a new centre than at the commercially important location at the mouth of the Danube? He penetrated deep into the Balkans, as far as the border of Thrace and, hence, as far as the border of the Eastern Empire. Puffed with success, he turned his army on the Byzantine Empire itself. The result was a crushing defeat for the Rus. To make peace, Svyatoslav and Emperor John Tzimisces met at the edge of the Danube. The Emperor rode to their meeting wearing golden armour and accompanied by a magnificent retinue, while Svyatoslav came as an oarsman, sitting on the bench of a boat, differentiated from the other Rus oarsmen only by the cleanness of his garment and by a bejewelled gold earring; a figure ridiculed by the Greeks but eminently worthy of his Viking ancestors. On his way home, probably in 972, Svyatoslav was slain by Pechenegs, and with him died the ambition of the Rus to control the lower Danube.

Svyatoslav's rejection of Christianity also died with him. When the blood had stopped running and the succession struggle ended, it was his son Vladimir who, with the help of a Swedish army, ruled this state which stretched from Lake Ladoga to the Black Sea and who, in time, was to bring his people into the Christian fold. The Russian *Chronicle* states that Vladimir considered the religion of Islam – which he rejected, it is said, because 'drinking is the joy of the Rus and we cannot live without this pleasure' – then he considered Judaism, then Latin Christianity, and finally Greek Christianity, which he accepted, we are told, because of the beauty and splendour of its liturgy. His gaining of the Emperor's sister as wife and lands in the Crimea as dowry no doubt provided additional persuasion. Whatever his motives, in 989 (or 990) the prince-leader of the Rus accepted the Christian faith. The *Chronicle* does not tell us what happened to the 300 concubines Vladimir had at Vijshgorod, the 300 at Belgorod, and the 200 at Berestovo. Before his conversion he had enjoyed an international reputation as a womanizer. The Russian *Chronicle* simply says – but with evident disapproval – that 'Vladimir was overcome by lust for women'. The German chronicler, Thietmar (975–1018), was more direct: '*erat enim fornicator immensus et crudelis*'. Once his conversion had been accomplished, Vladimir organized a mass baptizing of the Rus in the waters of the Dnieper at Kiev. Thus, there flowed into the land of the Rus the religion of the East and with it a cultural impact which is impossible to measure. The Greek language was not to be used in the liturgy – Slavonic became the language of religion – but the close religious ties with Byzantium were now made. Churches, monasteries and religious practices of every sort – indeed quickly acculturated to the Rus situation – were influenced by Constantinople, the very city which a Rus fleet of 1000 ships had severely threatened 130 years before. It was with good reason that the Rus gave to their principal church the title of Saint Sophia.

After his conversion, Vladimir sent 6000 fighting men to the emperor. Many observers have since seen in this deed the beginning of the famous Varangian Guard, the elite corps of Rus who guarded the person of the emperor. The use of foreign mercenaries by the imperial army was nothing new, and the use of Rus soldiers at this time indicates the normalization of relations between Rus and Greek. What is noteworthy, however, is the fact that sometime around the year 1000, a body of Rus formed the imperial palace guard. Their use for this purpose may not be traced back to Vladimir, but clearly by the turn of the millenium the force was in place. To be sure, the earliest reference to the 'Varangian Guard' by that name is not to be found until 1034, but that reference itself implies a brigade established for some time. Harald Hardrada, who was to become King of Norway and who nearly became King of England, served in this guard until 1042. A remarkable Greek work entitled *Advice to an Emperor*, which was written in the 1070s but which only came to light in 1881, described Harald as the son of a Varangian emperor and stated that he came into the Byzantine imperial force and that, for his great valour in a campaign in Bulgaria, he received the title 'spatharocandidate'. Although some Englishmen and Danes entered the Varangian Guard after 1066, it was probably still dominated by Varangians. They remained part of the Byzantine military establishment – the Danish King Eric I addressed them in Norse in 1103 – until 1204 when crusaders on their way to Jerusalem attacked, pillaged, ravaged and captured the

Christian city of Constantinople. Among those defending were the men of the Varangian Guard and, ironically, among the rapacious crusaders were the descendants of Vikings who had settled Normandy. The circle was complete.

The Rus and Islam

Commerce forged the link between the men of the north and the men of the book. There were hostile raids by the Rus in the lands of the Moslems, but their contacts were principally related to the business of business. The great wealth of Kufic coins in western Scandinavia tells only part of this story – 80,000 such coins have been found, half of them in Gotland – for large numbers of Kufic coins have also been found in Russia. The Rus merchants and the Moslem merchants met at the trading centres of the Volga: the road to Islam led inevitably along the Volga to the Caspian Sea. Near a bend in the Volga – close to modern Kazan – an international trading place existed at Bulgar, and here the merchants of many nations traded. The Rus traded principally in furs. Arabs who had been to the market at Bulgar in the tenth century remarked that the Rus dealt in a variety of furs: sable, fox, squirrel, ermine, marten, weasel and hare. Some of these skins came from Lappland and Finnmark, far to the north, on the edge of the Arctic Ocean. A constant, but probably small, marketing in slaves was part of the Rus commercial activity, although the Rus seem to have conducted this business privately and not in public markets. They would 'package' their slaves by dressing them in smart attire: the story is told of a Rus trader who was saddened when his favourite slave girl was bought, although he had dressed her in rags.

Shortly after the year 900 Ibn Rusteh, an Arab encyclopedist, noted how the Rus would keep the money they got for their furs and slaves in money-belts: in fact, he said, they did not keep fields or estates and lived by trade alone. They were neat and clean in appearance and wore baggy trousers gathered at the knees. They feared attack so much that one of them would not go outside to relieve himself without taking a bodyguard with him. It is not known where Ibn Rusteh obtained his information, but its reliability is not in question.

No witness of the Vikings anywhere or at any stage in their history provides a more detailed and vivid account than Ibn Fadlan, the ambassador from Baghdad to the Bulgars. His embassy left

Baghdad on 21 June 921 and passed through lands inhabited by Khwarizmians, Guzz Turks, Pechenegs and Bashkirs before reaching Bulgar on 12 May 922. Ibn Fadlan found no town there, only temporary booths and tents. It was his purpose to assist the Bulgars in fortifying their market. To paraphrase his account is merely to indicate something of its richness: its accuracy is uncontested and its importance obvious.

The Rus, he tells us, came as merchants to Bulgar, where they built wooden huts large enough to hold between ten and twenty persons. In order to ensure the sale of slaves or skins they set up wooden idols and left food and drink as an offering, and, if sales were moving too slowly, they returned and made further offerings. When all was sold, they came back to leave offerings of thanks. Never before had Ibn Fadlan seen such paragons of physical perfection: tall and blond and ruddy-complexioned. Each Rus man wore a garment that covered his body on one side and left one side free for action; he always carried an axe, a Frankish-type sword, and a knife with him. Tattoos covered him from fingertip to neck: trees and designs and the like. The women, in a way, also advertised the wealth of their husbands: the size and beauty of breast brooches and the number of neck rings were public indications of a husband's wealth. The women enjoyed wearing green-coloured beads and traded them among themselves. The Rus were a filthy people, like wild asses, for they eliminated bodily waste without modesty and did not wash after eating or after orgasm. When they washed, they did so from a basin – a habit repulsive to an Arab who used only running water for his toilet – and they took great care over their hair. They even copulated with their slave girls in the presence of companions and even slave-buyers. If any of the Rus was taken ill, he was removed to an isolated place and left with bread and water. If he recovered, he would return to his companions; if not, he would be cremated. Cremation usually took place ten days after death. During the interim, preparations would be made and the dead man's wealth divided in thirds: one-third for his family, one-third for his funeral garments, and one-third for drink.

Ibn Fadlan actually witnessed the funeral rites for a prominent Rus. As was the custom among these people, he said, the slaves of the deceased were asked which of them would die with their master. One volunteered, and she was put in the care of two young women, who waited on her. She spent ten days singing and drinking and indulging in other pleasures. On the day of cremation, the Rus

dragged the great man's ship onto the shore and built a wooden
scaffold for the ship; under it they placed firewood. Amidship a
couch covered in fabric was prepared for his body, and this area
was covered like a tent. The man's body was exhumed from its
temporary grave, dressed in fine garments and covered with a fur
piece. His companions placed his body on the couch and propped it
up with cushions and put food and drink at its feet. The weapons of
the deceased man were placed at his side. A number of animals – a
dog, two horses, two cows, a rooster and a hen – were killed, cut into
pieces, and placed in the ship. All that remained for his journey to
the other place was his slave girl. She went from tent to tent and the
master of each had intercourse with her and told her, 'Tell your lord
I have done this out of love for him.' She was then led to something
resembling a door frame. (Is this door frame not the 'pillars' used by
the Viking priest-paterfamilias, and known to us from their use in
Iceland and elsewhere?) She stood on the palms of the men's hands
and was raised so that she could see over the top. Three times it was
done. The first time she said, 'Behold, I see my father and mother';
the second time, 'I see all my dead relatives seated'; and the third
time, 'I see my master seated in paradise, and paradise is beautiful
and green; with him are men and boy servants; he is calling me; take
me to him.' And they did. Before she entered the burial
chamber-tent on her master's ship, she gave two gold bracelets to
the woman called 'Angel of Death' and a finger ring to each of her
two attendants. She drank and sang again, then hesitated at the
entrance to the chamber, but the 'Angel of Death' pushed her in.
The warriors gathered outside and struck their shields with their
swords so that the other servant girls would not hear her screams.
Six men entered the burial chamber after her, and each of them had
sexual intercourse with her. Then they placed her next to the body
of her dead master. Two of the men held her by the feet, two by the
hands, while the other two held the ends of a cord which they had
crossed about her neck. The 'Angel of Death' approached her, took
out a dagger, and, as the two men pulled the cord, she stabbed her
again and again in the chest until there was no life left in her. They
all withdrew from the burial chamber. Then the chief mourner
stood naked in front of the ship and lit a piece of wood with which he
set fire to the wood under the vessel. Each of the onlookers took a
lighted piece of wood and also put it on the firewood. Within an
hour the ship, the master, the slave girl and the wood were cinders
and ashes. A Rus, standing next to Ibn Fadlan, said through an

interpreter, 'You Arabs are fools; you take the people whom you love and respect most and put them in the ground where they are eaten by worms. We burn our loved one in a moment and he enters paradise at once.' The Rus built a small mound over the place, put a birch post in the middle, and wrote on it the man's name and the name of their king, who lived in a high place in their capital, which was called Kyawh (Kiev).

It was not merely the Moslem traveller visiting lands to the north on matters of commerce or diplomacy who knew of the Rus firsthand. Inhabitants along the shores of the Caspian Sea and even some distance inland knew of the Rus, not in their peaceful rituals of sending warrior–leaders to Valhalla but in the hostile rituals of attack, conquest and even slaughter. Six such attacks are known to us, and they reveal the extent and nature of the Rus activity east of the Dnieper. Preceding these attacks and, indeed, contemporary with them, trading contacts were established in the Caspian region. As early as the ninth century one well-informed Arab source described the Rus working the market areas of the lower Volga, where they bought goods from the Khazars, and the markets on the shores of the Caspian Sea, selling furs, sword-blades and spears. This same source says that they even took camels and followed the route to Baghdad, where they sold their wares, assisted by European slaves, who interpreted for them. There is the flavour of fact in all this, although some say (unconvincingly) that the author, Ibn Khurdadbeh (*c.* 820–911), had confused the Rus with Jewish Khazars. The author's mention of interpreters and his familiarity with Baghdad implies that the interpreters communicated the identity of these merchants from the north. What did these merchants from the north make of the greatest city in Islam? The transmission of Ibn Khurdadbeh's text contains problems, and, perhaps rightly, judgement should be reserved on the question of the Viking Rus having reached Baghdad in the ninth century. Even if they did reach the first city in Islam in the ninth century, it would only have been a small group that did so and, although appealing to romantic imagination, it is of little historical importance. Thus, there are no Viking adventures in *The Arabian Nights*, although one's fancy permits speculation about the source of Sinbad's nautical knowledge.

The passage to Islam was possible for the Rus only at the sufferance of the Khazars, that remarkable Turkish people, part Moslem, part Jewish and part Christian, who controlled the lower

Volga; a sufferance which was generally purchasable for a 10 per cent tax on the Rus goods. One Khazar leader is reported to have said, 'I do not permit the Rus who come in their ships to go by sea to attack the Arabs. . . . They would destroy the land of the Arabs as far as Baghdad.' Despite this boast the Rus did, indeed, pass through the lower Volga to the lands beyond. Sometime during the reign of Hasan Ibn Zaid, ruler of Tabaristan (864–84), the Rus sailed into the Caspian Sea and unsuccessfully attacked the eastern shore at Abaskun. This was probably a raid on a very small scale, and like the raid of 910 in which sixteen ships are reported to have pillaged along the Persian coast. Great raids, however, took place in about 913, in 943, 965 and in about 1041. In the first of these a fleet, numbering 500 ships, passed through the country of the Khazars, but their approach was not, as one might expect, down the Volga from Bulgar – the road to Islam – but from the Black Sea. These particular Rus, who were undoubtedly from the Dnieper Rus, sailed from the Black Sea into the Sea of Azov, then up the Don River past Sarkel, and then by a short portage reached the Volga, which led them into the Caspian Sea. In order to secure a peaceful passage through the land of the Khazars they promised the Khazars half of their booty. The Arabs were unprepared for such an attack: their sea had hitherto known only friendly ships intent on fishing and commerce. The Rus attacked in the Jurjan region around Abaskun, harassing the countryside as they went. Across the sea they raided at Baku in Azerbaijan, penetrating inland a distance of three days' journey. Everywhere they took what they could, including women and children as slaves. An attempt to check them as they lay in anchor near islands in the southwestern part of the Caspian Sea proved unsuccessful; and they were then able to roam and raid at will, a condition reminiscent of the Vikings at times in England and Francia. The news of their outrages preceded them as they headed homeward and, at the mouth of the Volga, despite the promise of the Khazar king, a large army of Moslem Khazars, enraged by the crimes committed against their fellow Moslems, met and devastated the Rus, only a remnant of whom escaped.

The Rus who came to the Caspian Sea in 943 might have intended to found a settlement on the Kiev pattern, but in this they were unsuccessful. This time the Rus, using the River Kura, penetrated deep into Azerbaijan, where, on a tributary, they captured Berda, the ancient capital of the region. The people of Berda were to be allowed to live in peace and to practise their Moslem faith as long as they agreed to recognize the Rus as their overlords. Stone-throwing and other abuse against the Rus broke the peace and, when the local people refused to accept an ultimatum to evacuate Berda (and here the source is an Arab one) the Rus began to kill the inhabitants and hold many for ransom. Negotiations became acrimonious and broke down, and a slaughter followed. Perhaps it was the Moslem women forced into slavery who poisoned the drinking water, or perhaps it was divine wrath, but, whatever the cause, the effect was that dysentery spread through the Rus ranks and the Rus, under the cover of darkness, rowed away. The Moslems then exhumed from the Rus graves the weapons which had been buried beside these warriors.

In 965 the adventurous Svyatoslav, perhaps provoked by the denial of passage by the Khazar king, attacked the great Khazar city of Itil near the mouth of the Volga. A great victory for the Rus ensued, thus avenging any past wrongs, and a visitor to Itil soon after remarked, 'The Rus attacked, and no grape or raisin remained, not a leaf on a branch'. Later, in the eleventh century, another adventure against the Moslems was undertaken on a grand scale. The fact that much legend is conflated with verifiable historical fact should not diminish the significance of this expedition from Sweden by Ingvar Vittfarne ('the widefarer') which went down the Volga into the land of the Saracens ('Serkland') in the mid eleventh century. The date of his death in this land, according to *Yngvar's Saga*, is 1041. There are no less than twenty-six runic stones – twenty-three of them in the Lake Mälar region of Uppland in Sweden – referring to Swedish warriors who went out with Ingvar on his expedition to the Saracen lands, an expedition whose purpose was probably to reopen old trade routes, now that the Bulgars and the Khazars no longer proved obstacles. A stone to Ingvar's brother indicates that he went east for gold but that he died in Saracen land, his body food for eagles. And with the death of Ingvar's brother and this Swedish expedition, the road between Baltic and Caspian became merely a context for Icelandic saga tellers.

Scandinavian to Slav

The controversies over the nature of the Rus and the origins of the Russian state have bedevilled Viking studies, and indeed Russian history, for over a century. It is historically certain that the Rus were Swedes. The evidence is uncontrovertible, and that a debate still rages at some levels of historical writing is clear evidence of the holding power of received notions and the fallibility, it must be reluctantly admitted, of historians. The debate over this issue – futile, embittered, tendentious and doctrinaire – has served to obscure the most serious and genuine historical problem which remains: the assimilation of these Viking Rus into the Slavic people among whom they lived. The principal historical question is not whether the Rus were Scandinavians or Slavs, but, rather, how quickly these Scandinavian Rus became absorbed into Slavic life and culture. The Slavicization of the Vikings paralleled their assimilation with the peoples of western Europe – in Ireland, England and Francia – and, as with the settlement of the Vikings in western Europe, issues concerning the settlement of the Vikings in Russia persist unresolved.

However one may view these unresolved issues, what is abundantly clear is that the Swedes who entered, settled and gave their name to that region of eastern Europe lost their Swedishness and left little material evidence of their having been there. Place-name evidence is extremely scanty and virtually non-existent once we mention the Dnieper rapids. The claim that the Swedes founded the Russian state overlooks in a grand way the fact that a state is not created, that it does not come into existence at a single moment in time. Dynamic factors contribute to the evolution of a state: among these factors, in the case of the Russian state, was the Swedish factor, which should neither be overlooked nor exaggerated. But why, in any case, assume that the 'founding' of a state is the central historical problem: this presupposes a view of society about which there is no unanimity or, for that matter, no consensus.

In 839 the Rus were Swedes; in 1043 the Rus were Slavs. Sometime between 839 and 1043 two changes took place: one was the absorption of the Swedish Rus into the Slavic people among whom they settled, and the second was the extension of the term 'Rus' to apply to these Slavic peoples by whom the Swedes were absorbed. The veil concealing this process is only intermittently lifted and then much too quickly dropped again. The Rus who, in 839, took the long way home from Constantinople via the court of Louis the Pious were clearly Swedes and, in the context, presumably first-generation Swedes living in north Russia. The Rus whom the Patriarch Photius decried in 860 must surely have been Scandinavians, although even at this time some of the crews might well have been Slavs. The leaders of the Rus retained Scandinavian personal names into the tenth century: the fifteen signatories of the treaty with the Greeks in 911 all had Scandinavian names, whereas among the signatories of the treaty of 945 there were some Slavonic names (three out of nineteen identifiable names). Liudprand of Cremona, who went to Constantinople twice (in 949 and 968), identified the Rus for his readers by saying that they were those people 'whom we call by another name, i.e., "northmen" ', the standard term used in the contemporary west to refer to the Scandinavians. Other contradictory signs appear. For example, the Russian *Chronicle* under the years 880–2 states that, when Oleg became Prince of Kiev, 'the Varangians, Slavs, and others who accompanied him were called Rus'. The dating in the *Chronicle* here, as elsewhere, is open to question, but it seems clear that by the end of the ninth century there was already some assimilation. The leadership, however, must have remained among those of Scandinavian ancestry for some time. The Slavic influence probably predominated by the time of the reign of Vladimir (*c.* 978–1015) in Kiev. The most telling indication that a new order had arrived was the acceptance of a Christianity, which was Byzantine in form but *Slavonic* in language. The language of the people was clearly Slavonic by 988, the date of Vladimir's conversion. What is even more remarkable is that virtually nothing of Old Norse penetrated into the Old Church Slavonic language or into modern Russian. Yet the link with Scandinavia persisted under Vladimir's successor, Yaroslavl, who came to power with the aid of Swedish warriors and who married a Swedish princess. He welcomed to his court such exiled Scandinavian leaders as Harald Hardrada and Magnus Olafsson and perhaps the latter's father, Olaf Haraldson, and gave his own daughter in marriage to Harald Hardrada; she came close to becoming Queen of England. The memory of the Scandinavian roots of Russia lived on in a romantic way, for the composers of the Icelandic sagas gave historical context and – who knows? – substance in tales told in the North Atlantic, tales of far-off places like Kiev and Constantinople and of long-dead heroes like Oleg and Harald Hardrada. Unfortunately romance is not the stuff of history. But history does indicate the striking rapidity with which the process of absorption took place: the Rus had become Slavs (i.e., Russians) in 150 years, a time-span comparable to the absorption periods in Ireland and England.

The last word on Russia belongs to the archaeologists, to whom our debt is great and of whom our expectations are high. The Leningrad school of archaeologists (Leo S. Klejn *et al.*) acknowledge the place of the Scandinavians among the ruling elite of the Rus easily. For them the process of assimilation should be viewed regionally, and northern Russia must be distinguished from Dnieper (or Kievan) Russia. In the northern part of what is now Russia, i.e., that part stretching from the region of Lake Ladoga eastward to the upper Volga, Finno-Ugric people lived before the coming of the Vikings, while some Balts and Slavs lived with the Finns in the Lake Ladoga area. The Scandinavians arrived in the early ninth century in the region near Lake Ladoga: cremation boat-burials of a type known only in central Sweden at that time have been found there. By the end of the tenth century towns were clearly emerging on the route east where the Rus met Finns, and some integration of the cultures occurred. The burial barrows left in the wake of these later movements conflate the Scandinavian and Finnish cultures: cremation boat-burials, weapons and other objects of Scandinavian type, as well as Finnish burial pyres in which the graves of men and women are separated. Evidence of such an integration can be found near Lake Ladoga and also at the cemeteries near Yaroslavl, about 300 miles to the east.

In the Dnieper region a similar story emerges. There the aboriginal Balts had already experienced the coming of Slavs before the movement or, more truly, the movements south of the Scandinavians. The principal meeting of Slav and Scandinavian took place in this region. To judge by the burial remains, graves of an unmistakably Scandinavian character appear in this region in about the year 900, but by the second half of the tenth century new rites with few Scandinavian features are to be found, and these were followed very quickly by warrior–graves bearing no Scandinavian features. Yet more Scandinavians arrived, often as mercenaries, in the last half of the tenth century to form part of the ruling class. For example, the funeral chambers near Chernigov bear striking similarities to those at Birka in central Sweden, but the funeral chambers of Vladimir's bodyguard, found in eastern Poland, reveal a mixture of Scandinavian and Kievan types of objects in the same barrows. Evidence of later burials which contain Scandinavian material refer almost exclusively to expensive articles imported from Gotland. In all this, the pickings are small, the argument necessarily thin, and the conclusions consequently probable rather than certain. Yet the chronology presented by the Leningrad archaeologists fits the facts as otherwise known and is not forced to stand alone. And perhaps it will be the archaeologists – too often, alas, the whipping boys of historians – who will at last bury the seemingly endless and tiresome argument about the Rus and Slav.

Selected further reading

Much of the pertinent source material has been translated into English, and the translations here have been based on these translations: S. H. Cross and O. P. Sherbowitz-Wetzer (trs. and eds.), *The Russian Primary Chronicle: Laurentian Text*, Cambridge, Mass.: Medieval Academy of America 1953; Cyril Mango (trs.), *The Homilies of Photius, Patriarch of Constantinople*, Cambridge, Mass.: Dumbarton Oaks Studies, no. 3, (1958); C. Moravcsik (ed.) and R. J. H. Jenkins (trs.), Constantine VII Porphyrogenitus, *De administrando imperio*, Washington: Dumbarton Oaks Texts, no. 1, 1967; H. M. Smysert, 'Ibn Fadlan's account of the Rus with some commentary and some allusions to *Beowulf*', in J. B. Bessinger and R. P. Creed (eds.), *Medieval and Linguistic Studies in Honour of Francis Peabody Magoun, Jr.,* Allen & Unwin 1965, pp. 92–119.

Among the so-called Normanist historians the work of Henryk Paszkiewicz presents that view in an exhaustive manner: *The Origin of Russia*, Allen & Unwin 1954, and *The Making of the Russian Nation*, Darton, Longman & Todd 1963. For the opposing view see N. V. Riasasnovsky, *A History of Russia*, Oxford University Press 1969. Over a hundred years old but still very useful are the Oxford lectures given by Vilhelm Thomsen, *The Relations Between Ancient Russia and Scandinavia and the Origin of the Russian State*, J. Parker 1877. More recent are *Varangian Problems*, in *Scando Slavica*, supplement 1, (1970), and H. R. Ellis Davidson, *The Viking Road to Byzantium*, Allen & Unwin 1976.

For a discussion of the river systems and portage routes see Robert J. Kerner, *The Urge to the Sea: The Course of Russian History,* Berkeley, Cal.: University of California Press 1942. Two works by A. A. Vasiliev examine aspects of the Rus and Byzantium: *The Russian Attack on Constantinople in 860*, Cambridge, Mass.: Medieval Academy of America, publication no. 46, (1946), and 'The second Russian attack on Constantinople', Cambridge, Mass.: *Dumbarton Oaks Papers*, no. 6 (1951), pp. 161–225. On other aspects of the Rus in Byzantium and the Balkans see Sir Steven Runciman, *The Emperor Romanus Lecapenus and His Reign*, Cambridge University Press 1929, and *A History of the First Bulgarian Empire*, G. Bell 1930. The conversion of the Rus is described in A. P. Vlasto, *The Entry of the Slavs into Christendom*, Cambridge University Press 1970. Two books on the Khazars are useful: D. M. Dunlop, *The History of the Jewish Khazars*, Princeton, NJ: Princeton University Press 1954, and Arthur Koestler, *The Thirteenth Tribe*, Hutchinson 1976. Recent excavations at

Novgorod are described by M. W. Thompson in *Novgorod the Great*, Evelyn, Adams & Mackay 1967. A summary of the extensive work of the Leningrad archaeologists can be found in articles in the *Norwegian Archaeological Review*, vols. 2 (1969), 3 (1970), 4 (1971), and 6 (1973).

8 Epilogue

The Vikings were to be found from Vinland to the Volga: a very large stage on which they acted out their historical roles. Two and a half centuries and it was over, ended by successful overseas settlements and the emergence of states in their peninsular homelands. Their string had run out as had that of the Persians, Greeks and Romans before them and so many others after them. The dynamics of history raise a people to a place of prominence – even dominance – and those same dynamics, still uncontrolled by human agencies including totalitarian governments and liberal institutions, bring about that people's decline. Strong states in western Europe, the reformed church, and new economic alliances provided a new shape to the Europe of the late eleventh century and after. The Viking ship had sailed its journey, and the setting northern sun was casting a long but fading sail–shadow upon lands to the west, to the south, and to the east. A new day would bring new things, but the Viking ship has left historians with problems still unresolved in its wake.

The historical questions which remain do *not* include such absurdities as 'The Vikings ... traders or pirates?', a false dichotomy if ever there was one. The largest question still outstanding despite attempts in these pages and elsewhere to answer it concerns the origins of the Viking period. Why in the decades surrounding the year 800 did Scandinavia erupt and send her sons forth in every direction except north? and what forces in Scandinavia kept this movement, once it had started, in motion? Strange as it may seem, the answer – or, rather, a part of it – may lie hidden under the permafrost of Greenland, thousands of miles west of Scandinavia. Scientists are not only beginning to chart the historical climate patterns of the world's largest island but also to relate the historical climate of Greenland to that of northern Europe. The permanence of the ice makes Greenland an ideal control place, and sophisticated modern techniques allow scientists to determine that a time lag of 250 years existed between the climate in Greenland and the climate in northern Europe during the pre-Viking and Viking ages. Thus, a study of the permafrost in Greenland reveals that Scandinavia experienced warm temperatures in the eighth century, which were followed by colder temperatures in the ninth century. In addition, protein analysis of soil samples in Denmark for the Viking age shows a clear intensification of the growing of plants high in protein (for example, cereals such as rye). Also, studies of animal bone samples dating from this period indicate that animals were decreasing in size. Further, it is known that more land was under cultivation. The land was being used in a very large measure to produce nutritional food for human consumption; a response, scientists argue, to increased demand due to a growth in population. The question of the origin of the Viking age remains far from settled, but, at least, directional signals are appearing, and it is the climatologist and the demographer who are giving them and coming to the aid of the historian.

The great obstacle – almost a smokescreen – for the historian concerned with Viking history must surely be the question of the Vikings and violence. Each generation of historians, it seems, is almost predetermined to reargue this issue. The menacing Viking, the raider of monasteries, and ravager of women certainly existed, and to find in him a peaceful farmer is to look with only half an eye or less. Yet the issue of the violence of the Vikings is, at best, a regional issue raised principally by English, French and Belgian historians. To be sure, no neutral reading of the sources for England for 1009, or for France in the late 850s, or for Belgium for 884 can deny the uncontrolled and barbaric violence unleashed by the men from the north, and, as a consequence of this violence, a widespread public fear, a profound unease, a massive psychological reaction. And other years can be easily added to these as can other places. The inquiring historian might ask: how violent were these Vikings? more violent than the Christians were to one another? violent only in the raiding and land-taking phases? truly sources of terror throughout these lands? These are serious questions, and the violence issue is not to be glossed over or laughed off; it is, however, an issue of the short range, one over which historians may appear to have gone berserk. Other questions, those of the long range, dealing with economic and anthropological issues, have suffered as a consequence of the violence question being given high priority in

Viking studies. Other questions demand and deserve attention.

The Hanseatic League, for example, which emerged in the late middle ages as a successful community of northern European merchant towns, was not created *ex nihilo* nor did it appear, like Melchisedek, without ancestors. Among its ancestors were the Viking merchants of the ninth, tenth and eleventh centuries. The island of Gotland is central to this genealogy, as to so much else in Viking history. Although the Viking age had ended and the Rus had become Slavs, the Gotlanders continued to trade. Their commercial activities kept them in contact with central Sweden, where Sigtuna had replaced Birka, with the Jutland neck, where Slesvig had replaced Hedeby, and with Novgorod, where a Gothic court had become established. Later, in the fourteenth and fifteenth centuries, Visby, the harbour on Gotland's western shore, became an important town in the Hanseatic community. The fact that the Hansa established a station at Novgorod was no accident, for the Hansa of the eastern Baltic owed much to the trading links set up long before by men from central Sweden and Gotland, whom contemporaries might have called Swedes or Goths or Varangians or Rus and whom we call Vikings.

The preoccupation with Viking violence obscures also the great problem of settlement: not the issues of how many and where and when and how long, but the more important phenomenon of the Vikings having been absorbed into native cultures. (Iceland and Greenland stand apart as uninhabited at the time of the Viking colonizing.) The fact remains that these vigorous, adventurous men from the north were absorbed by the Irish, the English, the French and the Slavs. They did not establish enduring enclaves in the Danelaw, in Normandy or in Russia. The enclaves established in Ireland (i.e., the towns) became Irish towns by the twelfth century, and the Norseman could not be seen then in the Celtic mass: he was part of it, indistinguishable from the rest. The process was accomplished so completely in France that precious little remains of their influence: a few place-names, a few specialized words relating to seafaring, and that is all. Even less remains in Russia. The impact on England, of course, was considerably greater, but, even there, absorption occurred, and, although traces can be found, they are but traces. In any case, once the Viking settlers in these lands were converted to Christianity, once intermarriage took place, and once local roots were put down, these people made no effort to stand apart. Thus, the Viking age, in a sense, ended in the fields of

Yorkshire and Lincolnshire, in the valley of the Seine, in the ports of Ireland, and along the portages of Russia, and it ended without a whimper. The roar that had come out of the north was now muted or, rather, it sounded new tones and new words. The world itself was new.

Index